London
GCSE MATHEMATICS

FOUNDATION COURSE

Heinemann

About this book

This book is designed to provide you with the best possible preparation for your London GCSE Mathematics Examination. The authors are examiners and coursework moderators themselves and have a good understanding of all the Examination Council's requirements.

Finding your way around

To help you find your way around when you are studying and revising use the:

- **edge marks** (shown on the front pages) – these help you get to the right unit quickly;
- **contents list** – this lists the headings that identify key syllabus ideas covered in the book so you can turn straight to them (Codes are included to show which part of the programmes of study and left-hand column of the syllabus these relate to. For example **S4d** means the content relates to Shape, space and measures section **4** understanding and using measures subsection **d**)

Remembering key ideas

We have provided clear explanations of the key ideas and techniques you need throughout the book. **Key points** you need to remember are listed in a **summary** at the end of each unit and marked like this where they appear in the units themselves:

■ **Each digit in a number has a face value and a place value.**

Exercises and examination questions

In this book questions are carefully graded so they increase in difficulty and gradually bring you up to examination standard.

- **past examination questions** are marked with an [L];
- **worked examples** and **worked examination questions** show you how to answer questions;
- **examination practice paper** – this is included to help you prepare for the examination itself;
- **answers** are included at the end of the book.

Investigations and information technology

Two units focus on particular skills required for your course and examination:

- using and applying mathematics (unit 12) – shows how investigative work is assessed, and the skills required to carry out such work;
- calculators and computers (unit 24) – shows you how to use a variety of methods of solving problems using calculators and computers.

Contents

1 Number

2 Algebra 1

3 Angles and turning

4 Fractions

5 Two-dimensional shapes

6 Decimals

7 Measure 1

8 Collecting and recording data

9 Algebra 2

10 Sorting and presenting data

11 Three-dimensional shapes

12 Using and applying mathematics

13 Measure 2

14 Percentages

15 Algebra 3

16 Pie charts

17 Ratio and proportion

18 Symmetry

19 Measure 3

20 Averages

21 Algebra 4

22 Transformations

23 Probability

24 Calculators and computers

Examination practice paper

Formulae sheet

Answers

Keith Pledger is **Project Director** for the London GCSE Mathematics series. He is subject officer for GCSE Mathematics at ULEAC and is also an OFSTED team inspector. Keith has worked in examining for over 21 years. Previously he was Head of Mathematics in three schools.

John Sylvester is **Series Editor** for the Foundation Book. He is an Examiner, Member of the Grading Committee and Coursework Moderator for GCSE Mathematics at ULEAC. He has been examining for over 25 years, chaired the subject committee and has been Head of Mathematics in two schools.

Christine Medlow is **Series Editor** for the Intermediate Book. She is Principal Examiner for GCSE Mathematics at ULEAC and has been examining with London for over 25 years. Christine has taught at a girls' Grammar School, a co-educational comprehensive school and in adult education.

David Kent is **Series Editor** for the Higher Book. He is Chair of Examiners for GCSE Mathematics and Principal Moderator for coursework at ULEAC. David has been a Head of Mathematics Departments and Adviser/ Inspector in three LEAs. He is at present an OFSTED team inspector.

Peter Jolly is **Consulting Editor** for the London GCSE Mathematics series. He is an examiner, a member of the subject advisory and grading committees, and a coursework moderator for GCSE Mathematics at ULEAC. Peter has worked in both grammar and comprehensive inner city schools.

Author team

John Casson
Tony Clough
Gareth Cole
Ray Fraser
Barry Grantham
John Hackney
Karen Hughes
Trevor Johnson
Andrew Killick
Graham Newman
Sally Russell
Rob Summerson
Roy Woodward

Publishing team

Editorial
Philip Ellaway
Juliet Smith

Design
Phil Richards
Colette Jacquelin
Fiona Reynolds

Production
David Lawrence
Lucy Wallis

Heinemann Educational Publishers
Halley Court, Jordan Hill, Oxford OX2 8EJ
a division of Reed Educational & Professional Publishing Ltd

OXFORD FLORENCE PRAGUE MADRID
ATHENS MELBOURNE AUCKLAND
KUALA LUMPUR SINGAPORE TOKYO
IBADAN NAIROBI KAMPALA JOHANNESBURG
GABORONE PORTSMOUTH NH (USA) CHICAGO
MEXICO CITY SAO PAULO

© Heinemann Educational Publishers

First published 1996

96 97 98 99 10 9 8 7 6 5 4 3 2 1

ISBN: 0435 532 022

Produced by Gecko Limited, Bicester, Oxon

Printed in Spain by Mateu Cromo S.A. Pinto (Madrid)

Acknowledgements

The publisher's and author's thanks are due to the University of London Examinations and Assessment Council (ULEAC) for permission to reproduce questions from past examination papers. These are marked with an [L]. The answers have been provided by the authors and are not the responsibility of the examining council.

p2 and 258: Frank Spooner Pictures; p3, 19, 40, 79: Tony Stone Worldwide; p19 ZEFA; p81: Tony Stone Images; p83 Vandystadt Agencie de Presse; p84 and 292 Associated Sports Photography; p134, 173 and 304 Topham Picture Point; p161 and 260 Richard Greenhill; p211 Rex Features London.

1 Number

1.1 Face value and place value

■ **Each digit in a number has a face value and a place value.**

The **face value** of this digit is 3

0	0	0	3	0

3 Tens = 30 seconds
before lift off

The **place value** of this digit is Ten

Look at this place value diagram:

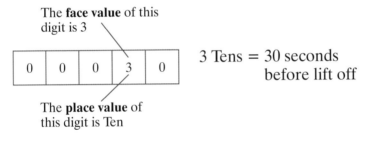

Here 8 means 8 Units = 8

Here 8 means 8 Tens = 80

386 has three digits. It is also called a three figure number.

Exercise 1A

1   Draw a place value diagram and write in:
   (a) a four figure number with a 4 in the Thousands column
   (b) a two figure number with a 3 in the Tens column

(c) a five figure number with a 1 in the Hundreds column
(d) a three figure number with a 9 in the Units column
(e) a four figure number with a 0 in the Tens column
(f) a five figure number with a 4 in the Hundreds column
(g) a three figure number with a 7 in every column
(h) a four figure number with a 6 in the first and last columns

1.2 Reading, writing and ordering numbers

Sometimes you will need to arrange numbers in order of size.

The size of a number depends on the face value and place value of its digits.

The three figure number 987 is smaller than the five figure number 16 412 even though the face value of its digits is greater.

16 412
↑
The thin space separates Thousands from Hundreds and makes it easier to read the number.

Numbers can be written in words like this:

Ten thousands	Thousands	Hundreds	Tens	Units	
		9	8	7	Nine hundred and eighty seven
1	6	4	1	2	Sixteen thousand four hundred and twelve

Two thousand eight hundred and twenty two women left the Armed Forces between 1978 and 1990.

Part of the thirty one thousand two hundred and fifty eight people at an outdoor rock concert.

The word numbers from the newspaper can be written in figures like this:

	Ten thousands	Thousands	Hundreds	Tens	Units	
Two thousand eight hundred and twenty two		2	8	2	2	or 2822
Thirty one thousand two hundred and fifty eight	3	1	2	5	8	or 31 258

Remember: zeros have a face value too.

Thousands	Hundreds	Tens	Units	
5	0	4	2	Five thousand and forty two
	4	0	6	Four hundred and six

Exercise 1B

1 Write these numbers in words:
(a) 36   (b) 95   (c) 598   (d) 246   (e) 5623
(f) There are 1251 people in James St. School.

2 Write these numbers in words:
(a) 709   (b) 890   (c) 6054   (d) 9201
(e) 26 007   (f) 40 200   (g) 32 000   (h) 70 090
(i) The number of school leavers in Axeshire last year
was 13 406.

3

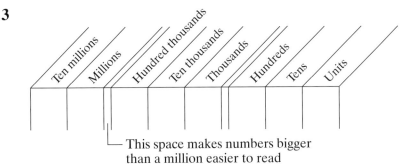

└─ This space makes numbers bigger
than a million easier to read

The table below gives the areas, in km^2, and the populations
of five member states of the European Union. Use the place
value diagram above to help you write the numbers in words.

	Country	Area	Population
(a)	Belgium	30 513	9 910 000
(b)	Luxembourg	2576	403 000
(c)	Spain	504 782	37 900 000
(d)	Portugal	92 082	9 913 000
(e)	France	547 026	54 200 000

4 Write the countries given in question **3** in order of size:
(a) by area
(b) by population.

5 Write the numbers below in figures:
  (a) The numbers of people employed by a local police authority were:
  - Traffic wardens: sixty nine
  - Civilian support staff: one thousand and ten
  - Police officers: two thousand three hundred and six

  (b) The tonnages of three cruise liners are:
  - Canberra: forty five thousand two hundred and seventy
  - QE 2: eighty three thousand six hundred and sixty three
  - Queen Mary: eighty thousand seven hundred and seventy four

  (c) The average daily readership of four newspapers was:
  - Financial Times: two hundred and ninety four thousand
  - Times: six hundred and eighty two thousand
  - Daily Mirror: two million six hundred thousand
  - Sun: three million nine hundred and ninety thousand

6 This table shows the numbers of people who died in road accidents in Britain:

Year	1961	1971	1976	1982	1984
Deaths	20 121	19 246	17 099	15 113	14 259

In which year did:
  (a) the smallest number of people die in road accidents
  (b) more than twenty thousand people die in road accidents
  (c) between fifteen and sixteen thousand people die in road accidents
  (d) less than fifteen thousand die in road accidents?

7 Write these numbers in figures:
(a) Sixty three
(b) Seven hundred and eight
(c) Seven thousand
(d) Eighteen thousand six hundred
(e) Seventy five thousand
(f) Eight hundred and nine thousand
(g) Four million
(h) One million one thousand
(i) Nine thousand and twenty
(j) Forty thousand six hundred

8 This table gives the prices of several popular motor cars:

Car	Price
Vauxhall Astra	£10 530
Volkswagen Polo	£9 110
Ford Granada	£20 270
Rover 623	£19 435
Citroen Xantia	£17 065
Jaguar Sport	£30 479
Mercedes Benz	£31 394
Marcos Mantera	£31 007
Volvo 940	£17 815
Ford Fiesta	£9 010

Rewrite the list in price order, starting with the least expensive.

9

(a) Put the numbers in the cloud in order. Start with the *smallest* number.
(b) Write the number 469 in words.

[L]

1.3 Combining numbers

This section will help you practise adding, subtracting, multiplying and dividing numbers.

You need to know:

- how to add (+) and subtract (−) two numbers in your head
- your multiplication tables up to 10 times 10.

Only use a calculator to check your answers when you have *finished* each exercise.

Adding

Here are some of the different ways of writing 6 add 9:

Find the **sum** of 6 and 9.
Work out 6 **plus** 9.
Find the **total** of 6 and 9.
Add 6 and 9.
Work out 6 **+** 9.

Exercise 1C

Work out the answer.

1 Find the total of 26 and 17.

2 Work out 58 plus 22.

3 Work out 236 + 95.

4 In four maths tests, Anna scored 61 marks, 46 marks, 87 marks and 76 marks.
   How many marks did she score altogether?

5 Find the sum of all the single figure numbers.

6 In a fishing competition, five competitors caught 16 fish, 31 fish, 8 fish, 19 fish and 22 fish.
   Find the total number of fish caught.

7 The number of passengers on a bus was 36 downstairs and 48 upstairs.
   How many passengers were on the bus altogether?

8 For her birthday party, Anna provided 86 bottles of cola, 58 bottles of orangeade and 72 bottles of mineral water.
   How many bottles did she provide in total?

9 Work out 38 + 96 + 127 + 92 + 48.

10 The numbers of caravans sold by the six branches of a nationwide caravan dealer were 86, 43, 75, 104, 38 and 70.
   What was the total number of caravans sold?

Subtracting

Here are some different ways of writing 38 subtract 16:

38 **minus** 16.
Take 16 **from** 38.
38 – 16
the **difference** between 38 and 16.
How many is 16 **less** than 38?
38 **take away** 16.

Exercise 1D

Work out the answer.

1 Take 1007 from 2010.

2 How much is 7260 minus 4094?

3 Work out 611 – 306.

4 Take 17 from 29.

5 When playing darts, James scored 111 with his first three darts, Iris scored 94 with her first three darts and Nadine scored 75 with her first three darts.
(a) How many more than Nadine did Iris score?
(b) What is the difference between James' and Iris' scores?
(c) How many less did Nadine score than James?

6 The winner of a darts match is the first one to score 601 points.
James has now scored 513, Iris 542 and Nadine 468.
(a) How many is James short of 601?
(b) How many more does Iris need to score to win?
(c) How many is Nadine's total less than 601?

Name	Score
James	513
Iris	542
Nadine	468

7 The 'thermometer' shows the yearly progress of a Cathedral Appeal towards a Target of £1 000 000.
(a) How much did the appeal raise between the end of 1988 and the end of 1989?
(b) How much money was raised between the end of 1989 and the end of 1990?
(c) At the start of 1991 how much was still needed to be raised to reach the target at the end of 1992?

	Target
1992	1 000 000
1991	82 126
1990	66 600
1989	43 640
1988	21 742

Cathedral Roof Repair Appeal

Multiplying

Here are some different ways of writing multiply 80×16.

Find the **product** of 80 and 16.
Times 16 by 80
Multiply 80 by 16.

Exercise 1E

Work out the answer.

1 Find the product of 36 and 30.

2 How many is 321 multiplied by 14?

3 Shirley Ltd bought 19 boxes of assorted CDs. Each box contained 24 CDs. How many did she buy?

4 Work out 106 times 43.

5 What is the product of 63 and 36?

6 Wasim and Jan are training for the school sports day.
During each session Wasim runs 50 metres 30 times and Jan runs 7 times round the 400 metre track.
(a) How far does Wasim run each session?
(b) How far does Jan run each session?
By sports day, Wasim has trained for 12 sessions and Jan for 20 sessions.
(c) How far has each run in training by sports day?

7 Packets of Cheese Flips come in three sizes.
There are 36 Cheese Flips in the Economy size, 3 times as many in the Large size and 6 times as many in the Family size.
How many Cheese Flips are in each size packet?

8 The distance from Mr. Singh's home to work is 17 miles.
He makes the journey 12 times a week.
How far does he travel:
(a) in one week
(b) in ten weeks
(c) in a year? (52 weeks make 1 year).

Dividing

Here are some of the different ways of writing 140 divided by 20.

Divide 140 by 20.
Share 140 by 20.
How many times does 20 go into 140?
Work out 140 ÷ 20.
Work out $\frac{140}{20}$.
How many 20s are there in 140?

Note: this is written
140 ÷ 20 not 20 ÷ 140.

Exercise 1F

Work out the answer.

1 (a) Work out 315 ÷ 15.
   (b) How many 50s make 750?
   (c) Work out $\frac{680}{17}$.
   (d) Work out 600 divided by 30.
   (e) Divide 8 into 112.

2 Five people shared a prize draw win of £2400 equally.
   How much did each person receive?

3 Edward packs books into boxes.
   Each box will hold 24 books.
   How many boxes will he need to pack:
   (a) 240 books
   (b) 720 books
   (c) 864 books?

4 A delivery van is used to carry crates of books
   from a printer to Heinemann's warehouse.
   The van can carry 18 crates at once.
   How many deliveries are needed to transfer:
   (a) 126 crates
   (b) 234 crates
   (c) 648 crates?

5 A packing case will hold 72 economy size boxes,
   24 large size boxes or 12 family size boxes.
   How many packing cases would be needed to pack:
   (a) 864 economy size boxes
   (b) 984 large size boxes
   (c) 960 family size boxes?

1.4 Solving number problems

Louise chooses 7 bath capsules.

She could find the cost by adding:

50p + 50p + 50p + 50p + 50p + 50p + 50p

or by multiplying:

50p × 7

Here multiplying is quicker than adding.

When you are solving number problems like this you need to choose whether to add, subtract, divide or multiply.

Example 1

We have won £2,000 in a lottery

We are having equal shares

How much is my share ?

The keys words here are **equal shares**. They tell you to **divide**:

£2000 ÷ 4 = £500

Exercise 1G

This exercise will help you choose whether to add, subtract, multiply or divide.

Look at the size of each answer when you have worked it out. This may help you check whether you have chosen + − × or ÷ correctly.

1 Owen keeps 12 pet hamsters and 21 pet rabbits.
How many pets has he altogether?

2 Ranjit and Jane both collect stamps.
Ranjit has 1310 stamps and Jane has 942 stamps.
How many more stamps has Ranjit than Jane?

3 42 packing cases of tins of beans are delivered to Simpsons Superstore. The packing cases each hold 48 tins of beans.
How many tins of beans are delivered altogether?

4 A librarian has 343 cassettes to display in the music library. They fill exactly 7 shelves.
How many cassettes are on each shelf?

5 Robina was given 20 face paints for her birthday. 4 of the paints were blue, 6 were green and 7 were red. The others were brown.
(a) How many of Robina's paints were brown?
(b) How many more green paints than blue paints did she have?
Robina gave 2 paints of each colour to her sister Amanda.
(c) How many paints did Robina give to Amanda altogether?
(d) How many paints did Robina have left?

6 Jason bought three boxes of toffees. There were 30 toffees in each box. Jason ate 14 toffees himself then shared all the rest equally between himself and his three sisters.
(a) How many toffees did Jason have to start with?
(b) When they were shared out, how many toffees did each person get?

7 This table shows the numbers of pupils in each year group at Gordon School:

Year 7	Year 8	Year 9	Year 10	Year 11
112	121	104	98	126

(a) How many pupils are at the school altogether?
(b) How many less pupils are in Year 10 than in Year 8?

Each class in Year 11 has 21 pupils.

(c) How many classes are there in Year 11?

(d) There are 3 times as many pupils in Bennett School as in Gordon School.
    How many pupils are in Bennett School?

8 A bus company owns twelve 48–seater coaches.
Every Saturday all the coaches are used to take people to the seaside.

(a) How many people can be carried at the same time in the 12 coaches?

One Saturday seven of the coaches each carried 39 people.
The other coaches each had 11 empty seats.

(b) How many people were carried altogether that Saturday?

1.5 Rounding numbers

Sometimes an exact answer is not needed because:

- an approximate answer is good enough;
- *or* an approximate answer is easier to understand than an exact answer;
- *or* there is no exact answer.

To give an approximate answer you can **round** to the nearest 10, 100, 1000 and so on.

■ **To round to the nearest 10:**
    look at the digit in the Units column.
    - If it is less than 5 round down
    - If it is 5 or more round up.

Example 2

Round 687 to the nearest ten.

687 to the nearest ten is 690.

There is a 7 in the Units column so round up to 690.

687 is closer to 690 than to 680.

■ **To round to the nearest 100:**
look at the digit in the Tens column.
- If it is less than 5 round down
- If it is 5 or more round up.

Example 3

Round 7650 to the nearest hundred.

7650 to the nearest hundred is 7700.

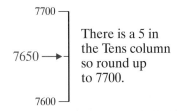

There is a 5 in the Tens column so round up to 7700.

■ **To round to the nearest 1000:**
look at the digit in the hundreds column.
- If it is less than 5 round down
- If it is 5 or more round up.

Example 4

Round 614 652 to the nearest thousand.

614 652 to the nearest thousand is 615 000.

Exercise 1H

1 Round to the nearest ten:
   (**a**) 57   (**b**) 63   (**c**) 185
   (**d**) 194   (**e**) 991   (**f**) 2407

2 Round to the nearest hundred:
   (**a**) 314   (**b**) 691   (**c**) 2406
   (**d**) 3094   (**e**) 8777   (**f**) 29 456

3 Round to the nearest thousand:
   (**a**) 2116   (**b**) 36 161   (**c**) 28 505
   (**d**) 321 604 (**e**) 717 171 (**f**) 2 246 810

4 For each of these liners, round:
   (**a**) the lengths to the nearest ten feet
   (**b**) the tonnages to the nearest hundred tonnes
   (**c**) the speeds to the nearest ten knots.

HOW IT COMPARES	Launched	Length	Tonnage	Speed
Queen Elizabeth	1938	1,029 ft	83,673	32 knots
Queen Mary	1934	1,019 ft	80,774	32 knots
New P&O cruise liner	(1994-5)	850 ft	67,000	24 knots
QE2	1967	963 ft	65,863	32.5 knots
United States	1951	990 ft	53,329	40 knots
Canberra	1960	820 ft	45,270	29.3 knots

Source: Great Passenger Ships of the world, A. Kludes

5 The table gives the areas and populations of five European Union states.

Country	Area (km²)	Population
Greece	131 944	9 804 266
Italy	301 225	57 436 280
Netherlands	33 812	14 292 416
Germany	356 733	80 180 660
Ireland	70 283	3 521 000

Round:
(a) the areas to the nearest thousand km²
(b) the populations to the nearest hundred thousand.

6 Give an approximate answer for each number below.
Explain why you chose your answer.
(a) James has a flock of 142 chickens.
(b) Mrs Wilson sold 306 portions of fish and chips.
(c) Asif needed 6318 bricks to build his new bungalow.
(d) A crowd of 35 157 spectators watched Chelsea last night.
(e) A pop group earned £45 376 290 in a year.
(f) Newhouse General Hospital treated 13 296 patients last year.

Is your answer reasonable?

When you do a calculation it helps to have a rough estimate of what answer to expect.

■ **Rounding is used to help you estimate an answer.**

Example 5

Estimate the answer to $\dfrac{289 \times 96}{184}$

Rounding each of the numbers to the nearest 100 gives:

$\dfrac{300 \times 100}{200}$

Working out the simplified calculation gives 150.

Example 6

Work out the exact value of $\dfrac{18 \times 104}{48}$ by calculator

Rough check your answer by estimating

$\dfrac{18 \times 104}{48}$ is about $\dfrac{20 \times 100}{50} \approx 40$

By calculator:

$\dfrac{18 \times 104}{48} = \dfrac{1872}{48} = 39$

Exercise 1I

1 Showing all your rounding, make an estimate of the answer to:

(a) $\dfrac{63 \times 57}{31}$ (b) $\dfrac{206 \times 311}{154}$ (c) $\dfrac{9 \times 31 \times 97}{304}$

(d) $\dfrac{2006}{12 \times 99}$ (e) $\dfrac{498}{11 \times 51}$ (f) $\dfrac{103 \times 87}{21 \times 32}$

2 For each of the following calculations:
  (i) Work out the exact values by calculator
  (ii) Rough check your answer by estimating.

(a) $\dfrac{201 \times 96}{51}$ (b) $\dfrac{11 \times 999}{496}$ (c) $\dfrac{146 \times 51}{69}$

(d) $\dfrac{1000}{9 \times 12}$ (e) $\dfrac{5206}{131 \times 7}$ (f) $\dfrac{913 \times 81}{39 \times 298}$

If you use your calculator to find an answer you can check it by estimating.

3 A football grandstand has 49 rows of seats. Each row seats 98 people.

(a) Estimate the capacity of the grandstand.
(b) Is your estimate bigger or smaller than the actual number? Explain your answer.

4   For Inglefield's school outing 1335 pupils went to the
     seaside by coach. Each coach carried 47 people.
     Estimate the number of coaches needed.

5   Thelma worked out the answer to the sum
     $916 \times 402 \div 1010$ on her calculator.
     Her answer was 36.458
     By estimating show whether her answer was right.

6   The Headteacher lives 16 miles from Inglefield School. He
     went to school on 195 days last year.
     Estimate how many miles he travelled to and from school.

7   A machine operator produces 121 memory chips every hour.
     He works 39 hours each week for 47 weeks in the year.
     Estimate the operator's annual chip production.

1.6 Even, odd and prime numbers

You need to be able to recognize these types of numbers:

- **Even** numbers – all divide exactly by 2:   2, 4, 6, 8, 10, . . .
- **Odd** numbers – none of these divide exactly by 2:   1, 3, 5, 7, . . .
- **Prime** numbers – only divide exactly by two numbers:
  themselves and 1:   2, 3, 5, 7, 11, . . .

Note: the number 1 is *not* a prime number because it can only
be divided exactly by *one* number – itself.

Exercise 1J

1   Write down any even numbers from the list:
     2, 18, 37, 955, 1110, 73 536, 500 000

2   Write down any odd numbers from the list:
     108, 537, 9216, 811, 36 225, 300 000

3   The first six prime numbers are
     2, 3, 5, 7, 11, 13.
     Write down the next seven prime numbers.

4   Here is a list of numbers.
     15, 20, 25, 30, 37, 39, 49, 69, 70, 71, 400, 450
     Write down:
     (a) the largest even number
     (b) the largest odd number
     (c) the largest prime number.

1.7 Factors and multiples

- A **factor** is a whole number which will divide into another whole number without a remainder.
  For example:
  1, 3, 5, 15 are all factors of 15 because they divide into 15 without a remainder.

- **Multiples** of 5 are made by multiplying the whole numbers 1, 2, 3 . . . by 5 like this:

$$\left. \begin{array}{l} 1 \times 5 = \ \mathbf{5} \\ 2 \times 5 = \mathbf{10} \\ 3 \times 5 = \mathbf{15} \end{array} \right\} \text{ These are multiples of 5.}$$

  Multiples of 7 are 7, 14, 21 . . .

Exercise 1K

1 Find one factor other than 1 of:
   (a) 9   (b) 24   (c) 32   (d) 55   (e) 108   (f) 625

2 Find all six factors of 12.

3 Find all the factors of:
   (a) 32   (b) 200   (c) 340   (d) 1000

4 Find three multiples of 9.

5 Find the nearest number to 100 that is a multiple of 9.

6 Find:
   (a) three multiples of 6 that are bigger than 50.
   (b) three multiples of 20 that are between 1000 and 2000.
   (c) three multiples of 15 that are bigger than 100.

7 Write down:
   (a) three numbers that have a factor of 8.
   (b) three numbers that have a factor of 150.
   (c) three numbers that only have odd number factors.

8 **(a)** Copy this number square:

10	20	30	40	50
60	70	80	90	100
110	120	130	140	150
160	170	180	190	200
210	220	230	240	250

(b) Draw a line — through any number with a factor of 3.
(c) Draw a line | through any number with a factor of 20.
(d) Draw a line \ through any multiples of 30.
(e) Draw a line / through any multiples of 90.
(f) Which number do all four lines pass through?

1.8 Squares and cubes

- A **square number** is the result of multiplying one number by itself.
  49 is a square number because $7 \times 7 = 49$
  Sometimes 7×7 is written as 7^2 (seven squared).

  This is a 3 by 3 square :

  $3 \times 3 = 3^2 = 9$
  is a square number.

- A **cube number** is the result of multiplying one number by itself, then multiplying by the number again.
  343 is a cube number because $7 \times 7 \times 7 = 343$
  Sometimes $7 \times 7 \times 7$ is written as 7^3 (seven cubed).

- $8 \times 8 = 64$
  8 is the **square root** of 64
  The square root sign $\sqrt{\ }$ is used like this:
  $\sqrt{64}$ means the square root of 64, so $\sqrt{64} = 8$
  $\sqrt{25} =$ so 5 is the square root of 25

Exercise 1L

1 Find:
(a) the next three square numbers after 1, 4, 9, —, —, —.
(b) the square numbers represented by:
    (i) 10^2 **(ii)** 20^2 **(iii)** 30^2
(c) the square number nearest to:
    (i) 80   **(ii)** 150   **(iii)** 200
(d) the next three cube numbers after 1, 8, 27, —, —, —.
(e) the cube numbers represented by:
    (i) 8^3 **(ii)** 10^3 **(iii)** 20^3
(f) the cube number nearest to:
    (i) 80   **(ii)** 150   **(iii)** 200

2 (a) Draw a number square from 1 to 100 on squared paper.
 (b) Draw a ○ round all the square numbers in the square.
 (c) Draw a — through all the cube numbers in the square.
 (d) Which two numbers are both square and cube numbers?

1.9 Negative numbers

The temperature here is 31 degrees below zero Celsius.

● We use negative numbers to represent quantities that are less than zero.

  −31 °C is 31 degrees below zero.

This thermometer is showing a temperature of −5 °C

The Dead Sea is the lowest place on Earth. It is 396 m below sea level.

−396 m is 396 m below sea level.

Exercise 1M

1 Write down the largest and the smallest number in each list.
(a) 5, –10, –3, 0, 4
(b) –7, –2, –9, –13, 0
(c) –3, 6, 13, –15, –6
(d) –13, –2, –20, –21, –5

2 Write the missing two numbers in each sequence.
(a) 4, 3, 2, 1, —, —, –2
(b) 10, 7, 4, 1, —, —, –8
(c) –13, –9, –5, –1, —, —, –13
(d) 13, 8, 3, –2, —, —, –17
(e) 21, 12, 3, –6, —, —, –33
(f) –13, –10, –7, –4, —, —, 5

3 Use this number line to find the number that is:
(a) 5 more than 2   (b) 4 more than –7
(c) 7 less than 6   (d) 2 less than –3
(e) 6 less than 0   (f) 10 more than –7
(g) 6 more than –6   (h) 4 less than –3
(i) 10 less than 5   (j) 1 more than –1

9
8
7
6
5
4
3
2
1
0
–1
–2
–3
–4
–5
–6
–7

4 What number is:
(a) 30 more than –70   (b) 50 less than –20
(c) 80 greater than –50   (d) 90 smaller than 60
(e) 130 smaller than –30   (f) 70 bigger than 200
(g) 170 bigger than –200   (h) 100 bigger than –100
(i) 140 more than –20   (j) 200 less than –200?

5 The table gives the highest and lowest temperatures in several cities during one year.

	New York	Brussels	Tripoli	Minsk	Canberra
Highest temperature	27 °C	32 °C	34 °C	28 °C	34 °C
Lowest temperature	–9 °C	–6 °C	8 °C	–21 °C	7 °C

(a) Which city recorded the lowest temperature?
(b) Which city recorded the biggest difference between its highest and lowest temperatures?
(c) Which city recorded the smallest difference between its highest and lowest temperatures?

6 The temperature of the fridge compartment of a fridge–freezer is set at 8 °C. The freezer compartment is set at –10 °C.
What is the difference between these temperature settings?

7 The deep freeze of a freezer shop should be set at –12 °C. It is set to –18 °C by mistake.
What is the difference between these temperature settings?

Summary of key points

1 Each digit in a number has a face value and a place value.

The face value of this digit is 3.

325

The place value of this digit is Hundred.

2 To round to the nearest 10 look at the digit in the Unit column:

- If it is less than 5 round down.
- If it is 5 or more round up.

3 To round to the nearest 100 look at the digit in the Tens column:

- If it is less than 5 round down.
- If it is 5 or more round up.

4 To round to the nearest 1000 look at the digit in the hundreds column:

- If it is less than 5 round down.
- If it is 5 or more round up.

5 Rounding is used to help you estimate an answer.

2 Algebra 1

2.1 Using letters to represent numbers

Algebra is the branch of mathematics in which letters are used to represent numbers.

This can help solve some mathematical problems.

 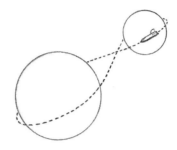

If you know how fast a cyclist is travelling you can use this algebra to work out how far she will get in a given time:

$$s = v \times t$$

(distance = velocity × time)

Very complicated algebra is used to calculate the right orbit for a spacecraft to visit the moon. Luckily you don't have to do this in your GCSE course!

You can use letters even when you do not know the number itself.

Example 1

Peter has some records. How many records has he got?

You do not know how many records Peter has, but using algebra you could say:

'Peter has x records.'

Example 2

If Peter buys 3 more records, how many will he have altogether?

x records and 3 records is $x + 3$ records.

Example 3

Ann used 6 thank-you cards to thank friends for her Birthday presents. How many thank-you cards has she got left?

You do not know how many thank-you cards she had to start with, but you can say she had y. After using 6 she will have $y - 6$ left.

Example 4

Yasmin has some sweets. So has Ali. How many sweets do they have altogether?

Use two different letters: x for Yasmin's sweets and y for Ali's.

Altogether they have $x + y$ sweets.

Exercise 2A

Use algebra to write:

1	3 more than a	**2**	x with 4 added
3	x more than 7	**4**	2 less than b
5	c with 3 taken away	**6**	p less than q
7	x more than y	**8**	4 together with a
9	$3b$ with 6 subtracted		

2.2 Adding with letters

In algebra you can add letters that are the same. For example:

$a + a$ can be written as $2a$ a means $1a$
$a + a + a$ can be written as $3a$ so $1a + 1a = 2a$

Exercise 2B

Write these in a shorter form. The first one is done for you:

1 $a + a + a + a + a + a = 6a$ **2** $p + p + p + p$

3 $b + b + b + b + b$ **4** $q + q + q + q + q + q$

5 $c + c$ **6** $n + n + n$

7 $w + w + w + w + w$ **8** $y + y + y + y + y$

9 $z + z + z + z + z + z + z$ **10** $a + a + a + a + a + a + a$

11 $b + b + b + b + b$ **12** $p + p + p + p + p + p + p + p$

Write these out in a longer form. The first one is done for you:

13 $4a = a + a + a + a$ **14** $2p$

15 $5p$ **16** $7a$ **17** $2y$ **18** $4q$ **19** $3c$

20 $5d$ **21** $10a$ **22** $5h$ **23** $6g$ **24** $4z$

2.3 Expressions and terms

■ **An algebraic expression is a collection of letters and symbols.** For example:

$$a + 3b - 2c \text{ is an \textbf{algebraic expression}}$$

These are each called **terms**.

Terms which use the same letter or arrangement of letters are called **like terms.**

a and $3a$ are like terms

$2g$ and $8g$ are like terms

Sometimes you can make algebraic expressions simpler by adding or subtracting like terms:

■ **You can combine like terms by adding them:**

$2a + 3a = 5a$

$3b + 4b + b = 8b$

■ **You can combine like terms by subtracting them:**

$5a - 3a = 2a$

$7a - a = 6a$ (Remember: this is $7a - 1a$)

Exercise 2C

Make these expressions simpler by adding or subtracting like terms:

1 $2a + 4a$ **2** $3b + 4b$ **3** $5c + 2c$

4 $5d - 3d$ **5** $7e - 3e$ **6** $5f - f$

7 $3a + 2a + 2a$ **8** $2a + 5a + a$ **9** $5c + 3c + 4c$

10 $6g + 7g + g$ **11** $7g - 3g$ **12** $9s - 6s$

13 $15q - q$ **14** $3p + 7p + 8p$ **15** $12p - 6p$

2.4 Collecting like terms

■ **You can simplify algebraic expressions by collecting like terms together.** For example:

$$2a - 4b + 3a + 5b$$

collect the
a terms $2a + 3a - 4b + 5b$ collect the
                                                                           b terms

combine the   combine the
a terms $5a + b$ *b* terms

Notice that the + or − sign is part of each term.
The minus sign is part of the term − 4*b*

Here are some more examples:

$3a + 5b + 3b + a$	simplifies to:	$4a + 8b$
$5p + 3q - 2p + q$	simplifies to:	$3p + 4q$
$5a + 7 - 3a - 4$	simplifies to:	$2a + 3$

Exercise 2D

Simplify these expressions by collecting like terms:

1 $3a + 4b + 4a + 2b$ **2** $6m + 5n + 3m + 2n$

3 $2p + 3q - p + 2q$ **4** $8e + 6c + 8e$

5 $5y + 7p - 3y + 5p$ **6** $2a + 8g + 3a + 5g - a$

7 $4k + 3q + 5k - 2q$ **8** $9d + 7f - 8d + 3f$

9 $5h + 8 - 2h + 2$ **10** $3f + 2f + 4e - 2e$

11 $7g + 8n - 3g - n$ **12** $5 + g + 2 + 3g - 3 - 2g$

13 $2a + 3a + 4a + 5a$ **14** $3b + b + 5b - 4b$

15 $7c + 8c - 5c - 6c$ **16** $5d + 4d - 3d + 6d - 7d$

17 $2a + 7b + 5a - 6b$ **18** $2c + 4b + 6c - 3b + 7b - 2c$

19 $3p + 2p - 4p + 3 - 2$ **20** $7y + 4z + 2y - 3z + 5y + 3z$

21 $12a - 7a + 9a - 2a + 5a$ **22** $3p + 4p + 5p - 8p - 4p$

23 $6s + 4s - 3s + 5s - 5s$ **24** $3a + 2 + 5a - 1 - 7a - 1$

2.5 Multiplying with letters and numbers

Remember $2a$ is $a + a$ and $3a$ is $a + a + a$, but:

$2a$ also means 2 lots of a or 2 multiplied by a or $2 \times a$

$3a$ means   3 lots of a or 3 multiplied by a or $3 \times a$

In algebra when you want to multiply two items you just write them next to each other like this:

$2 \times a$ is written $2a$ $c \times d$ is written cd

$a \times b$ is written ab $3 \times e \times f$ is written $3ef$

Don't forget that $12ab$ is $12 \times a \times b$ *not* $1 \times 2 \times a \times b$!

Exercise 2E

Use multiplication signs to write these expressions out in a longer form. The first one is done for you:

1 $pq = p \times q$ **2** rst **3** $2ef$ **4** $5abc$

5 $7klm$ **6** $9ab$ **7** $15abc$ **8** $3pqrs$

9 $16st$ **10** $6yz$ **11** $8defg$ **12** $20abcd$

Write these expressions in a simpler form. The first one is done:

13 $p \times q = pq$ **14** $e \times f \times g$ **15** $r \times s \times t$

16 $2 \times e \times f$ **17** $2 \times c \times d$ **18** $h \times d \times s$

19 $2 \times s \times f$ **20** $3 \times d \times e \times f$ **21** $4 \times p \times q$

22 $3 \times h \times j$ **23** $5 \times k \times v$ **24** $12 \times r \times s \times t$

2.6 Multiplying algebraic expressions

Sometimes you can simplify algebraic expressions, such as $2a \times 3b$, by multiplying them by each other:

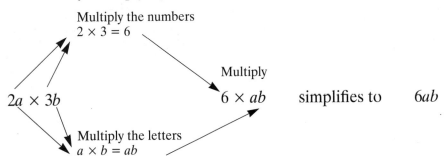

Multiply the numbers
$2 \times 3 = 6$

Multiply

$2a \times 3b$ $6 \times ab$ simplifies to $6ab$

Multiply the letters
$a \times b = ab$

Here are some more examples:

$5a \times 4b$ so $5 \times 4 = 20$
$a \times b = ab$ and $20 \times ab = 20ab$

$3p \times 4q$ so $3 \times 4 = 12$
$p \times q = pq$ and $12 \times pq = 12pq$

Exercise 2F

Simplify these expressions by multiplying them by each other.
The first one is done for you:

1 $2a \times 4b = 8ab$ **2** $3c \times 5d$ **3** $3p \times 4q$

4 $5s \times 4t$ **5** $6f \times 5g$ **6** $7p \times 4q$

7 $9m \times 4n$ **8** $3a \times 4b \times 2c$ **9** $3r \times 4s \times 2t$

10 $5p \times 4q$ **11** $2a \times 6b$ **12** $5p \times 4q \times 2r$

13 $3t \times 4s$ **14** $4p \times 7t$ **15** $9e \times 5c$

16 $8g \times 4q \times 2r$ **17** $4d \times 12r$ **18** $12s \times 5t$

19 $5y \times 6t$ **20** $2s \times 4t \times 5r$

2.7 Using powers to multiply letters

When you want to multiply two letters that are the same
together you can write them as powers:

	How you write it:	How you say it:	
$a \times a$	a^2	a to the power 2	usually called a squared
$a \times a \times a$	a^3	a to the power 3	usually called a cubed
$a \times a \times a \times a$	a^4	a to the power 4	often called a to the fourth
$a \times a \times a \times a \times a$	a^5	a to the power 5	often called a to the fifth

You can use powers for numbers too:

	How you write it:	How you say it:	
3×3	3^2	3 to the power 2	usually called 3 squared
$3 \times 3 \times 3$	3^3	3 to the power 3	usually called 3 cubed
$3 \times 3 \times 3 \times 3$	3^4	3 to the power 4	often called 3 to the fourth

Exercise 2G

1 Write these expressions in a simpler way using powers.
For example: $d \times d = d^2$
(a) $b \times b \times b$ (b) $p \times p$
(c) $r \times r \times r \times r \times r \times r \times r$ (d) $s \times s \times s \times s \times s$
(e) $q \times q \times q \times q$ (f) $c \times c \times c \times c \times c$

2 Simplify these expressions using powers:
(a) $a \times a \times a \times a$ (b) $s \times s \times s$
(c) $t \times t \times t \times t \times t \times t$ (d) $v \times v \times v$
(e) $f \times f \times f \times f \times f$ (f) $y \times y \times y \times y \times y$

3 Write out these expressions in full.
For example: $c^2 = c \times c$
(a) a^3 (b) a^4 (c) d^2 (d) e^5
(e) f^4 (f) p^5 (g) a^7 (h) s^2
(i) k^6 (j) n^3 (k) n^7 (l) a^{12}

4 Write in a simpler form:
(a) a to the power 5   (b) c to the power 6
(c) d squared   (d) e cubed
(e) f to the power 7

5 Find the values of these powers.
For example: $6^2 = 6 \times 6 = 36$
(a) 3^2 (b) 2^3 (c) 4^2 (d) 5^4
(e) 2^5 (f) 4^3 (g) 2^4 (h) 2^7
(i) 6^3 (j) 5^3 (k) 5^2 (l) 10^5

2.8 Putting in the punctuation

In maths brackets help show the order in which you should
carry out the operations $\div \times + -$ For example:

$$2 + (3 \times 4) \quad \text{is different from} \quad (2 + 3) \times 4$$

even though they both use the same numbers and the $+ \times$
symbols in the same order.

Always deal with the operations in brackets first.
Then $\div$ and $\times$. Then $+$ and $-$.

■ **BoDMAS is a made-up word to help you remember the
order of operations:**

BoDMAS

Brackets   of   Divide   Multiply   Add   Subtract

Here are some examples:

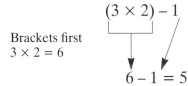

Brackets first
$3 \times 2 = 6$

Brackets first
$2 - 1 = 1$

This one has no Brackets or Divide, so start with Multiply, then Add, then Subtract.

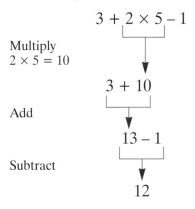

Multiply
$2 \times 5 = 10$

Add

Subtract

■ **When the signs are the same you do them in the order they appear.**

$16 \div 4 \div 2$
$= 4 \div 2$
$= \quad 2$

Exercise 2H

1 Use BoDMAS to help you find the value of these expressions:

(a) $5 + (3 + 1)$ (b) $5 - (3 + 1)$

(c) $5 \times (2 + 3)$ (d) $5 \times 2 + 3$

(e) $3 \times (4 + 3)$ (f) $3 \times 4 + 3$

(g) $20 \div 4 + 1$ (h) $20 \div (4 + 1)$

(i) $6 + 4 \div 2$ (j) $(6 + 4) \div 2$

(k) $24 \div (6 - 2)$ (l) $24 \div 6 - 2$

(m) $7 - (4 + 2)$ (n) $7 - 4 + 2$

(o) $(15 - 5) \times 4 \div (2 + 3) \times 2$

2 Make these expressions correct by replacing the • with $+$ or $-$ or $\times$ or $\div$ and using brackets if you need to. The first one is done for you:

(a) $4 \cdot 5 = 9$ becomes $4 + 5 = 9$ (b) $4 \cdot 5 = 20$

(c) $2 \cdot 3 \cdot 4 = 20$ (d) $3 \cdot 2 \cdot 5 = 5$

(e) $5 \cdot 2 \cdot 3 = 9$ (f) $5 \cdot 2 \cdot 3 = 30$

(g) $5 \cdot 4 \cdot 5 \cdot 2 = 27$ (h) $5 \cdot 4 \cdot 5 \cdot 2 = 23$

2.9 Using brackets in algebra

Brackets are often used in algebra. For example:

$2 \times (a + b)$ means add a to b *before* multiplying by 2

Usually this is written: $2(a + b)$ without the $\times$. This avoids confusion with the letter x which is used a lot in algebra.

$2(a + b)$ means $2 \times a + 2 \times b = 2a + 2b$

Working this out is called **expanding the brackets**. Actually the brackets disappear!

Here are some more examples of expanding the brackets:

$$3(b + c) = 3 \times b + 3 \times c = 3b + 3c$$
$$3(2a - b) = 3 \times 2a + 3 \times -b = 6a - 3b$$

Exercise 2I

Expand the brackets in these expressions.

1 $2(p + q)$	**2** $3(c + d)$	**3** $5(y - n)$
4 $3(t + u)$	**5** $7(2p + q)$	**6** $2(3a - 2b)$
7 $4(2a + b)$	**8** $3(a - 2b)$	**9** $3(4r - 5s)$
10 $10(a - 7b)$	**11** $4(6s + 4t)$	**12** $5(6p + 4q - 2r)$
13 $12(3a + 4b)$	**14** $7(4s - 5t)$	**15** $3(5a - 4b + 2c)$

Adding expressions with brackets

Example 5

Expand the brackets in the expression $2(a + 3b) + 5(2a - b)$.
Then collect like terms.

$$2\,(a + 3b) \quad + \quad 5\,(2a - b)$$

$$2 \times a + 2 \times 3b \quad + \quad 5 \times 2a + 5 \times -b$$

$$2a + 6b \quad + \quad 10a - 5b$$

Collect the a terms
$2a + 10a = 12a$

Collect the b terms
$6b - 5b = 1b = b$

$$12a \quad + \quad b$$

Exercise 2J

Expand the brackets in these expressions and then collect like terms.

1 $2(a + b) + 3(a + b)$

2 $3(a - 2b) + 4(2a + 3b)$

3 $5(2a - b) + 4(2a + b)$

4 $3(p + q) + 4(p + q)$

5 $4(5a + c) + 2(3a - c)$

6 $3(p + 2q) + 3(5p - 2q)$

7 $5(4t - 3s) + 8(3t + 2s)$

8 $7(2d + 3e) + 6(2e - 2d)$

9 $5(3z + b) + 4(b - 2z)$

10 $2(a + b + 2c) + 3(2a + 3b - c)$

11 $3(4a - 2b) + 5(a + b)$

12 $6(p + 2q + 3r) + 2(3p - 4q - 9r)$

13 $4(3a + 5b) + 5(2a - 4b)$

14 $5(5g + 4h) + 4(h - 5g)$

15 $2(a + 2b - 3c) + 3(5a - b + 4c) + 4(a + b + c)$

> **Remember:**
> $4a$ means $a + a + a + a$
> and $4 \times a$
> $3ab$ means $3 \times a \times b$
> p^4 means $p \times p \times p \times p$
> $3(c + d)$ means $3c + 3d$

Subtracting expressions with brackets

Example 6

Expand the brackets in the expression $15 - (6 + 2)$

Remember: the minus sign belongs with the term so:

$15 - (6 + 2)$ means 15 $+$ $-1 \times (6 + 2)$

$= 15 - 6 - 2$

$= 7$

Example 7

Expand $-(a + b)$

$-(a + b)$ means $-1 \times (a + b)$

$= -a - b$

$-1 \times b = -b$

Example 8

Expand $-(a - b)$

$-(a - b)$ means $-1 \times (a - b)$

$= -a + b$

$-1 \times -b = +b$

> **Remember:**
> When you multiply:
> like signs give +
> $2 \times 3 = 6$
> $-2 \times -3 = 6$
> unlike signs give −
> $2 \times -3 = -6$
> $-2 \times 3 = -6$

Exercise 2K

1 Work out:
   (a) $10 - (3 + 2)$ **(b)** $20 - (5 - 2)$ **(c)** $12 - (6 - 4)$
   (d) $10 - (3 \times 2)$ **(e)** $12 - (5 + 3)$ **(f)** $6 - (7 - 5)$
   (g) $14 - (8 + 6)$ **(h)** $15 - (3 - 2)$

2 Remove the bracket in these expressions:
   (a) $-(p + q)$ **(b)** $-(p - q)$ **(c)** $-(a + b + c)$
   (d) $-(a + b - c)$ **(e)** $-(r + s)$ **(f)** $-(r - s)$
   (g) $-(p + q - r)$ **(h)** $-(p - q + r)$

Example 9

Write $3a + 2b - (a + b)$ as simply as possible.

$$3a + 2b - (a + b) \quad = 3a + 2b - a - b$$
$$= 2a + b$$

Exercise 2L

Write these expressions as simply as possible:

1 $4a + 3b - (a + b)$

2 $5p + 2q - (p + q)$

3 $3(2a + 4) - (3a + 5)$

4 $2y - 3z - (y + z)$

5 $3(3r + 4s) - 2(r + s)$

6 $3(2a + 5) - 2(3a + 4)$

7 $5(2s + 3t) - 4(s + 2t)$

8 $4(3a + b) - 3(2a + 5b)$

9 $2(m + 3n) - (2m + n)$

10 $5(8h - 3k) - 4(7h + 2k)$

11 $3(c + 2d) - 2(c + 3d)$

12 $4a - (3a + 5b)$

Example 10

Write $3a + 2b - 2(a - b)$ as simply as possible. Watch out for the $-$ sign *inside* the bracket.

Multiplying gives
$-2 \times -b = +2b$

$$3a + 2b - 2(a - b) \quad = 3a + 2b - 2a + 2b$$
$$= a + 4b$$

Exercise 2M

Simplify these expressions. They *all* have – signs inside brackets.

1 $4a + 3b - (a - b)$ **2** $5p + 2q - (p - q)$

3 $3(2a + 4) - (3a - 5)$ **4** $2y - 3z - (y - z)$

5 $3(3r + 4s) - 2(r - s)$ **6** $3(2a + 5) - 2(3a - 4)$

7 $5(2s + 3t) - 4(s - 2t)$ **8** $4(3a + b) - 3(2a - 5b)$

9 $2(m + 3n) - (2m - n)$ **10** $5(8h - 3k) - 4(7h - 2k)$

11 $3(c + 2d) - 2(c - 3d)$ **12** $4a - (3a - 5b)$

Exercise 2N: Mixed questions

Simplify these expressions as much as you can:

1 $a + a + a + a + a$ **2** $a \times a \times a \times a \times a \times a$

3 $p + p + p + p + p + p$ **4** $p \times p \times p \times p \times p$

5 $2p + 4p + 5p$ **6** $8k - 4k + 3k$

7 $9s - 3s + 5s$ **8** $6t + 8t - t$

9 $3d - 5d$ **10** $4j - 7j$

11 $2(a + b)$ **12** $5(3p - q)$

13 $4(s + 2t)$ **14** $4(9p - 2q + 5r)$

15 $2(4m + 2n) + 3(5m + 3n)$ **16** $3(4s + 2t) + 2(3s - 2t)$

17 $3(2a - 5b) + 2(3a - 4b)$ **18** $5(2p + 3d) - 2(3p + 2d)$

19 $5(3a - 2b) - 2(3a - 4b)$

20 $2(3a - 4b) + 2(a + 4b) - 4(2a - b)$

21 $3(2t - 50) + 2(3t + 50) - t + 20$

22 $5(3p - 2q) - 4(3p - q) + 2(p - 3q)$

23 $2(5m + 3n) - 3(2m - n) - 4(m + n)$

24 $3(3a - 4b) + 2(4a + b) + 4(2a - 3b)$

25 $5(2b - 3a) - 3(2a + 3b) - 4(2b - 5a)$

2.10 Number patterns

Sometimes you will need to find the missing numbers in a number pattern like this one:

2, 4, 6, 8, 10, —, —, 16, 18

Algebra can help you do this. But first let's explore some number patterns.

2, 4, 6, 8, 10, —, —, 16, 18

The two missing numbers are 12 and 14.

The rule for this pattern is: **add 2 each time**. This pattern is also the two times table, and all the members are multiples of 2.

The rule for this pattern is: **add 4 each time**.

0, 4, 8, 12, 16, —, —, 28, 32

The two missing numbers are 20 and 24.

Exercise 20

Find the two missing numbers in these number patterns. Write down the rule for each pattern too.

1 3, 6, 9, —, —, 18, 21

2 5, 10, 15, 20, —, —, 35, 40

3 1, 2, 3, 4, —, —, 7, 8

4 7, 14, 21, 28, —, —, 49, 56

5 0, 6, 12, —, —, 30, 36

6 10, 20, 30, —, —, 60, 70

7 5, 7, 9, 11, —, —, 17, 19

8 4, 7, 10, 13, —, —, 22, 25

9 3, 8, 13, 18, —, —, 33, 38

10 1, 5, 9, 13, —, —, 25, 29

Smaller and smaller

Sometimes the numbers in a pattern get smaller each time.
The rule for this pattern is: **take away 2 each time**.

42, 36, 30, —, —, 12

The rule for this pattern is — I eat six of them each time!

18, 16, 14, 12, —, —, 6, 4, 2, 0

The missing numbers are 10 and 8.

Exercise 2P

Find the two missing numbers in these number patterns. Write
down the rule for each pattern too.

1 21, 18, 15, 12, —, —, 3   **2** 24, 20, 16, —, —, 4, 0

3 30, 25, 20, —, —, 5, 0   **4** 49, 42, 35, 28, —, —, 7

5 28, 25, 22, 19, 16, —, —, 7   **6** 37, 32, 27, 22, —, —, 7

7 19, 17, 15, —, —, 9, 7   **8** 25, 21, 17, —, —, 5, 1

9 33, 28, 23, —, —, 8, 3   **10** 45, 38, 31, 24, —, —, 3

Larger and larger

Example 11

Find the missing numbers in this number pattern:

1, 2, 4, 8, —, —, 64, 128

The missing numbers are 16 and 32.

The rule for this pattern is: **multiply by 2 each time.**

The numbers in the pattern are also all powers of 2:

1, 2, 4, 8, 16, 32, 64, 128

$$2 = 2^1$$
$$2 \times 2 = 2^2$$
$$2 \times 2 \times 2 = 2^3$$

Exercise 2Q

Find the missing numbers in these number patterns. Write
down the rule for each pattern too.

1 1, 3, 9, —, —, 243   **2** 1, 4, 16, —, 256

3 1, —, 25, 125, —, 3125   **4** 1, 10, 100, —, —, 100 000

5 3, 6, 12, —, —, 96   **6** 2, 6, 18, —, —, 486

7 2, 8, 32, —, —, 2048   **8** 2, 20, 200, —, —, 200 000

9 2, 10, 50, —, 1250   **10** 3, 15, 75, —, 1875

Example 12

Find the missing number in this number pattern:

243, 81, 27, —, 3, 1

The missing number is 9.

The rule for this pattern is: **divide by 3 each time**.

The numbers in the pattern are also all powers of 3:

$$243 = 3 \times 3 \times 3 \times 3 \times 3 = 3^5$$
$$81 = 3 \times 3 \times 3 \times 3 = 3^4$$
$$27 = 3 \times 3 \times 3 = 3^3$$
$$9 = 3 \times 3 = 3^2$$
$$3 = 3 = 3^1$$

Exercise 2R

Find the missing numbers in these number patterns.

1 128, 64, 32, —, 8, 4, —, 1

2 256, 64, —, 4, 1

3 100 000, 10 000, —, —, 10

4 625, 125, —, 5, 1

5 96, 48, 24, —, —, 3

6 486, 162, 54, —, —, 2

7 2048, 512, 128, —, —, 2

8 200 000, 20 000, 2000, —, —, 2

9 1250, 250, 50, —, 2

10 1875, 375, 75, —, 3

2.11 Finding the rule for a number pattern

Here are some more difficult number patterns with some hints on how to find their rules:

Example 13

Pattern: 1, 4, 7, 10, 13, ...

Differences between each pair of numbers: + 3 + 3 + 3 + 3 +3

The rule is: **add 3 each time**.
So the next number is 16.

Example 14

Pattern: 1,   4,   9,   16,   25,   . . .

Difference: + 3   + 5   + 7   + 9

The rule is: **add the next odd number each time.**
The *difference* goes up by 2 each time.

Example 15

Pattern: 1,   1,   2,   3,   5,   8,   13,   . . .

Difference: + 0   + 1   + 1   + 2   + 3   + 5

The rule is: **add the previous two numbers each time.**
The *difference has the same pattern* as the pattern itself.

Exercise 2S

Write out each pattern in the same way as Examples 13, 14 and 15. Find the differences and rule for each one, and the next number.

1 1, 3, 5, 7, 9, . . .   **2** 1, 5, 9, 13, 17, . . .

3 1, 8, 27, 64, 125, . . .   **4** 2, 4, 8, 10, 12, . . .

5 2, 5, 8, 11, 14, . . .   **6** 3, 7, 11, 15, 19, . . .

7 2, 2, 4, 6, 10, 16, . . .   **8** 3, 3, 6, 9, 15, 24, . . .

9 3, 5, 7, 9, 11, 13, . . .   **10** 4, 7, 10, 13, 16, . . .

11 2, 7, 12, 17, 22, . . .   **12** 3, 8, 13, 18, 23, . . .

2.12 Using algebra to write the rule for a number pattern

You can use algebra to write a rule to find any number in a pattern.

Each number in a pattern is called a **term**:

      2,   4,   6,   8,   10, ...

This is the **first term**, or term number 1.   The **fourth term**, or term number 4.   The nth number in the pattern is called the **nth term** or term number n.

> **The term: term**
> **Term** is also used for the parts of an algebraic expression. There is more about this on page 24.

To find the 20th number in a pattern you need a rule to find the **20th term**.

Start by writing the pattern next to the term numbers in a table:

+2

Pattern			2	4	6	8	10	...
Term number			1	2	3	4	5	

This pattern is easy to spot. It is the two times table. The rule for finding the *next* number is: add 2 each time.

The rule to find any term is: **multiply 2 by the term number.** So the **third term** should be:

term number × 2

$3 \times 2 = 6$

The ***n*th term** will be:

term number × 2

$n \times 2 = 2n$

The general rule for the *n*th term of this pattern is:
*n*th term = $2n$

Example 16

Find the general rule for the *n*th term in this pattern:
1, 4, 7, 10, 13, ...

Use your rule to find the 20th term.

Write the pattern next to the term numbers in a table:

+ 3

Pattern			1	4	7	10	13	...
Term number			1	2	3	4	5	

The rule for finding the *next* number is: add 3 each time.

The rule to find any term is: **multiply 3 by the term number then take away 2.**

So the fourth term should be:

(term number × 3) – 2

$(4 \times 3) - 2 = 10$

The *n*th term will be:

$(n \times 3) - 2$ which simplifies to: $3n - 2$

So the general rule for the *n*th term is: *n*th term = $3n - 2$

The 20th term will be: $(3 \times 20) - 2 = 58$

Exercise 2T

Write each pattern in a table in the same way as Example 16.
Find the general rule for the nth term. Then use your rule to
find the 20th term.

1 3, 6, 9, 12, 15, 18, 21, . . .   **2** 5, 10, 15, 20, 25, 30, 35, 40, . . .

3 1, 2, 3, 4, 5, 6, 7, 8, . . .   **4** 7, 14, 21, 28, 35, 42, 49, 56, . . .

5 0, 6, 12, 18, 24, 30, 36, . . .   **6** 10, 20, 30, 40, 50, 60, 70, . . .

7 5, 7, 9, 11, 13, 15, 17, 19, . . .   **8** 4, 7, 10, 13, 16, 19, 22, 25, . . .

9 3, 8, 13, 18, 23, 28, 33, 38, . . .   **10** 1, 5, 9, 13, 17, 21, 25, 29, . . .

Summary of key points

1 An algebraic expression is a collection of letters and
symbols:

$$a + 3b - 2c \quad \text{is an algebraic expression}$$

These are each called terms.

2 You can combine like terms by adding or subtracting
them:

$2a + 3a = 5a$ and $3b + 4b - b = 6b$

3 You can simplify algebraic expressions by collecting
like terms together:

$2a - 4b + 3a + 5b$ simplifies to: $5a + b$

4 BoDMAS is a made-up word to help you remember
the order of operations:

BoDMAS

Brackets of Divide Multiply Add Subtract

5 When the signs are the same you can do them in the
order they appear.

3 Angles and turning

3.1 Turning

The big wheel is turning . . .

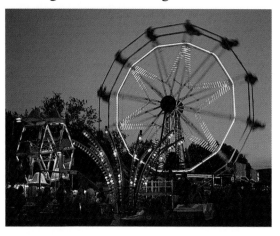

You can show clockwise ↻ and anticlockwise ↺ turns like this:

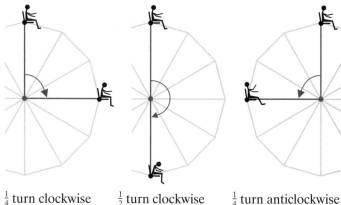

$\frac{1}{4}$ turn clockwise $\frac{1}{2}$ turn clockwise $\frac{1}{4}$ turn anticlockwise

Example 1

An aeroplane is flying North. In which direction will it be flying after:
(a) a $\frac{1}{4}$ turn clockwise
(b) a $\frac{1}{2}$ turn clockwise
(c) a $\frac{1}{4}$ turn anticlockwise?

(a) a $\frac{1}{4}$ turn clockwise   (b) a $\frac{1}{2}$ turn clockwise   (c) a $\frac{1}{4}$ turn anticlockwise

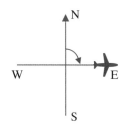

It will be flying East.

It will be flying South.

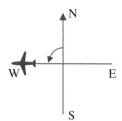

It will be flying West.

Exercise 3A

1   Write down which of these are turning movements:
    (a) a door opening   **(b)** a ship changing direction
    (c) opening a book   **(d)** a person crossing the road
    (e) a skier skiing down a mountain
    (f) a weather vane as the wind changes

2   Lisa is facing East. Which way will she be facing after:

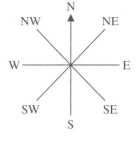

    (a) a quarter turn clockwise

    (b) a $\frac{1}{4}$ turn anticlockwise

    (c) a $\frac{1}{2}$ turn clockwise

    (d) a $\frac{1}{2}$ turn anticlockwise?

3   Ajay is walking South-West. Which direction is he walking in after:

    (a) a $\frac{1}{4}$ turn clockwise

    (b) a half turn

    (c) a $\frac{1}{4}$ turn anticlockwise?

4   How much does the hour hand of a clock turn between:

    (a) 3pm and 6pm   **(b)** 1pm and 7pm

    (c) 11am and 2pm?

3.2 Measuring angles

■ **An angle is a measure of *turn*. It is a change of direction. There is no change of position.**

■ **An angle which is a $\frac{1}{4}$ turn is called a right angle.**

■ **An angle which is less than a $\frac{1}{4}$ turn is called an acute angle.**

■ **An angle which is more than a $\frac{1}{4}$ turn is called an obtuse angle.**

Example 2

Name the different types of angles in this diagram:

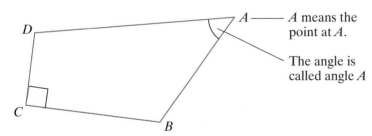

A —— A means the point at A.

The angle is called angle A

Angle A is less than a $\frac{1}{4}$ turn. It is an **acute angle**.

Angle B is more than a $\frac{1}{4}$ turn. It is an **obtuse angle**.

Angle C is a quarter turn. It is a **right angle**.

Angle D is more than a $\frac{1}{4}$ turn. It is an **obtuse angle**.

Measuring angles in degrees

So far angles have been described as $\frac{1}{4}$ and $\frac{1}{2}$ turns. You will need to measure smaller and larger turns than these. The unit for measuring angles is called a **degree**.

90° is a quarter turn.

180° is a half turn.

■ **There are 360 degrees in a full turn.**
The sign for a degree is °.

Exercise 3B

In questions **1–6** write down whether the marked angles are acute, obtuse or right angles.

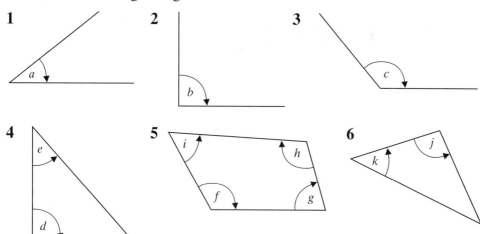

In questions 7–12 estimate the size of the marked angle in degrees.

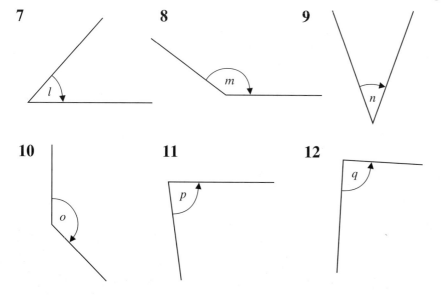

3.3 Naming angles

You can use letters to name the sides and angles of shapes.
This shape is named *ABCD* using the letters for the corners
and going round clockwise:

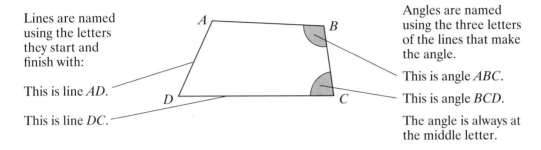

Lines are named
using the letters
they start and
finish with:

This is line *AD*.

This is line *DC*.

Angles are named
using the three letters
of the lines that make
the angle.

This is angle *ABC*.

This is angle *BCD*.

The angle is always at
the middle letter.

Exercise 3C

Use letters to identify the lines and shaded angles in each
diagram:

3.4 Measuring angles with a protractor

You can use a **protractor** to measure angles accurately.

Protractor

Use the inside
scale to measure
anticlockwise
turns.

Place the cross
at the point of
the angle you
are measuring.

Use the outside
scale to measure
clockwise turns.

Angle measurer

You can use an angle measurer
instead of a protractor.

The cross
is at the centre.

Example 3

Use a protractor to measure the angle *CBA*.

Here the lines of angle *CBA* are long enough to reach the outer edge of the protractor.

The angle is 57°.

Example 4

Use a protractor to measure the angle *BCD*.

Use the inside scale to measure Angle *BCD*.

When the line is too short to reach the scale, extend it with a straight edge like this piece of paper.

The angle is 103°.

Exercise 3D

Measure and name these angles:

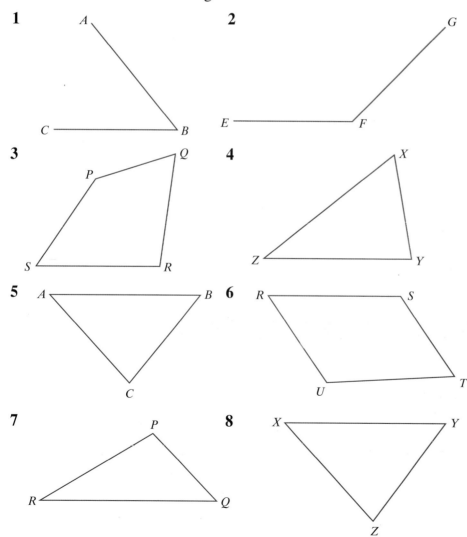

1

2

3

4

5

6

7

8

3.5 Drawing angles

You need to be able to draw angles which are accurate to within two degrees.

Example 5

Draw these two angles on a line DE which is 8 cm long:

(a) a clockwise angle
$DEF = 79°$

(b) an anticlockwise angle
$EDC = 123°$

(a) Drawing angle DEF:

Draw DE 8 cm long.

Put the protractor cross at E. Mark the point F at a clockwise turn of 79°.

Join the points E and F to give the angle DEF.

(b) Drawing angle EDC:

 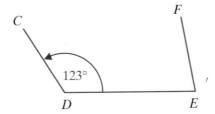

Put the protractor cross at D. Mark the point C at an anticlockwise turn of 123°.

Join the points D and C to give the angle EDC.

Exercise 3E

You need a protractor, ruler and pencil.

1   Draw and label these angles:
    (a) $ABC = 40°$ (b) $DEF = 65°$ (c) $GHK = 125°$
    (d) $LMN = 34°$ (e) $OPQ = 136°$ (f) $RST = 162°$
    (g) $UVW = 78°$ (h) $XYZ = 97°$

2 Make accurate drawings of these diagrams.

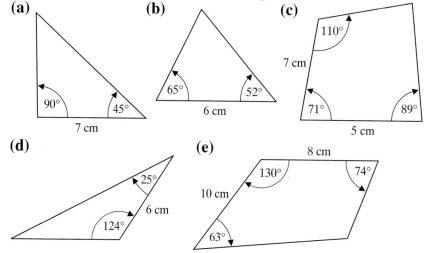

(a) **(b)** **(c)**

(d) **(e)**

3.6 Angles on a straight line

Here are two angles *ABC* and *CBD*.   Joined together they make the angle *ABD* which is a straight line.

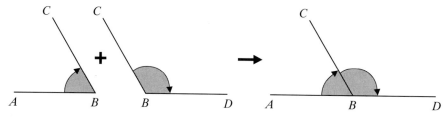

These two angles add up to 180°:

angle *ABC* + angle *CBD* = 180°

■ **The angles on a straight line add up to 180°.**

Example 6

(a)   What size is angle *a*?   (b)   What size is angle *b*?

    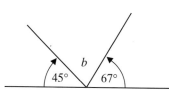

The angles make a straight line so:

$58 + a = 180$

$a = 180 - 58 = 122°$

The 3 angles make a straight line so:

$45 + b + 67 = 180$

$b = 180 - 45 - 67 = 68°$

This can also be written
$b = 180 - (45 + 67) = 68°$

Exercise 3F

In each question find the value of the letter.

1

2

3

4

5

6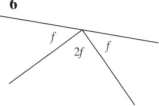

3.7 Angles meeting at a point

■ **The angles at a point add up to 360°.**

■ **Where two straight lines cross, the opposite angles are equal. They are called vertically opposite angles.**

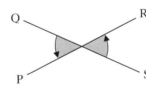

The shaded angles opposite each other are the same.

To see why, imagine that line *QS* has turned anticlockwise to give line *PR*. Both 'ends' of the line have moved through the same angle.

Example 7

Find all the angles in this diagram. Give reasons for your answers.

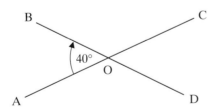

Angle $AOB = 40°$

So angle $COD = 40°$ (vertically opposite angle AOB)

Angle $AOD = 180 - 40 = 140°$ (the angles make a straight line)

So angle $BOC = 140°$ (vertically opposite angle AOD)

Give reasons for your answers when you can.

Exercise 3G

Find the angles represented by letters in these questions:

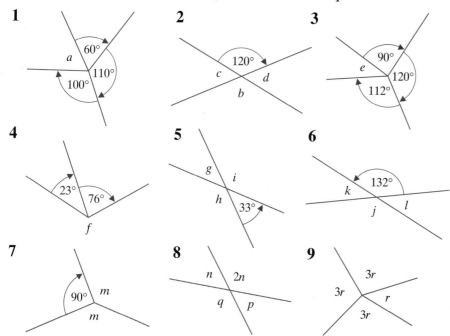

1   **2**   **3**

4   **5**   **6**

7   **8**   **9**

3.8 Sums of angles for triangles and quadrilaterals

■ **The interior angles of a triangle always add up to 180°.**

You can see this by checking that the angles in these triangles add up to 180°.

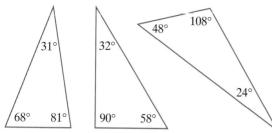

Another way to see this is to cut out a triangle and tear the corners off like this:

Tear these corners off.

Put three corners together. They make a straight line which is an angle of 180°.

■ **The interior angles of a quadrilateral (a four-sided shape) always add up to 360°.**

You can see this by measuring the angles . . .

. . . or by dividing the quadrilateral into two triangles . . .

The anges of the two triangles add up to:

180° + 180° = 360°

. . . or by tearing off the four corners:

Put the angles together. They make a full turn of 360°.

Example 8

(a) Work out the missing angle in this triangle.

(b) Find the missing angle of this quadrilateral.

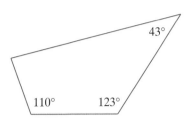

(a) Two of the angles add up to 130°. The third angle must be

$180° - 130° = 50°$.

(b) The 3 angles marked add up to 276°. So the missing angle must be

$360° - 276° = 84°$.

Exercise 3H

Work out the missing angles in these triangles and quadrilaterals.

1

2

3

4

5

6

7

8

9

3.9 Parallel lines

The distance between the two edges of a ruler is the same all the way along it. Similarly the distance between the two rails of a train track is the same wherever it is measured.

■ **Lines which remain the same distance apart are called** *parallel lines*. **On diagrams this is shown by marking the parallel sides with arrows.**

If there is a second pair of parallel lines in one diagram these are marked with double arrows.

Exercise 3I

1 Find and name as many pairs of parallel lines as you can in this diagram.

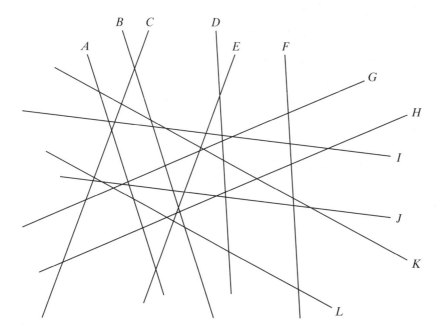

2 Here is the logo of the 'Flying A' pizza company.
On a copy of the drawing mark:
   (a) a right angle with an R
   (b) two parallel lines each with a P
   (c) an obtuse angle with an O.

(L)

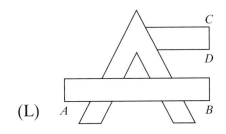

Summary of key points

1 An angle is a measure of turn. It is a change of direction. There is no change of position.

2 An angle which is a $\frac{1}{4}$ turn is called a right angle.

3 An angle which is less than a $\frac{1}{4}$ turn is called an acute angle.

4 An angle which is more than a $\frac{1}{4}$ turn is called an obtuse angle.

5 There are 360 degrees in a full turn.
The sign for a degree is °.

6 The angles on a straight line add up to 180°.

7 The angles at a point add up to 360°.

8 When two straight lines cross, the opposite angles are equal. They are called vertically opposite angles.

9 The interior angles of a triangle always add up to 180°.

10 The interior angles of a quadrilateral always add up to 360°.

11 Lines which remain the same distance apart are called parallel lines.
On diagrams this is shown by marking the parallel sides with arrows.

4 Fractions

4.1 Fractions from pictures

All these things can be divided into parts called **fractions**:

This football pitch has two halves.

One part is **one half** or $\frac{1}{2}$ of the pitch.

This computer disc has eight sectors.

One part is **one eighth** or $\frac{1}{8}$ of the disc.

This chessboard has 64 small squares.

One part is **one sixty fourth** or $\frac{1}{64}$ of the board.

Using numbers to represent fractions

I am going to eat three quarters or $\frac{3}{4}$ of this cake.

- The top number shows how many parts I will eat.

  The top number is called the **numerator**.

  $$\frac{3}{4}$$

  The bottom number shows how many parts the cake is divided into.

  The bottom number is called the **denominator**.

Two thirds or $\frac{2}{3}$ of these parking spaces are occupied.

Two spaces have cars in them.

The car park is divided into three spaces.

$$\frac{2}{3}$$

Exercise 4A

1   Copy these shapes into a table like this. The first one is done for you.

Shape	Fraction shaded	Fraction not shaded
◐	$\frac{1}{2}$	$\frac{1}{2}$

2 Make four copies of this shape. Shade them to show these fractions:

(a) $\frac{1}{16}$ (b) $\frac{3}{16}$ (c) $\frac{8}{16}$ (d) $\frac{16}{16}$

3 Make three copies of this shape. Shade them to show these fractions:

(a) $\frac{1}{6}$ (b) $\frac{3}{6}$ (c) $\frac{1}{2}$

4.2 Fractions from words

Sometimes you will need to use fractions to solve problems given in words.

Example 1

John has a collection of 1000 stamps. 113 are British stamps. The others are foreign.

What fraction of John's collection is:

(a) British (b) foreign?

(a) 113 of the 1000 stamps are British.

The fraction is: $\frac{113}{1000}$

(b) 1000 – 113 = 887 stamps are foreign.

The fraction is: $\frac{887}{1000}$

Exercise 4B

1 There are 28 people on a bus. 13 are female and 15 are male. What fraction of the people are:
(a) male (b) female?

2 Flora has 28 heavy metal CDs and 47 rock and roll CDs.
(a) How many CDs does she have altogether?
(b) What fraction of her collection is heavy metal?
(c) What fraction of her collection is rock and roll?

3 A transport company has a fleet of 51 vehicles. 37 are lorries, 10 are vans and 4 are cars.
What fraction of the fleet is:
(a) lorries (b) vans (c) cars?

4 A plumber's weekly earnings are £217 per week. £198 is basic pay and £19 is bonus pay.
What fraction of weekly earnings is:
(a) basic pay   (b) bonus pay?

5 At a dog show the total entry was 7 Alsatians, 3 Corgis, 5 Spaniels and 1 Labrador.
(a) How many dogs were entered?
What fraction of the entries were:
(b) Alsatians   (c) Corgis   (d) Spaniels   (e) Labradors?

6 An electrical superstore sold 5 CD players, 6 cassette players, 4 refrigerators and 2 deep freezers.
(a) How many items were sold altogether?
What fraction of the items sold were:
(b) CD players   (c) cassette players   (d) refrigerators   (e) deep freezers?

7 A taxi driver works 11 hours a day. She spends 6 hours driving, 4 hours waiting for passengers and 1 hour on paperwork.
What fraction of her day is spent:
(a) driving   (b) waiting   (c) on paperwork?

4.3 Improper fractions and mixed numbers

These fractions are **top heavy**:

$\frac{11}{9}$ is top heavy because 11 is greater than 9

$\frac{18}{5}$ is top heavy because 18 is greater than 5

■ **Top heavy fractions are also called improper fractions.**

■ **An improper fraction can also be written as a mixed number – a mixture of a whole number and a fraction.**

improper fraction $\frac{11}{9} = \frac{9}{9} + \frac{2}{9} = 1\frac{2}{9}$ mixed number

YOU SAY THIS :
"9 GOES INTO 11
ONE REMAINDER
2 OVER 9"

■ **A mixed number can also be written as an improper fraction:**

mixed number $1\frac{3}{11} = \frac{14}{11}$ improper fraction

Here is how to do this for $1\frac{3}{11}$. Change the mixed number to elevenths.

1 can be written $\frac{11}{11}$ So: $1\frac{3}{11} = \frac{11}{11} + \frac{3}{11} = \frac{14}{11}$

Here is how to write $5\frac{3}{7}$ as an improper fraction. Change the mixed number to sevenths.

5 can be written $\frac{5\times7}{7} = \frac{35}{7}$ So: $5\frac{3}{7} = \frac{35}{7} + \frac{3}{7} = \frac{38}{7}$

Exercise 4C

1 Change these improper fractions to mixed numbers.

(a) $\frac{5}{2}$ (b) $\frac{7}{4}$ (c) $\frac{9}{7}$ (d) $\frac{11}{8}$

(e) $\frac{9}{8}$ (f) $\frac{16}{5}$ (g) $\frac{23}{10}$ (h) $\frac{24}{5}$

(i) $\frac{16}{7}$ (j) $\frac{12}{5}$ (k) $\frac{20}{3}$ (l) $\frac{16}{9}$

(m) $\frac{39}{4}$ (n) $\frac{27}{5}$ (p) $\frac{26}{9}$ (q) $\frac{17}{10}$

2 Change these mixed numbers to improper fractions.

(a) $1\frac{1}{2}$ (b) $5\frac{1}{2}$ (c) $2\frac{3}{4}$ (d) $1\frac{2}{3}$

(e) $3\frac{1}{4}$ (f) $4\frac{2}{5}$ (g) $3\frac{7}{10}$ (h) $5\frac{1}{5}$

(i) $7\frac{3}{4}$ (j) $2\frac{1}{4}$ (k) $1\frac{9}{10}$ (l) $9\frac{1}{3}$

(m) $2\frac{5}{6}$ (n) $5\frac{3}{8}$ (p) $3\frac{5}{8}$ (q) $1\frac{9}{100}$

4.4 Simplifying fractions

■ **Fractions can be simplified if the numerator (top) and denominator (bottom) have a common factor.** For example:

$$\frac{4}{8}$$

The numerator will divide by 4

The denominator will divide by 4

These are equivalent fractions:

$\frac{4}{8}$

$\frac{1}{2}$

$\frac{4}{8}$ 4 divided by 4 is 1 $\frac{1}{2}$ so $\frac{4}{8}$ can be simplified to $\frac{1}{2}$

8 divided by 4 is 2

$\frac{4}{8}$ and $\frac{1}{2}$ are **equivalent fractions**. They represent the same value. To simplify a fraction you find an equivalent fraction that has smaller numbers on the top and bottom.

Example 2

Simplify $\frac{9}{15}$ by finding a common factor.

3 is a common factor of 9 and 15.

$\frac{9}{15}$ 9 divided by 3 is 3 $\frac{3}{5}$

15 divided by 3 is 5

Factors of 9 are: 1, 3, 9
Factors of 15 are: 1, 3, 5, 15

3 is a common factor

$\frac{9}{15}$ is the same as $\frac{3}{5}$

Example 3

Simplify $\frac{24}{30}$ by finding a common factor.

3 is a common factor of 24 and 30.

$$\frac{24}{30} \quad \boxed{\begin{array}{l} \text{24 divided by 3 is 8} \\ \text{30 divided by 3 is 10} \end{array}} \quad \frac{8}{10}$$

$\frac{8}{10}$ can also be simplified. 2 is a common factor of 8 and 10.

$$\frac{8}{10} \quad \boxed{\begin{array}{l} \text{8 divided by 2 is 4} \\ \text{10 divided by 2 is 5} \end{array}} \quad \frac{4}{5}$$

$\frac{4}{5}$ cannot be simplified any more. This fraction is in its **simplest form**.

Exercise 4D

Simplify these fractions by finding common factors:

1   (a) $\frac{4}{6}$ (b) $\frac{3}{6}$ (c) $\frac{2}{4}$ (d) $\frac{3}{9}$
    (e) $\frac{4}{10}$ (f) $\frac{8}{12}$ (g) $\frac{14}{21}$ (h) $\frac{15}{20}$
    (i) $\frac{14}{22}$ (j) $\frac{24}{28}$ (k) $\frac{27}{36}$ (l) $\frac{25}{30}$

2   Copy these shapes into a table like this.
    For each shape use two **equivalent fractions** to describe
    how much is shaded.
    The first one is done for you.

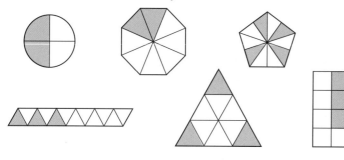

Shape	Fraction	Fraction
	$\frac{2}{4}$	$\frac{1}{2}$

In questions **3**, **4** and **5** write your answers as fractions in their simplest form.

3   A car salesman sold 6 new cars and 15 secondhand cars.
    What fraction of the cars was:
    (a) new   (b) secondhand?

4   Sîan has collected autographs from:
    16 pop stars   28 footballers   12 athletes
    What fraction of her autographs are:
    (a) pop stars'   (b) footballers'   (c) athletes'?

5 Here are Form 11B's traffic survey results:
What fraction of the vehicles were:
(a) Private cars   (b) Vans
(c) Lorries   (d) Buses?

TRAFFIC SURVEY RESULTS
Private cars 64
Vans   20
Lorries   24
Buses   12

4.5 Finding a fraction of a quantity

You need to be able to do calculations like these:

$\frac{3}{4}$ of £60 $\frac{5}{8}$ of 160

Example 4

Find $\frac{3}{4}$ of £60.

Multiply the numerator 3 by the quantity 60: $\frac{3 \times 60}{4} = \frac{180}{4}$ Another method: one quarter is

Divide the result 180 by the denominator 4: $\frac{180}{4} = 45$ $\frac{60}{4} = £15$

So $\frac{3}{4}$ of £60 is £45.

Three quarters is
$3 \times 15 = £45$

Example 5

Find $\frac{5}{8}$ of 160.

$$\frac{5 \times 160}{8} = \frac{800}{8}$$

$$\frac{800}{8} = 100$$

So $\frac{5}{8}$ of 160 is 100.

Exercise 4E

1 Find:
(a) $\frac{1}{2}$ of 70   (b) $\frac{2}{5}$ of £65   (c) $\frac{3}{10}$ of 80 kg
(d) $\frac{2}{3}$ of 96   (e) $\frac{3}{8}$ of £56   (f) $\frac{3}{4}$ of 60p
(g) $\frac{1}{4}$ of £6.80   (h) $\frac{7}{10}$ of 90p   (i) $\frac{7}{8}$ of £3.20

2 A superstore employs 85 people. $\frac{2}{5}$ are men.
(a) How many men does the store employ?
(b) How many women does the store employ?

3 A mail order company prints 200 000 catalogues. $\frac{13}{20}$ are sent to customers. $\frac{3}{20}$ are sent to agents. $\frac{1}{5}$ are sent to shops.
How many catalogues are sent to:
(a) customers   (b) agents   (c) shops?

4 A chain store closed $\frac{2}{15}$ of its 345 shops.
How many shops were closed?

5   A factory worker is paid £186 per week. $\frac{2}{5}$ is deducted for tax and national insurance.
How much is deducted?

6   The metal parts of a car weigh 1250 kg. $\frac{3}{10}$ of the metal is recycled.
How much does the recycled metal weigh?

7   Stan sold 560 sandwiches today. $\frac{1}{4}$ were ham sandwiches, $\frac{2}{5}$ were salad, $\frac{1}{8}$ were tuna and the rest were cheese.
How many of each type did Stan sell?

8   A building company built 3050 houses. $\frac{1}{10}$ had four bedrooms, $\frac{7}{50}$ had two bedrooms. The rest had three bedrooms.
How many houses had:
(a) four bedrooms   **(b)** two bedrooms
(c) three bedrooms?

9   A department store had 480 customers last Saturday. $\frac{2}{3}$ paid by credit card, $\frac{1}{4}$ paid by cheque and the others paid by cash.
How many customers paid by:
(a) credit card   **(b)** cheque   **(c)** cash?

4.6 Equivalent fractions

Here is a block of fudge divided in three different ways:

$\frac{1}{4}$ $\frac{2}{8}$ $\frac{4}{16}$

The fractions $\frac{1}{4}$, $\frac{2}{8}$ and $\frac{4}{16}$ all represent the same amount of the fudge.

$\frac{1}{4}$, $\frac{2}{8}$ and $\frac{4}{16}$ are **equivalent fractions**.

■   **Equivalent fractions are fractions that have the same value.**

Simplifying to find equivalent fractions

You can see this by simplifying $\frac{4}{16}$.

Divide the numerator and the   Then do this again:
denominator by the common factor 2:

$$\frac{4}{16} \quad \boxed{\begin{array}{l}\text{4 divided by 2 is 2} \\ \text{16 divided by 2 is 8}\end{array}} \quad \frac{2}{8} \qquad\qquad \frac{2}{8} \quad \boxed{\begin{array}{l}\text{2 divided by 2 is 1} \\ \text{8 divided by 2 is 4}\end{array}} \quad \frac{1}{4}$$

So $\frac{4}{16} = \frac{2}{8} = \frac{1}{4}$ These are equivalent fractions.

Multiplying to find equivalent fractions

Another way of finding equivalent fractions is to *multiply* the numerator and denominator by the same (common) number:

For example:

$$\frac{3}{4} \quad \boxed{\begin{array}{l}\text{3 multiplied by 6 is 18}\\ \text{4 multiplied by 6 is 24}\end{array}} \quad \frac{18}{24}$$

You can keep doing this:

$$\frac{18}{24} \quad \boxed{\begin{array}{l}\text{18 multiplied by 2 is 36}\\ \text{24 multiplied by 2 is 48}\end{array}} \quad \frac{36}{48}$$

So $\frac{3}{4} = \frac{18}{24} = \frac{36}{48}$ These are equivalent fractions.

Example 6

Change $\frac{3}{7}$ to any equivalent fraction.

Multiply the numerator and denominator by, say, 5.

$$\frac{3}{7} = \frac{3 \times 5}{7 \times 5} = \frac{15}{35}$$

So $\frac{3}{7}$ and $\frac{15}{35}$ are equivalent fractions.

> **Remember**
>
> $\dfrac{3}{7}$ ── numerator
>   ── denominator

Example 7

Change $\frac{5}{8}$ to an equivalent fraction with the denominator 48.

To change the denominator from 8 to 48, multiply 8 by 6.

To get an equivalent fraction multiply the numerator 5 by 6 too.

$$\frac{5}{8} = \frac{5 \times 6}{8 \times 6} = \frac{30}{48}$$

So $\frac{5}{8}$ and $\frac{30}{48}$ are equivalent fractions.

Example 8

Complete this set of equivalent fractions: $\frac{2}{5} = \frac{}{10} = \frac{}{15}$

To get from $\frac{2}{5}$ to $\frac{}{10}$ multiply top and bottom by 2:

$$\frac{2}{5} \quad \boxed{\begin{array}{l}\text{2 multiplied by 2 is 4}\\ \text{5 multiplied by 2 is 10}\end{array}} \quad \frac{4}{10}$$

To get from $\frac{2}{5}$ to $\frac{}{15}$ multiply top and bottom by 3:

$$\frac{2}{5} \quad \boxed{\begin{array}{l}\text{2 multiplied by 3 is 6}\\ \text{5 multiplied by 3 is 15}\end{array}} \quad \frac{6}{15}$$

So the set of equivalent fractions is $\frac{2}{5} = \frac{4}{10} = \frac{6}{15}$

Exercise 4F

1 Copy these sets of fractions. Fill in the missing numbers to make the fractions equivalent:

(a) $\frac{1}{2} = \frac{}{10} = \frac{}{100} = \frac{}{8} = \frac{}{12} = \frac{3}{}$

(b) $\frac{2}{3} = \frac{}{6} = \frac{}{9} = \frac{}{60} = \frac{}{90} = \frac{20}{}$

(c) $\frac{7}{10} = \frac{}{20} = \frac{}{50} = \frac{}{100} = \frac{}{2000} = \frac{28}{}$

(d) $\frac{3}{4} = \frac{}{16} = \frac{}{20} = \frac{}{28} = \frac{}{400} = \frac{90}{}$

(e) $\frac{1}{8} = \frac{}{24} = \frac{}{32} = \frac{}{64} = \frac{}{480} = \frac{7}{}$

2 Write down five other fractions equivalent to:

(a) $\frac{1}{5}$ (b) $\frac{2}{5}$ (c) $\frac{5}{6}$ (d) $\frac{7}{8}$ (e) $\frac{3}{20}$

3 (a) Give an equivalent fraction to $\frac{1}{2}$ and an equivalent fraction to $\frac{1}{3}$ so that the denominators of the two new fractions are equal.

(b) Repeat part (a) for:

(i) $\frac{2}{5}$ and $\frac{3}{6}$ (ii) $\frac{1}{10}$ and $\frac{1}{7}$ (iii) $\frac{1}{4}$ and $\frac{5}{6}$

(iv) $\frac{1}{2}$ and $\frac{3}{5}$ (v) $\frac{2}{3}$ and $\frac{1}{8}$ (vi) $\frac{3}{4}$ and $\frac{3}{5}$

4.7 Putting fractions in order of size

Which is larger: $\frac{3}{4}$ or $\frac{3}{5}$?   Equivalent fractions can help you decide.

First make lists of equivalent fractions for $\frac{3}{4}$ and $\frac{3}{5}$:

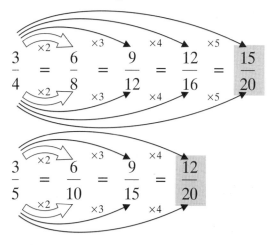

Compare the lists. Find fractions with the same denominator (bottom)

$\frac{15}{20}$ is larger than $\frac{12}{20}$ (Imagine a cake divided into 20 parts and getting either 12 or 15 slices.)

As $\frac{15}{20}$ is equivalent to $\frac{3}{4}$ and $\frac{12}{20}$ is equivalent to $\frac{3}{5}$

$\frac{3}{4}$ must be *larger* than $\frac{3}{5}$

Exercise 4G

1 Which is larger:
    (a) $\frac{2}{5}$ or $\frac{3}{6}$ **(b)** $\frac{1}{10}$ or $\frac{1}{7}$ **(c)** $\frac{1}{4}$ or $\frac{5}{6}$
    (d) $\frac{1}{2}$ or $\frac{3}{5}$ **(e)** $\frac{2}{3}$ or $\frac{1}{8}$ **(f)** $\frac{3}{4}$ or $\frac{3}{5}$

2 Put these fractions in order of size starting with the smallest:
    $\frac{2}{5}$ $\frac{1}{2}$ $\frac{7}{3}$ $\frac{3}{4}$ $\frac{2}{10}$

Using fractions in your examination

In your examination fractions will usually appear in the context of a number problem or in questions on probability, areas or volumes. You need to be able to add, subtract, multiply and divide fractions in such problems. The rest of this unit shows you how to do this.

4.8 Adding fractions

It is easy to add fractions when the denominator (bottom) is the same:

Easy to add:

$$\frac{1}{4} + \frac{2}{4} = \frac{3}{4}$$

denominators the same

Harder to add:

$$\frac{1}{2} + \frac{2}{3} = \ ?$$

denominators different

Adding fractions with the same denominator

$$\frac{7}{10} + \frac{2}{10} = \frac{9}{10}$$

Add the numerators (top).

Write them over the **same** denominator (bottom).

Adding fractions with different denominators

$$\frac{1}{2} + \frac{2}{3} = \ ?$$

Find equivalent fractions to these that have the same denominator (bottom).

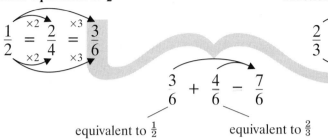

Fractions equivalent to $\frac{1}{2}$

$$\frac{1}{2} = \frac{2}{4} = \frac{3}{6}$$

Fractions equivalent to $\frac{2}{3}$

$$\frac{2}{3} = \frac{4}{6}$$

These fractions have the same denominators (bottom).
Now they are easy to add.

$$\frac{3}{6} + \frac{4}{6} - \frac{7}{6}$$

equivalent to $\frac{1}{2}$ equivalent to $\frac{2}{3}$

So $\frac{1}{2} + \frac{2}{3} = \frac{7}{6}$

$\frac{7}{6}$ is top heavy. It is usually written as a mixed number: $1\frac{1}{6}$

■ **To add fractions find equivalent fractions that have the same denominator (bottom).**

Example 9

Work out $\frac{5}{8} + \frac{3}{7}$

Find equivalent fractions to these that have the same denominator (bottom).

An easy way to do this is:

$$\frac{5}{8} \xrightarrow{\times 7} \frac{35}{56} \qquad \frac{3}{7} \xrightarrow{\times 8} \frac{24}{56}$$

same denominators
now you can add the numerators

$$\frac{35}{56} + \frac{24}{56} = \frac{59}{56}$$

So $\frac{5}{8} + \frac{3}{7} = \frac{59}{56}$

$\frac{59}{56}$ is top heavy. It is usually written as a mixed number: $1\frac{3}{56}$

Example 10

Work out $\frac{2}{3} + \frac{7}{12}$

Find equivalent fractions to these that have the same denominator (bottom).

$$\frac{2}{3} + \frac{7}{12} = ?$$

Notice that
$3 \times 4 = 12$

So you only need to change one of the fractions:

$$\frac{2}{3} \xrightarrow{\times 4} \frac{8}{12}$$

Now both have the same denominator:

$$\frac{8}{12} + \frac{7}{12} = \frac{15}{12}$$

equivalent to $\frac{2}{3}$

So $\frac{8}{12} + \frac{7}{12} = \frac{15}{12}$

$\frac{15}{12}$ is top heavy. It is usually written as a mixed number: $1\frac{3}{12}$
This simplifies to $1\frac{1}{4}$

Example 11

Work out $2\frac{1}{4} + 3\frac{1}{5}$

These are **mixed numbers**. First add the whole numbers: $2 + 3 = 5$

Then add the fractions:

$$\frac{1}{4} + \frac{1}{5} = ?$$

Change both denominators (bottom) to 20
because $4 \times 5 = 20$

$$\frac{1}{4} \overset{\times 5}{\underset{\times 5}{=}} \frac{5}{20} \qquad\qquad \frac{1}{5} \overset{\times 4}{\underset{\times 4}{=}} \frac{4}{20}$$

$$\frac{5}{20} + \frac{4}{20} = \frac{9}{20}$$

same denominator
now add the numerators

Now put the whole numbers and the fractions back together:
$5 + \frac{9}{20}$ is $5\frac{9}{20}$
So $2\frac{1}{4} + 3\frac{1}{5} = 5\frac{9}{20}$

Exercise 4H

1   Work out:
(a) $\frac{3}{8} + \frac{4}{8}$ (b) $\frac{2}{9} + \frac{5}{9}$ (c) $\frac{5}{12} + \frac{1}{12}$ (d) $\frac{5}{18} + \frac{11}{18}$
(e) $\frac{1}{2} + \frac{1}{4}$ (f) $\frac{1}{4} + \frac{3}{8}$ (g) $\frac{1}{2} + \frac{7}{8}$ (h) $\frac{2}{3} + \frac{1}{6}$
(i) $\frac{5}{6} + \frac{1}{3}$ (j) $\frac{2}{5} + \frac{3}{10}$ (k) $\frac{7}{12} + \frac{3}{4}$ (l) $\frac{3}{4} + \frac{7}{20}$

2   Work out:
(a) $\frac{1}{6} + \frac{5}{8}$ (b) $\frac{3}{4} + \frac{1}{10}$ (c) $\frac{4}{9} + \frac{5}{12}$ (d) $\frac{7}{8} + \frac{9}{10}$
(e) $\frac{3}{10} + \frac{4}{15}$ (f) $\frac{5}{6} + \frac{1}{4}$ (g) $\frac{3}{8} + \frac{7}{12}$ (h) $\frac{1}{6} + \frac{8}{9}$

3 Work out:

(a) $\frac{1}{2} + \frac{1}{3}$ (b) $\frac{2}{5} + \frac{1}{6}$ (c) $\frac{5}{8} + \frac{1}{5}$ (d) $\frac{3}{4} + \frac{1}{9}$

(e) $\frac{5}{6} + \frac{3}{7}$ (f) $\frac{9}{10} + \frac{2}{7}$ (g) $\frac{2}{3} + \frac{7}{10}$ (h) $\frac{3}{5} + \frac{3}{4}$

4 Work out:

(a) $2\frac{1}{2} + \frac{2}{3}$ (b) $3\frac{1}{4} + 2\frac{1}{2}$ (c) $1\frac{1}{4} + 2\frac{7}{8}$ (d) $3\frac{1}{3} + 5\frac{3}{4}$

(e) $3\frac{5}{16} + 1\frac{7}{8}$ (f) $2\frac{11}{12} + \frac{3}{4}$ (g) $\frac{5}{6} + 6\frac{1}{3}$ (h) $2\frac{2}{3} + 4\frac{3}{5}$

5 In a market garden: $\frac{1}{4}$ of the garden is used for potatoes, $\frac{3}{20}$ is used for beans and $\frac{1}{10}$ is used for cabbages. What fraction of the garden is used to grow these vegetables altogether?

6 John gave away his old record collection to his brother and two sisters. The elder sister received $\frac{3}{10}$ of them and the younger sister $\frac{5}{16}$ of them. The brother received the rest. What fraction of the collection did the sisters receive altogether?

I said you could have $\frac{5}{16}$ of the records not $\frac{5}{16}$ of each one!

4.9 Subtracting fractions

It is easy to subtract fractions when the denominator (bottom) is the same:

Easy to subtract:

$$\frac{7}{12} - \frac{2}{12} = \frac{5}{12}$$

denominators the same

Harder to subtract:

$$\frac{5}{9} - \frac{1}{4} = ?$$

denominators different

Example 12

Work out $\frac{5}{9} - \frac{1}{4}$

Find equivalent fractions to these that have the same denominator (bottom):

An easy way is: change both denominators to 36 because $9 \times 4 = 36$

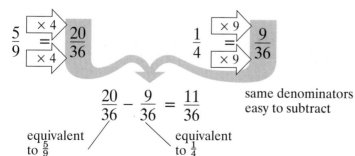

$$\frac{5}{9} \xrightarrow[\times 4]{\times 4} \frac{20}{36} \qquad \frac{1}{4} \xrightarrow[\times 9]{\times 9} \frac{9}{36}$$

$$\frac{20}{36} - \frac{9}{36} = \frac{11}{36}$$

same denominators
easy to subtract

equivalent to $\frac{5}{9}$ equivalent to $\frac{1}{4}$

So $\frac{5}{9} - \frac{1}{4} = \frac{11}{36}$

Example 13

Work out $4\frac{1}{2} - 1\frac{5}{11}$

These are **mixed numbers**.

First subtract the whole numbers: $4 - 1 = 3$

$\qquad 4\frac{1}{2} - 1\frac{5}{11} \qquad$ is the same as: $\qquad 3\frac{1}{2} - \frac{5}{11}$

Then find equivalent fractions to $\frac{1}{2}$ and $\frac{5}{11}$ that have the same denominator (bottom).

Change both denominators to 22 because $2 \times 11 = 22$

$$\frac{11}{22} - \frac{10}{22} = \frac{1}{22}$$

same denominators
easy to subtract

Now put the whole numbers and fractions back together:
3 and $\frac{1}{22}$ is $3\frac{1}{22}$

So $4\frac{1}{2} - 1\frac{5}{11} = 3\frac{1}{22}$

Example 14

Work out $2\frac{3}{12} - \frac{8}{12}$

$\frac{3}{12}$ is smaller than $\frac{8}{12}$ so you can't just subtract the fractions on their own.

Change the mixed number $2\frac{3}{12}$ into a top heavy (or improper) fraction.

$2\frac{3}{12} \quad = \quad \frac{24}{12} + \frac{3}{12} \quad = \quad \frac{27}{12}$

So: $\quad 2\frac{3}{12} \quad - \quad \frac{8}{12} \quad = \quad \frac{27}{12} - \frac{8}{12}$

$\qquad\qquad\qquad = \quad \frac{19}{12} \quad$ usually written as a mixed number: $1\frac{7}{12}$

■ **To subtract fractions find equivalent fractions that have the same denominator (bottom).**

Exercise 4I

1 Work out:
   (a) $\frac{5}{11} - \frac{3}{11}$ **(b)** $\frac{7}{9} - \frac{5}{9}$ **(c)** $\frac{7}{8} - \frac{1}{8}$ **(d)** $\frac{7}{12} - \frac{5}{12}$

2 Work out:
   (a) $\frac{1}{2} - \frac{1}{4}$ **(b)** $\frac{7}{8} - \frac{3}{4}$ **(c)** $\frac{5}{8} - \frac{1}{2}$ **(d)** $\frac{3}{4} - \frac{1}{8}$
   (e) $\frac{5}{6} - \frac{1}{3}$ **(f)** $\frac{7}{12} - \frac{1}{3}$ **(g)** $\frac{9}{10} - \frac{2}{5}$ **(h)** $\frac{1}{4} - \frac{1}{20}$

3 Work out:
(a) $\frac{5}{8} - \frac{1}{6}$ (b) $\frac{7}{10} - \frac{1}{4}$ (c) $\frac{7}{9} - \frac{5}{12}$ (d) $\frac{5}{6} - \frac{4}{9}$
(e) $\frac{7}{10} - \frac{4}{15}$ (f) $\frac{3}{4} - \frac{7}{20}$ (g) $\frac{3}{4} - \frac{3}{10}$ (h) $\frac{7}{8} - \frac{7}{10}$

4 Work out:
(a) $\frac{2}{3} - \frac{1}{2}$ (b) $\frac{5}{8} - \frac{1}{3}$ (c) $\frac{1}{5} - \frac{1}{6}$ (d) $\frac{3}{5} - \frac{1}{3}$
(e) $\frac{4}{5} - \frac{2}{3}$ (f) $\frac{3}{4} - \frac{3}{5}$ (g) $\frac{7}{10} - \frac{1}{3}$ (h) $\frac{9}{10} - \frac{3}{4}$

5 Work out:
(a) $5\frac{1}{4} - \frac{1}{10}$ (b) $7\frac{1}{2} - \frac{1}{3}$ (c) $6\frac{1}{2} - 5\frac{1}{4}$ (d) $9\frac{1}{2} - 7\frac{3}{10}$
(e) $4 - 1\frac{3}{10}$ (f) $4\frac{4}{5} - 3\frac{9}{10}$ (g) $1\frac{2}{3} - \frac{11}{12}$ (h) $5\frac{3}{4} - 2\frac{19}{20}$

6 In a school, $\frac{7}{16}$ of the students are girls.
What fraction of the students are boys?

7 $\frac{2}{5}$ of the students at Hay College wear contact lenses.
What fraction of the students do not wear them?

8 The garden of Granny Smith's house measures $1\frac{1}{3}$ acres.
Sharkey Estates buy $1\frac{1}{4}$ acres of the garden to build new
homes.
What fraction of the garden does Granny Smith have left?

4.10 Multiplying fractions

How to multiply two fractions:

Multiply the numerators (top)

$$\frac{5}{8} \times \frac{7}{10} = \frac{35}{80}$$

Multiply the denominators (bottom)

So $\frac{5}{8} \times \frac{7}{10} = \frac{35}{80}$ This simplifies to $\frac{7}{16}$ (by dividing top and
bottom of $\frac{35}{80}$ by 5).

Another way of doing this is to simplify the fractions *before*
you multiply them:

$$\frac{5}{8} \times \frac{7}{10} = \frac{5 \times 7}{8 \times 10}$$

You can simplify here by
dividing the top and
bottom by 5.

$$\frac{(5 \times 7) \div 5}{(8 \times 10) \div 5} = \frac{7}{8 \times 2} = \frac{7}{16}$$

This gives the same answer $\frac{7}{16}$ as the first method.

This method is less obvious than the first one. Ask your
teacher if you need help to understand it.

How to multiply a fraction by a whole number:

$$\frac{7}{10} \times 4 = ?$$

You can write 4 as the **top heavy** (or improper) fraction $\frac{4}{1}$

Multiply the numerators (top)

$$\frac{7}{10} \times \frac{4}{1} = \frac{28}{10}$$

Multiply the denominators (bottom)

So $\frac{7}{10} \times 4 = \frac{28}{10}$ This is usually written as a mixed number: $2\frac{8}{10}$

The fraction part of $2\frac{8}{10}$ simplifies (by dividing top and bottom by 2) so $2\frac{8}{10} = 2\frac{4}{5}$

How to multiply two mixed numbers:

$$3\frac{1}{4} \times 2\frac{4}{5} = ?$$

Change both mixed numbers to top heavy (or improper) fractions:

$$3\frac{1}{4} = \frac{12}{4} + \frac{1}{4} = \frac{13}{4} \qquad\qquad 2\frac{4}{5} = \frac{10}{5} + \frac{4}{5} = \frac{14}{5}$$

Multiply

$$\frac{13}{4} \times \frac{14}{5} = \frac{182}{20}$$

Multiply

So $3\frac{1}{4} \times 2\frac{4}{5} = \frac{182}{20}$ This is usually written as a mixed number: $9\frac{2}{20}$

The fraction part of $9\frac{2}{20}$ simplifies (by dividing top and bottom by 2) so $9\frac{2}{20} = 9\frac{1}{10}$

Exercise 4J

1   Work out:
(a) $\frac{1}{2} \times \frac{3}{4}$ (b) $\frac{3}{8} \times \frac{1}{4}$ (c) $\frac{2}{5} \times \frac{4}{5}$ (d) $\frac{3}{8} \times \frac{3}{4}$
(e) $\frac{5}{12} \times \frac{1}{3}$ (f) $\frac{7}{10} \times \frac{3}{4}$ (g) $\frac{3}{10} \times \frac{3}{5}$ (h) $\frac{2}{3} \times \frac{2}{3}$

2 Work out:

(a) $\frac{1}{2} \times \frac{4}{5}$ (b) $\frac{3}{4} \times \frac{4}{5}$ (c) $\frac{5}{6} \times \frac{3}{5}$ (d) $\frac{4}{5} \times \frac{3}{10}$

(e) $\frac{5}{6} \times \frac{3}{4}$ (f) $\frac{7}{12} \times \frac{3}{14}$ (g) $\frac{8}{9} \times \frac{3}{10}$ (h) $\frac{3}{4} \times \frac{16}{21}$

3 Work out:

(a) $\frac{1}{2} \times 7$ (b) $\frac{2}{3} \times 5$ (c) $6 \times \frac{4}{5}$ (d) $8 \times \frac{3}{4}$

(e) $\frac{7}{10} \times 20$ (f) $9 \times \frac{2}{3}$ (g) $10 \times \frac{2}{5}$ (h) $\frac{5}{6} \times 12$

4 Work out:

(a) $3\frac{1}{4} \times \frac{1}{2}$ (b) $\frac{2}{3} \times 4\frac{1}{2}$ (c) $\frac{5}{6} \times 1\frac{1}{3}$ (d) $2\frac{1}{2} \times \frac{7}{10}$

(e) $3\frac{1}{2} \times 1\frac{1}{2}$ (f) $2\frac{1}{3} \times 2\frac{3}{8}$ (g) $1\frac{4}{5} \times 2\frac{1}{3}$ (h) $3\frac{3}{4} \times 1\frac{2}{5}$

5 On Monday to Friday inclusive Jamie spends $2\frac{1}{4}$ hours on his homework but his sister Claire spends only $1\frac{3}{4}$ hours each day on hers.

How long in a week does each one spend on homework?

6 A machine takes $5\frac{1}{2}$ minutes to produce a special type of container.

How long would the machine take to produce 15 containers?

> Area of rectangle is length × width
> Volume of box is length × width × depth

7 Calculate the area of a rectangle of length $3\frac{1}{4}$ cm and width $2\frac{1}{4}$ cm.

8 A hand-made chocolate box is 6 inches long by $3\frac{1}{2}$ inches wide by $2\frac{1}{4}$ inches deep.
Calculate the volume of the box.

9 One way to calculate the circumference of a circle is to use the formula: Circumference = diameter $\times 3\frac{1}{7}$

Calculate the circumference of a circle with diameter:

(a) 4 cm   (b) $6\frac{1}{2}$ cm   (c) $\frac{3}{4}$ cm

4.11 Dividing fractions

Turn the ÷ sign into a × sign.

$$\frac{1}{4} \div \frac{3}{5} = ?$$

$$\frac{1}{4} \times \frac{5}{3} = \frac{5}{12}$$

So $\frac{1}{4} \div \frac{3}{5} = \frac{5}{12}$

Turn the fraction you are dividing by upside down.

This is called **inverting** the fraction

Why inverting works
A fraction like $\frac{3}{4}$ is the same as:

$$3 \div 4$$

or $3 \times \frac{1}{4}$

But $\frac{1}{4}$ is $\frac{4}{1}$ inverted.

So dividing is the same as multiplying by the inverted number.

$$12 \div 3 = 4$$
$$12 \times \frac{1}{3} = 4 \text{ too}$$

How to divide mixed numbers:

$$3\tfrac{1}{2} \div 4\tfrac{3}{4} = ?$$

Change mixed numbers to top heavy (or improper) fractions.

$$\frac{7}{2} \div \frac{19}{4}$$

Turn ÷ into ×

Invert the dividing fraction.

$$\frac{7}{2} \times \frac{4}{19} = \frac{28}{38}$$

So $3\tfrac{1}{2} \div 4\tfrac{3}{4} = \frac{28}{38}$ This simplifies to $\frac{14}{19}$ (by dividing top and bottom by 2).

How to divide a fraction by a whole number

$$\frac{15}{16} \div 5 = ?$$

Turn ÷ into ×

Invert the dividing number

$$\frac{15}{16} \times \frac{1}{5} = \frac{15}{80}$$

So $\frac{15}{16} \div 5 = \frac{15}{80}$ This simplifies to $\frac{3}{16}$ (by dividing top and bottom by 5).

Remember:
$5 = \dfrac{5}{1}$
so inverting gives
$\dfrac{1}{5}$

■ **To divide fractions, invert the dividing fraction (turn it upside down) and multiply.**

Exercise 4K

1 Work out:
 (a) $\frac{1}{3} \div \frac{1}{4}$ (b) $\frac{1}{4} \div \frac{1}{3}$ (c) $\frac{3}{4} \div \frac{1}{2}$ (d) $\frac{1}{2} \div \frac{7}{10}$
 (e) $\frac{2}{3} \div \frac{1}{5}$ (f) $\frac{5}{8} \div \frac{1}{3}$ (g) $\frac{5}{6} \div \frac{3}{4}$ (h) $\frac{7}{10} \div \frac{4}{5}$

2 Work out:
 (a) $2\tfrac{1}{2} \div \tfrac{1}{2}$ (b) $3\tfrac{1}{4} \div 2\tfrac{1}{2}$ (c) $3\tfrac{3}{4} \div 2\tfrac{1}{4}$ (d) $1\tfrac{5}{8} \div 3\tfrac{1}{6}$
 (e) $3\tfrac{2}{3} \div 7\tfrac{1}{3}$ (f) $5\tfrac{1}{2} \div 2\tfrac{3}{4}$ (g) $1\tfrac{7}{10} \div 2\tfrac{7}{10}$ (h) $\tfrac{7}{8} \div 1\tfrac{2}{3}$

3 Work out:
 (a) $\frac{3}{4} \div 8$ (b) $\frac{5}{6} \div 2$ (c) $\frac{3}{5} \div 6$ (d) $\frac{4}{5} \div 5$
 (e) $1\tfrac{1}{3} \div 4$ (f) $3\tfrac{1}{4} \div 6$ (g) $2\tfrac{5}{6} \div 10$ (h) $2\tfrac{1}{2} \div 15$

4 Work out:
 (a) $8 \div \frac{1}{2}$ (b) $12 \div \frac{3}{4}$ (c) $6 \div \frac{3}{5}$ (d) $8 \div \frac{7}{8}$
 (e) $4 \div \frac{4}{5}$ (f) $1 \div \frac{7}{12}$ (g) $5 \div \frac{1}{3}$ (h) $6 \div \frac{1}{4}$

Summary of key points

1 Fraction words you need to know:

$\dfrac{3}{4}$ ——— numerator

——— denominator

2 Top heavy fractions like $\frac{11}{9}$ are also called improper fractions.

3 An improper fraction like $\frac{11}{9}$ can be written as a mixed number: $1\frac{2}{9}$

4 Fractions can be simplified if the numerator (top) and denominator (bottom) have a common factor:

$\dfrac{8}{12}$ simplifies to $\dfrac{2}{3}$ ÷4 the common factor is 4

5 Equivalent fractions are fractions that have the same value:

$\dfrac{8}{12} = \dfrac{4}{6} = \dfrac{2}{3}$

6 To add fractions find equivalent fractions that have the same denominator (bottom):

$\dfrac{1}{2} + \dfrac{4}{6}$

$\dfrac{3}{6} + \dfrac{4}{6} = \dfrac{7}{6}$

7 To subtract fractions find equivalent fractions that have the same denominator (bottom):

$\dfrac{4}{6} - \dfrac{1}{2}$

$\dfrac{4}{6} - \dfrac{3}{6} = \dfrac{1}{6}$

8 To multiply two fractions:

Multiply numerators (top)

$\dfrac{3}{4} \times \dfrac{4}{7} = \dfrac{12}{28}$

Multiply denominators (bottom)

9 To divide fractions, invert the dividing fraction (turn it upside down) and multiply:

$\dfrac{1}{4} \div \dfrac{2}{5}$

Turn ÷ into ×   Invert (turn upside down)

$\dfrac{1}{4} \times \dfrac{5}{2}$

5 Two-dimensional shapes

This design for a bathroom tile is made from three different types of shape: triangles, squares and rectangles.

On paper the design is flat and has no thickness. It is a two-dimensional (or 2-D) shape.

■ **2-D shapes are flat; they have no thickness.**

This unit shows you how to recognize and draw some common 2-D shapes.

5.1 Recognizing triangles and quadrilaterals

■ **A triangle is a three-sided shape.**

You need to be able to recognize these special types of triangles:

Shape					
Name	Isosceles triangle	Equilateral triangle	Right-angled triangle	Obtuse-angled triangle	Scalene triangle
Properties	2 equal sides	3 equal sides	one angle 90°	one angle greater than 90°	no special features
	2 equal angles	all angles equal 60°			

Dashes show equal sides

These show equal angles

This is a right angle (90°)

■ **A quadrilateral is a four-sided shape.**

You need to be able to recognise these special types of quadrilateral.

Name	Shape	Properties
Trapezium		1 pair of parallel sides.
Parallelogram		2 pairs of parallel sides, opposite sides equal. opposite angles equal
Rhombus		2 pairs of parallel sides, all sides equal, diagonals cross at right angles.
Rectangle		all angles are 90°, opposite sides equal and parallel, diagonals equal.
Square		all angles 90°, all sides equal, opposite sides parallel, diagonals equal and cross at right angles,
Kite		two pairs of adjacent sides (next to each other) equal, 1 pair opposite angles equal, diagonals cross at 90°.

Sides marked with the same number of arrows are parallel.

Sides marked with the same number of dashes are equal.

Exercise 5A

1 Copy and complete these sentences. Use numbers, and the correct word chosen from:

> **equal** **opposite** **parallel** **sides**

The first two have been done for you.

(a) A **triangle** has _3_ sides and _3_ angles.

(b) An **equilateral triangle** has <u>equal</u> sides. Each angle measures <u>60</u>°.

(c) An **isosceles triangle** has ____ equal sides and ____ angles which are equal.

(d) The largest angle in a **right-angled triangle** always measures ____ .

(e) **Quadrilaterals** have ____ sides and angles.

(f) The angles in a **rectangle** are all ____ . Opposite sides are ____ .

(g) All the sides of a **square** are ____ and the angles are all ____ .

(h) A **kite** has 2 pairs of equal ____ and one pair of ____ angles.

(i) ____ sides and angles of a **parallelogram** are ____ .

____ sides are parallel.

(j) A **rhombus** has 4 equal ____ and opposite angles are

____ .

____ sides are parallel.

(k) A **trapezium** has 1 pair of ____ sides.

2 Name these special quadrilaterals:

(a)

(b)

(c)

(d)

(e)

(f)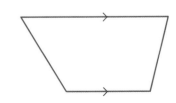

3   You will need a ruler and a protractor.

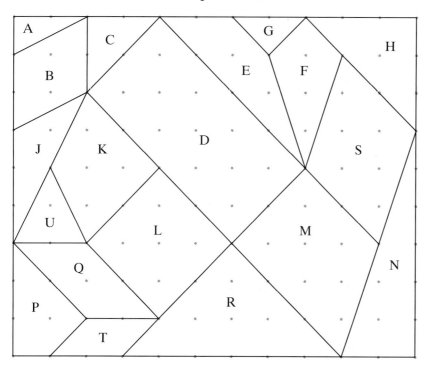

Copy and complete these statements about the 2-D shapes
in the picture.
Use a ruler and protractor to help you.
The first one has been done for you.

(a) Shapes <u>A, C, G, H, N and R</u> are all right-angled triangles.

(b) Shape _____ is a square.

(c) Shapes _____ are all parallelograms.

(d) Shape D is a _____ .

(e) Shapes _____ and _____ are trapeziums.

(f) The kites are shapes _____ and _____ .

(g) Shape _____ is an ordinary quadrilateral.

(h) Shape U is an _____ triangle.

(i) The only rhombus in the picture is shape _____ .

(j) Shapes _____ are isosceles triangles.

5.2 Drawing 2-D shapes on squared paper

Squared paper makes it easier to draw some 2-D shapes.
Parallel lines and lines at right angles are easily drawn, and
lengths are easily measured.

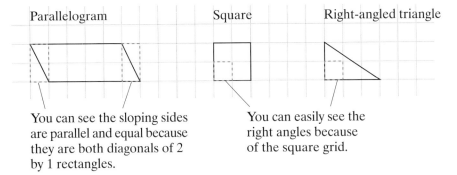

Parallelogram

Square

Right-angled triangle

You can see the sloping sides
are parallel and equal because
they are both diagonals of 2
by 1 rectangles.

You can easily see the
right angles because
of the square grid.

1   On squared paper draw:
   (a) a rectangle with sides 2 cm and 3 cm
   (b) a right-angled triangle with base 3 cm and height 2 cm
   (c) a square with sides 3 cm long

2   On squared paper draw:
   (a) an isosceles triangle with a base of 5 cm and a height
         of 3 cm
   (b) a parallelogram with the longest sides 5 cm
   (c) a trapezium with parallel sides that add up to 9 cm and
         with height 3 cm

3   Design some square tiles using quadrilaterals and
      triangles. Do not use too many different shapes in any one
      design. Here are two designs from the floor of a Roman
      Villa:

5.3 Drawing more complicated shapes

Sometimes you will need to draw more complicated shapes accurately using a ruler, protractor and compasses.

Example 1

Draw a triangle *PQR* with sides *PQ* = 7 cm, *PR* = 5 cm and *QR* = 9 cm.

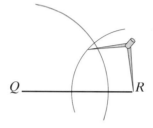

Point *P* is 7 cm from *Q* and 5 cm from *R*.

Draw the line *QR* = 9 cm.   Use compasses to draw the points 7 cm from *Q*.   Use compasses to draw points 5 cm from *R*.   Join *P* to *Q* and *P* to *R* to make a triangle *PQR*.

Exercise 5C

Use a protractor and compasses to help you do these questions.

1 Draw:
  (a) an equilateral triangle with sides 5 cm long.
  (b) a triangle with sides 6 cm, 5 cm and 7 cm long.
  (c) the isosceles triangle with sides 6 cm, 5 cm and 5 cm.

2 Draw these shapes accurately:

(a)   **(b)**   **(c)**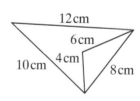

Make accurate drawings of:

3 **(a)**   **(b)** **(c)**

4 A parallelogram *PQRS* where *PQ* = *RS* = 8 cm, *PS* = *QR* = 5 cm, angle *QPS* = 60° and angle *PQR* = 120°.

5   A rhombus *DEFG* with sides of 6 cm and angle
       DEF = 35°.

6   A right-angled triangle *EFG* with the right angle at *F* and
       with *EF* = 4 cm and *FG* = 3 cm. Measure *EG*.

7   A triangle *XYZ* where *XY* = 6 cm, angle *XYZ* = 65° and
       angle *YXZ* = 45°. Measure *XZ* and *YZ* as accurately as
       you can.

5.4   Congruent shapes

These triangles are facing different ways but they are all exactly
the same shape and size. We say that **corresponding sides** are
the same length. **Corresponding angles** are also equal.

■   **Shapes which are exactly the same size and shape are
congruent.**

Example 2

Which of these triangles are congruent?

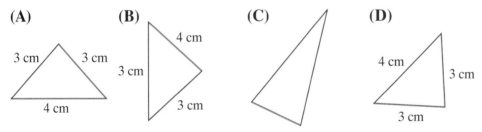

All the triangles are isosceles but **(C)** is longer and thinner
than the others.

(A), **(B)** and **(D)** each have sides 3 cm, 3 cm and 4 cm. Their
angles are the same as well.

(A), **(B)** and **(D)** are **congruent**.

Exercise 5D

Write down the letters of the shapes which are congruent.

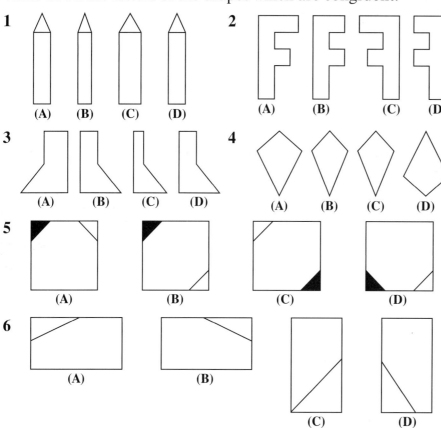

5.5 Polygons

All these shapes are polygons:

Not all sides of a polygon need to be the same.

Polygons can have sides which point inwards.

Polygons are closed shapes – there are no gaps in the perimeter.

■ **Polygon is the general name for a 2-D shape with straight sides.**

You need to know the names of some special polygons:

- A polygon with 5 sides is a **pentagon**. (penta = 5; a modern pentathlon has 5 events)
- A polygon with 6 sides is a **hexagon**. (hex = 6)
- A polygon with 8 sides is an **octagon**. (octo = 8; an octopus has 8 tentacles)
- A polygon with 10 sides is a **decagon**. (deca = 10; a decathlon has 10 events)

Regular polygons

■ **A polygon is a *regular polygon* if its sides are all the same length and its angles are all the same size.**

Equilateral triangles and squares are regular polygons. Here are some others you will use:

This pentagonal building occupied by the US defence department is a regular polygon.

Interior and exterior angles of polygons

When you extend a side of a polygon you get two angles. One inside the polygon and one outside.

Learn these two rules:

■ **For a polygon: interior angle + exterior angle = 180°**

■ **The exterior angles of a polygon always add up to 360°.**

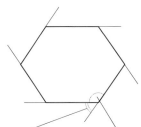

The angle outside is called the exterior angle.

The angle inside is called the interior angle.

Example 3

Find the sum of:
    (a) interior angles of a pentagon
    (b) the exterior angles of a pentagon.

(a) The inside of the pentagon can be divided into three triangles. The angles of a triangle always add up to 180°, so the angles of a pentagon add up to $3 \times 180° = 540°$

(b) The exterior angles are marked on this pentagon. Start at one corner and work clockwise ↻ around the pentagon.

At each corner you turn clockwise.

By the time you have gone past every corner you will have turned one full turn, so the sum of the exterior angles is 360°.

Exercise 5E

1   Draw the different types of polygons listed in this table. For each one extend the sides to show the exterior angles. Then:
   - Measure the interior and exterior angles and record them in your table.
   - Complete the table to show the sum of the interior angles and the sum of the exterior angles.

   The first one is done for you.

Type of polygon	Interior angles	Sum	Exterior angles	Sum
Triangle	43° + 122° + 15° =	180°	137° + 58° + 165° =	360°
Equilateral triangle				
Isosceles triangle				
Parallelogram				
Pentagon				

Example 4

Work out the exterior angle of a regular hexagon and use it to find the interior angle.

The hexagon has 6 sides.
The exterior angles add up to 360°
So each exterior angle is 360° ÷ 6 = 60°

Each interior angle is 180° − 60° = 120°

There are six equal exterior angles of 60°

Each interior angle is 180° – 60° = 120°

Exercise 5F

1   Work out:
   (a) the exterior angle of a regular octagon
   (b) the interior angle of a regular pentagon
   (c) the interior angle and exterior angle of a regular decagon.

2   A regular polygon has an exterior angle of 24°. Work out how many sides it has.

3   A regular polygon has an interior angle of 172°. Find the
    exterior angle and work out how many sides it has.

4   Draw a regular hexagon with sides 6 cm long.
    - Join all the vertices (corners).
    - Identify as many of the special types of quadrilaterals
      from page 72 as you can find in your hexagon.

5   Repeat question **4** for a regular pentagon.
    - Identify different congruent shapes and say how many
      of each of them there are.
    - Present your answers in a table.
    - Find and mark this shape in your pentagon: ▲
      It is called an arrowhead.

5.6 Tessellations

■   **A pattern of shapes which fit together without leaving any
    gaps or overlapping is called a tessellation.**

You can tessellate some shapes to cover a flat surface. It is
easier to show this if you work on dotted grid paper.

Example 5

Tessellate this trapezium on a grid.

There are three possible ways of doing this. They are:

    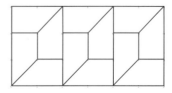

Exercise 5G

You will need dotted grid paper.

1   Show how each of these shapes tessellate.

2   Make some interesting patterns using combinations of different shapes that tessellate together.

3   See if you can invent some shapes with curved sides that tessellate.

Summary of key points

1   2-D shapes are flat. They have no thickness.

2   A triangle is a three-sided shape.

3   A quadrilateral is a four-sided shape.

4   Shapes which are exactly the same size and shape are congruent.

5   Polygon is the general name for a 2-D shape with straight sides.

6   A polygon is a regular polygon if its sides are all the same length and its angles are all the same size.

7   For a polygon: interior angle + exterior angle = 180°.

8   The exterior angles of a polygon always add up to 360°.

9   A pattern of shapes which fit together without leaving gaps or overlapping is called a tessellation.

6 Decimals

6.1 Understanding place value

Some things in life have whole number values.

There are a *whole* number of people and animals

Other items do not have whole number values.
The weight of a packet of sugar is 2.2 lbs.
The height of a person may be 1.76 metres.

These are *decimal* numbers. Decimals are used when you need to record a value more accurately than a whole number.

■ **In a decimal number the decimal point separates the whole number from the decimal places.**

Example 1

A Formula One Grand Prix driver has his lap time recorded as 53.398 seconds.

You can understand better what 53.398 seconds really means by drawing a decimal place value diagram.

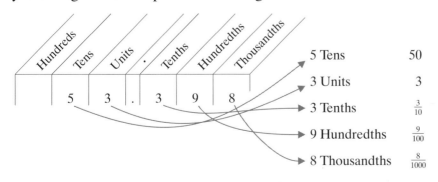

							5 Tens	50
							3 Units	3
							3 Tenths	$\frac{3}{10}$
							9 Hundredths	$\frac{9}{100}$
							8 Thousandths	$\frac{8}{1000}$

2.2 is read as two point two.
1.76 is read as one point seven six.

Read the whole number and then read the digits in order.
Fifty three point three nine eight

Example 2

A woman 400 m hurdler's time is 56.08 seconds. Draw up a place value table.

5 Tens	50
6 Units	6
Zero Tenths	$\frac{0}{10}$
8 Hundredths	$\frac{8}{100}$

BENZ

Even though there are zero *tenths* the 0 has to be recorded to keep the 8 in its correct place value position.

Example 3

Write down the place value of the digit underlined in each number

(a) 3<u>2</u>.8   (b) 0.38<u>5</u>   (c) 10.0<u>3</u>
(d) 4.2<u>9</u>0

(a) 2 units   (b) 5 thousandths   (c) 0 tenths
(d) 9 hundredths

Exercise 6A

1   Draw a place value diagram like the one in Examples 1 and 2 and write in these numbers.
     (**a**) 41.6   (**b**) 4.16   (**c**) 34.6   (**d**) 1.463
     (**e**) 0.643   (**f**) 1.005   (**g**) 5.01   (**h**) 0.086

2   What is the place value of the digit underlined in each number?
     (**a**) 2<u>5</u>.4   (**b**) 2.<u>5</u>4   (**c**) 25.4<u>6</u>   (**d**) 3.5<u>4</u>6
     (**e**) <u>1</u>8.07   (**f**) 9.66<u>9</u>   (**g**) 216.0<u>3</u>1   (**h**) 2.135<u>7</u>
     (**i**) 9.1<u>0</u>2   (**j**) 3.<u>3</u>36   (**k**) 2.59<u>1</u>   (**l**) 0.0<u>2</u>7

3   The table gives the price of a pack of Sudso soap powder in different shops:

Shop	Stall	Corner	Market	Main	Store	Super
Price	£1.29	£1.18	£1.09	£1.31	£1.20	£1.13

Write the list of prices in order starting with the lowest price.

4 The table gives the height in metres of six girls:

Rachel	Ira	Sheila	Naomi	Latif	Jean
1.56	1.74	1.78	1.65	1.87	1.7

Write the list of names in descending order of height, starting with the tallest.

5 The fastest lap times (in minutes) of six drivers was:

Ascarino	53.072	Bertolini	53.207
Rascini	52.037	Alloway	57.320
Silverman	53.027	Killim	53.702

Write down the drivers' times in order, fastest first.

6 A new cereal gives the weights per 100 g of vitamins and minerals:

Fibre	1.5 g	Iron	0.014 g
Vitamin B6	0.002 g	Thiamin B1	0.0014 g
Riboflavin B2	0.0015 g	Sodium	0.02 g

Write down the weights in order starting with the lowest.

6.2 Rounding decimal numbers

As with ordinary numbers, it is sometimes helpful to round a decimal number and give the result correct to the nearest whole number or correct to so many decimal places (d.p.).

Example 4

Round £5.11 to the nearest pound.

■ **To round to the nearest whole number, look at the figure in the tenths column or first decimal place. If it is 5 or more round the whole number up. If it is less than 5 do not change the whole number.**

In this example the first decimal place is **less** than 5 so you do not change the whole number

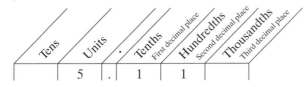

£5.11 to the nearest pound is £5

Example 5

Round 7.815 to the nearest whole number.

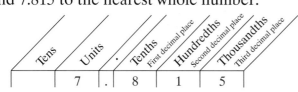

Tens	Units	.	Tenths	Hundredths	Thousandths
	7	.	8	1	5

7 is in the units column
8 is in the first decimal place
1 is in the second decimal place
5 is in the third decimal place

8 in the first decimal place is more than 5 so you round up.

7.815 is rounded to 8.

Example 6

Terry spent £47.52 on a new video game. Round the cost to the nearest pound.

Because the figure in the first decimal place is 5 (or more), the whole number is rounded to £48.

■ **To round a decimal correct to one place of decimals (1d.p.) you look at the second place of decimals. If it is 5 or more you round up, if it is less you leave this and any remaining numbers out.**

To correct to *two* places of decimals you look at the third place.
To correct to three places of decimals you look at the fourth place . . .

Example 7

Round the following numbers correct to *one* place of decimals.

(a) 25.27　　　(b) 25.72　　　(c) 25.55　　　(d) 25.528

(a) The second decimal place is 7 which is 5 or more so round the 2 up to 3. The answer is 25.3.

(b) The second decimal place is 2 which is less than 5 so leave this number out. The answer is 25.7.

(c) The second decimal place is 5 which is 5 or more so round the 5 up to 6. The answer is 25.6.

(d) The second decimal place is 2 which is less than 5 so leave this and any other numbers out. The answer is 25.5.

Exercise 6B

1　Round to the nearest whole number:
　(a) 7.8　　　　(b) 13.29　　　(c) 14.361　　(d) 5.802
　(e) 10.59　　　(f) 19.62　　　(g) 0.771　　　(h) 20.499
　(i) 0.89　　　　(j) 100.09　　(k) 19.55　　　(l) 1.99

2 Round these numbers correct to one place of decimals:
   (a) 3.6061   **(b)** 5.3391   **(c)** 0.0901   **(d)** 9.347
   (e) 10.6515   **(f)** 7.989   **(g)** 2.0616   **(h)** 0.4999
   (i) 2.45   **(j)** 125.67   **(k)** 0.05   **(l)** 9.890

3 Round:
   (a) 13.6 mm to the nearest mm
   (b) 80.09 m to the nearest m
   (c) 0.907 kg to the nearest kg
   (d) £204.49 to the nearest £
   (e) 3.601 lb to the nearest lb
   (f) 0.299 tonnes to the nearest tonne
   (g) 10.5001 g to the nearest g
   (h) 8.066 mins to the nearest min

6.3 Adding and subtracting with decimals

Example 8

Two children weigh 24.5 kg and 35.75 kg. What is their combined weight?

Combined weight is 24.5 kg + 35.75 kg

Keep numbers in their columns like in a place value diagram.

Put the decimal points under each other.

$$24.5$$
$$35.75$$

Decimal point in the answer will be in line.

Then add:

$$
\begin{array}{r}
24.5 \\
+\ 35.75 \\
\scriptstyle 1\ 1 \\
\hline
60.25
\end{array}
$$

Example 9

Add 13.6 and 125.403

$$
\begin{array}{r}
13.6 \\
+\ 125.403 \\
\scriptstyle 1 \\
\hline
139.003
\end{array}
$$

Exercise 6C

Work these out **without a calculator**, showing all your working.

1 1.5 + 4.6	**2** 3 + 0.25	**3** 26.7 + 42.2
4 125.7 + 0.32	**5** 0.1 + 0.9	**6** 16.1 + 2.625
7 9.9 + 9.9	**8** 10 + 1.001	**9** 156.3 + 1.84
10 0.005 + 1.909	**11** 117 + 1.17	**12** 4.56 + 0.751

Exercise 6D

Work these out **without a calculator**, showing all your working.

1 6.3 + 17.2 + 8.47	**2** 13.08 + 9.3 + 6.33
3 0.612 + 3.81 + 14.7	**4** 8.6 + 3.66 + 6.066
5 7 + 3.842 + 0.222	**6** 23.43 + 5.36 + 2.216
7 3.07 + 12 + 0.0276	**8** 5.02 + 31.5 + 142.065

Example 10

Bill earns £124.65 per week but loses £33.40 in tax and national insurance. What does he take home?

£124.65 − £33.40

$$
\begin{array}{r} 124.65 \\ -\ \ 33.40 \\ \hline \quad . \quad \end{array}
$$

Remember to put the decimal points under each other.

$$
\begin{array}{r} 1^{1}24.65 \\ -\ \ 33.40 \\ \hline 91.25 \end{array}
$$

Bill takes home £91.25

Exercise 6E

Work these out **without a calculator**, showing all your working.

1 19.9 − 13.7	**2** 5.84 − 1.7	**3** 23.5 − 9.4
4 100.7 − 3.4	**5** 0.59 − 0.48	**6** 1 − 0.65
7 16.9 − 10.71	**8** 21.64 − 10.5	**9** 2.5 − 1.6
10 5.84 − 1.77	**11** 23.5 − 9.47	**12** 14 − 0.75
13 6.125 − 4.9	**14** 14.01 − 2.361	**15** 3.29 − 1.036
16 204.06 − 35.48		

■ **When working out a decimal addition or subtraction sum always put the decimal points under each other.**

6.4 Multiplying decimals

Example 11

Find the cost of 5 books at £4.64 each.

```
   464
×    5
  ₃ ₂
  2320
```

Multiply the numbers together ignoring the decimals.

0d.p.   +   2d.p.   = 2d.p.

Count the total number of decimal places (d.p.) in the numbers you are multiplying.

2320 must have 2d.p.

The answer must have the same number of decimal places.

Answer is £23.20

Example 12

0.52×0.4

```
    52
×    4
   208
```

0.52   ×   0.4

2d.p.   +   1d.p.   = 3d.p.

The answer must have 3d.p. so is 0.208

■ **When multiplying decimals the answer must have the same number of decimal places as the total number of decimal places in the numbers being multiplied.**

Exercise 6F

Work these out **without a calculator**, showing all your working.

1 Find the cost of:
   (a) 6 books at £2.25 each
   (b) 4 tins of biscuits at £1.37 each
   (c) 8 ice creams at £0.65 each
   (d) 1.5 kilos of pears at £0.80 per kilo.

2 **(a)** 7.6×4 **(b)** 0.76×4 **(c)** 0.76×0.4
   (d) 2.25×5 **(e)** 2.25×0.5 **(f)** 0.225×0.5
   (g) 22.5×0.05 **(h)** 2.25×0.005 **(i)** 0.225×0.005

3 **(a)** 24.6×7 **(b)** 3.15×0.03 **(c)** 0.12×0.12
   (d) 0.2×0.2 **(e)** 1.5×0.6 **(f)** 0.03×0.04

4 **(a)** 6.42×10 **(b)** 64.2×10 **(c)** 0.642×10
   (d) 56.23×10 **(e)** 5.623×10 **(f)** 0.05623×10

Look carefully at your answers to question **4**. What do you notice?

5   (a) 0.045×100 (b) 0.45×100 (c) 4.5×100
      (d) 0.0203×100 (e) 0.203×100 (f) 2.03×100

     What do you notice about your answers to question **5**?

6.5 Division with decimals

Example 13

Five friends win £216.35 in a charity lottery. They share the money equally. How much do they each get?

$216.35 \div 5$ Put the decimal points in line.

$$
\begin{array}{r}
43.27 \\
5\,\overline{)21^16.^13^35}
\end{array}
$$

> Because 5 is a whole number divide straight away.

Work out **without a calculator**, showing all your working.

1   (a) $64.48 \div 4$ (b) $3.165 \div 5$ (c) $133.56 \div 9$
      (d) $205.326 \div 6$ (e) $35.189 \div 7$ (f) $0.0368 \div 8$

2   (a) $34.5 \div 10$ (b) $3.45 \div 10$ (c) $0.345 \div 10$
      (d) $78 \div 10$ (e) $7.8 \div 10$ (f) $0.78 \div 10$
      (g) $65 \div 10$ (h) $65 \div 100$ (i) $65 \div 1000$

     Write down anything you notice about your answers to question **2**.

3   How many 3 litre jugs would be needed to hold 43.5 litres of lemonade?

4   Seven people share £107.80 equally. How much will each receive?

Example 14

1.2 metres of fabric costs £1.56. What is the cost per metre?

£1.56 ÷ 1.2   not a whole number

> If the number you are dividing by is **not** a whole number change it to a whole number.

To change 1.2 to a whole number multiply by 10

$$1.2 \times 10 = 12$$

Do the same to £1.56 $1.56 \times 10 =$ £15.6
The sum becomes   £15.6 ÷ 12

$$
\begin{array}{r}
1.3 \\
12\,\overline{)15.^36}
\end{array}
$$
Answer is 1.3 which in money terms is £1.30

Exercise 6H

Work out **without a calculator**, showing all your working.

1	$7.75 \div 2.5$	**2**	$7.92 \div 2.2$	**3**	$9.86 \div 5.8$
4	$18.9 \div 12.6$	**5**	$0.129 \div 0.03$	**6**	$0.27 \div 0.1$
7	$6.634 \div 0.62$	**8**	$0.2121 \div 0.21$	**9**	$3.5 \div 1.4$
10	$353.6 \div 6.8$				

6.6 Fractions and decimals

Fractions can be changed into decimals by dividing the numerator by the denominator.

Example 15

Change $\frac{3}{4}$ into a decimal.

$\frac{3}{4}$ means $3 \div 4$ (numerator ÷ denominator)

$$4 \overline{\smash{)}\, 3.^30^20} \quad \begin{array}{c} 0.75 \end{array}$$

Put extra '0' here.

Answer is 0.75

To remind yourself about numerators and denominators look back at Unit 4.

Some fractions which you often use are shown in this table along with their decimal conversion equivalents:

Fraction	Decimal
$\frac{3}{10}$	0.3
$\frac{2}{5}$	0.4
$\frac{1}{4}$	0.25
$\frac{1}{2}$	0.5
$\frac{3}{4}$	0.75
$\frac{1}{8}$	0.125
$\frac{1}{3}$	0.3333 . . .

Decimals can be changed into fractions by using a place value table.

Example 16

Change 0.763 into a fraction.

The place value table shows 0.763 is 7 tenths, 6 hundredths and 3 thousandths which is the same as 763 thousandths, so you can write the decimal as a fraction like this:

$$\frac{763}{1000}$$

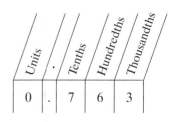

Example 17

Write as a fraction: (a) 0.7   (b) 0.59   (c) 0.071

Answers using the place value table:

(a) 7 tenths $= \frac{7}{10}$

(b) 59 hundredths $= \frac{59}{100}$

(c) 71 thousandths $= \frac{71}{1000}$

■ **Fractions can be changed into decimals by dividing the numerator by the denominator. Decimals can be changed into fractions by using a place value table.**

Exercise 6I

1   Change these fractions to decimals. Show your working.

    (a) $\frac{3}{5}$ (b) $\frac{1}{2}$ (c) $\frac{7}{10}$ (d) $\frac{7}{20}$

    (e) $\frac{4}{25}$ (f) $\frac{3}{50}$ (g) $\frac{7}{8}$ (h) $\frac{9}{20}$

    (i) $\frac{19}{25}$ (j) $\frac{5}{16}$ (k) $\frac{1}{8}$ (l) $\frac{27}{50}$

    (m) $\frac{9}{100}$ (n) $\frac{13}{200}$ (o) $\frac{2}{3}$ (p) $\frac{19}{20}$

2   Change these decimals to fractions.

    (a) 0.3   (b) 0.37   (c) 0.93   (d) 0.137

    (e) 0.293   (f) 0.07   (g) 0.59   (h) 0.003

    (i) 0.00003   (j) 0.0013   (k) 0.77   (l) 0.077

    (m) 0.39   (n) 0.0041   (o) 0.019   (p) 0.031

Summary of key points

1   In a decimal number the decimal point separates the whole number from the decimal places.

2   To round a decimal to the nearest whole number, look at the first decimal place. If it is 5 or more round the whole number up, if it is less than 5 do not change the whole number.

3   To round a decimal correct to one place of decimals look at the second place. If it is 5 or more round up, if it is less leave this and any remaining numbers out.

4   When making a decimal addition or subtraction sum always put the decimal points under each other.

5   When multiplying decimals the answer must have the same number of decimal places as the total number of decimal places in the numbers being multiplied.

6   Fractions can be changed into decimals by dividing the numerator by the denominator. Decimals can be changed into fractions by using a place value table.

7 Measure 1

7.1 Estimating

In real-life situations people are estimating all the time. How long will it take me to walk to the shops? Have I got time for another cup of tea? Is there enough milk in the fridge for the rest of the week?

Here are some measures that you have to estimate in real life:

You need to be able to estimate measurements in metric units and the old style Imperial units such as gallons, miles, and pounds.

Some Imperial measures
12 inches	= 1 foot
3 feet	= 1 yard
1760 yards	= 1 mile
8 pints	= 1 gallon

7.2 Estimating lengths

■ **Lengths and distances are measured in these metric and Imperial units:**
  metric: **kilometres (km), metres (m), centimetres (cm), millimetres (mm)**
  Imperial: miles, yards, feet, inches

Here are some estimates of distances in real life:

A 30 cm ruler is about 1 foot long.

A door is 2 m high or about $6\frac{1}{2}$ feet.

A long stride is 1 m long or about 3 feet.

$2\frac{1}{2}$ times around the track is 1 km or about $\frac{5}{8}$ mile.

Exercise 7A

Look at this picture, then write down an estimate for each of the following:

1 The height of the:
   (a) man   **(b)** girl
   (c) bus   **(d)** car

2 The length of the:
   (a) car   **(b)** bus
   (c) wall

3 The height of the:
   (a) house   **(b)** tree
   (c) wall

4 The width of the:
   (a) drive   **(b)** garage
   (c) house

7.3 Estimating capacities

■ **Capacity is a measure of the amount a container can hold.
It is measured in these units:**
metric: litres (*l*), centilitres (*cl*), millilitres (m*l*)
Imperial: gallons, pints

A milk carton holds
1 pint or 570 m*l*.

A petrol can holds
1 gallon or 4.5 litres.

A mug and a can of
cola hold about ½ pint
or about 300 m*l*.

Exercise 7B

Look at this picture, then copy and complete the table with
your estimates for each of the following.
Give your answers in metric and Imperial units.

	Amount of	Metric	Imperial
1	milk in a full carton		
2	milk in the carton		
3	cola in a full can		
4	cola in the glass		
5	coffee in the jug		
6	petrol in a full tank		
7	water in a full bucket		
8	water in a full paddling pool		

7.4 Estimating weights (masses)

■ **Weight is measured in these units:**
**metric: tonnes (t), kilograms (kg), grams (g),
          milligrams (mg)
Imperial: tons, hundredweight, stones, pounds, ounces**

A $\frac{1}{4}$ pound packet of
tea weighs about 100 g.

A 1 kg bag of
sugar weighs
about 2.2 pounds.

A 50 kg bag of
cement weighs
about 110 pounds.

Exercise 7C

Look at this picture, then copy and complete the table with
your estimates.

Give your answer in metric and Imperial units.

	Weight of the	Metric	Imperial
1	bag of potatoes		
2	block of butter		
3	bag of apples		
4	packet of coffee		
5	loaf of bread		
6	packet of cereal		
7	bottle of squash		
8	packet of biscuits		
9	packet of crisps		
10	box of soap powder		

Example 1

My car is 20 m long.

This is not very sensible because that means the car would be
over 60 feet long or about as long as an articulated lorry.

A sensible answer would be about 4 or 5 m.

Exercise 7D

For each of these statements say whether the measurements are sensible or not. If the statement is not sensible then give a reasonable estimate for the measurement.

1   (a) My teacher is 20 m tall.
    (b) My father is 20 cm tall.
    (c) The classroom measures 2 m by 3 m.
    (d) I bought 2 g of potatoes at the supermarket.
    (e) A can of cola holds 3 l of liquid.
    (f) A house is 10 m high.

2   (a) The tallest boy in school is 2 m tall.
    (b) John can just lift 50 kg.
    (c) Jane has to walk 1 km to school each day.
    (d) A cup full of tea contains 2 l of liquid.
    (e) The river Thames is 20 km long.
    (f) A 50 p piece weighs 0.5 kg.

3   (a) A box of chocolates weighs 500 g.
    (b) A 50 cc moped can travel at 150 miles per hour.
    (c) A pint glass will hold 1 l of liquid.
    (d) The capacity of the petrol tank in my car is 5 l.

4   (a) My new sports car can travel at 100 miles per hour.
    (b) The Eiffel Tower in Paris is more than 200 m high.
    (c) The capacity of the petrol tank in my car is 50 gallons.
    (d) A packet of tea weighs 50 g.
    (e) A kilo bag of sugar weighs 2 pounds.

7.5 Choosing appropriate units of measure

When you want to measure something you have to choose the most appropriate units to use. For example, to measure how long it takes to run 100 m you use seconds. To measure how long it takes to run a 26 miles marathon you would need to use hours, minutes and seconds.

SHOULD I USE HOURS, MINUTES OR SECONDS TO TIME THE 400 METRE RACE

Exercise 7E

Copy and complete this table with appropriate units for each measurement. Give both metric and Imperial units of measurement.

		Metric	Imperial
1	The length of your classroom		
2	The width of this book		
3	The distance of Edinburgh from London		
4	The length of a double decker bus		
5	The weight of a sack of potatoes		
6	The weight of a packet of sweets		
7	The weight of a lorry full of sand		
8	The amount of petrol in a car's petrol tank		
9	The amount of liquid in a full cup of tea		
10	The amount of medicine in a medicine spoon		
11	The amount of water in a raindrop		
12	The amount of water in a reservoir		
13	The time it takes to boil an egg		
14	The time it takes to run 400 metres		
15	The time it takes to walk 20 miles		
16	The time it takes to sail from Southampton to New York		
17	The length of a pencil		
18	The thickness of a page in this book		
19	The weight of 30 of these books		
20	The time it takes to travel from Earth to Mars		

7.6 Measuring time

You need to be able to:
- read the time using digital and analogue clocks
- use 12-hour and 24-hour clock times and convert from one type to the other.

■ **Digital clocks have a number display:**

■ **Analogue clocks have hands:**

Reading the time from an analogue clock

When you *say* the time you use phrases such as 'half past four' and 'ten to five'.

This clock shows the key phrases you need to know:

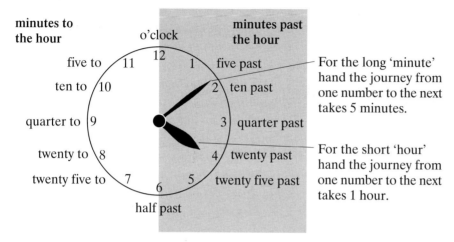

For the long 'minute' hand the journey from one number to the next takes 5 minutes.

For the short 'hour' hand the journey from one number to the next takes 1 hour.

Exercise 7F

1 Write down the times shown by these clocks as you would say them.

2 Draw six clock faces and mark these times on them:
   (a) seven o'clock   (b) ten past eight
   (c) quarter to five   (d) twenty to three
   (e) quarter past nine   (f) twenty five past four

Reading the time from a digital clock

Digital clocks make it easy to say the time:

The colon : keeps
the hours and minutes apart.

 9:20   means 20 minutes past 9.
You can also say: nine twenty.

9:40   means 40 minutes past 9, or twenty minutes to 10.
You can also say: nine forty.

Exercise 7G

1   Write these times as you would *say* them:
   (a) 8:30   **(b)** 10:10   **(c)** 11:05
   (d) 4:45   **(e)** 3:55

2   Draw five digital watches and show the following times on
   them:
   (a) quarter past 9   **(b)** half past 3   **(c)** twenty to 5
   (d) quarter to 7   **(e)** five o'clock

You need to be able to tell the difference between times such
as 2 o'clock in the morning and 2 o'clock in the afternoon.
Here are two ways of doing this.

12-hour clock times use **am** or **pm** to show whether a time is before or after midday:

24-hour clock times number the hours from **1** to **24**

Morning	Afternoon
The time shown by these clocks is	The time shown by these clocks is
9:25 am or 09:25	1:35 pm or 13:35

Changing 12-hour clock times to 24-hour clock times

Up to 12 noon the times are the same:

12-hour → 24-hour

9:35 am → 09:35

\ A digital clock
shows a zero here.

After 12 noon add 12 to the hour number:

12-hour → 24-hour

1:45 pm → 13:45

+ 12

Exercise 7H

1   Change these times from 12-hour clock times (am and pm)
    to 24-hour clock times.
    (a) 10:00 am   **(b)** 10:00 pm   **(c)** 9:30 am
    (d) 9:30 pm   **(e)** 8:20 pm   **(f)** 8:20 am
    (g) 7 am   **(h)** 8 pm   **(i)** 3:30 pm
    (j) 4:40 am   **(k)** 1:08 am   **(l)** 1:08 pm
    (m) 5:50 pm   **(n)** 5:50 am   **(o)** 11 pm
    (p) 8 am
    (q) Quarter past 8 in the morning
    (r) Quarter to 9 in the evening
    (s) Five to three in the afternoon
    (t) Twenty to seven in the morning

2   Change these times from 24-hour clock times to 12-hour
    clock times (am or pm).
    (a) 08:00   **(b)** 09:20   **(c)** 21:30   **(d)** 13:10
    (e) 12:10   **(f)** 00:20   **(g)** 01:40   **(h)** 08:00
    (i) 15:45   **(j)** 18:00   **(k)** 16:30   **(l)** 21:10
    (m) 23:55   **(n)** 14:02   **(o)** 06:25   **(p)** 00:00
    (q) 24:00   **(r)** 12:00   **(s)** 10:55   **(t)** 20:55

7.7 Reading scales

You need to be able to read these types of scales:

. . . a ruler to measure
lengths.

This line is 4 cm long.

. . . weighing scales

This scale shows 30 g.

. . . a measuring jug to measure
capacity

This jug contains 20 ml of liquid.

Exercise 7I

1   Write down the readings on these scales.

(a)

(b)

(c)

(d)

(e)

(f)

2   Draw diagrams to show these readings on a scale.
   (a) 5 cm   (b) 20 ml   (c) 50 g
   (d) 3 cm   (e) 25 ml   (f) 250 g

Using the marks on a scale

Here is how to read measurements that are in between the numbers marked on a scale:

This pencil ends between the 5 and the 6.

This pointer is between 20 and 30.

This reading is between 150 and 200.

There are 10 spaces between the 5 and the 6 so each mark shows $\frac{1}{10}$ or 0.1

There are 10 spaces between 20 and 30 so each mark shows 1 unit.

There are 5 spaces marked between 150 and 200 so each mark shows 10 units.

As the pencil ends on the third mark it must be 0.3 or $\frac{3}{10}$ more than 5.

As the pointer is on the seventh mark it must be 7 more than 20.

The reading is 170 units.

The pencil is 5.3 units long.

The reading is 27 units.

Exercise 7J

Write down the reading on these scales.

1

5   6   7   8
cm

2

190
180
170
cm

3

mph
40   50

4

40
30
20
10 ml

5

mph
10   20   30   40

6

7   8   9
cm

Estimating from a scale

Some scales have no helpful marks on them so you have to estimate a reading.

The only helpful mark on this scale is halfway between 4 and 5 at 4.5.

As the pointer is a little more than halfway between 4.5 and 5 a good estimated reading is 4.8 units.

4   5

Exercise 7K

Write down the measurements on these scales.

1

5   6   7   8

2

3   4   5   6
cm

3

mph
20   30   40   50

4

mph
70   80   90   100

5

4   5   6   7   8

6

2   3   4   5

Post Office scales

Post Office scales weigh letters and parcels and also show you how much it costs to post them.

This scale shows that for a letter weighing up to about 60 g the cost of postage is 19p second class and 26p first class.

Exercise 7L

1   Write down the cost of posting these letters:

(a)   (b)   (c)

2   Draw a scale showing letters with the following weights.
   (a) 30 g   (b) 50 g   (c) 100 g   (d) 200 g

Measuring lines accurately

When you measure the length of a line remember to start
measuring from the 0 on the scale you are using, *not the end* of
the ruler.

Start measuring
from the zero mark.

This line measures 3.7 cm.

Exercise 7M

1   Measure and write down the lengths of these lines in
   centimetres:

(a) ────────

(b) ──────────────

(c) ─────────────────────

(d) ──────────────────────────────────

(e)

(f)

(g) ────────

(h) ──────────────────────────

2 Draw and label lines with lengths:
  (a) 4 cm   (b) 6 cm   (c) 2.5 cm   (d) 5.7 cm
  (e) 4.8 cm   (f) 3.2 cm   (g) 8.3 cm   (h) 10.2 cm
  (i) 4.6 cm   (j) 3.9 cm   (k) 6.4 cm   (l) 7.2 cm

3 Draw and label lines with lengths:
  (a) 20 mm   (b) 35 mm   (c) 55 mm   (d) 100 mm
  (e) 74 mm   (f) 8 mm   (g) 18 mm   (h) 68 mm

Exercise 7N

1 (a) What metric unit of length would you use
      to measure the length of a large coach?
  (b) Using the unit you gave in part (a)
      estimate the length of a large coach.

[L]

2 The world record time for running 100 metres is about
  10 seconds.
  (a) Estimate the fastest time a sixteen-year-old boy could
      run 100 metres.
  (b) How long would it take the Prime Minister to *walk*
      400 metres? Give your answer in minutes.

[L]

3 The scale diagram shows a
  man and a dinosaur called
  a velociraptor.

  The man is 6 ft tall.

  Estimate the height of the
  velociraptor
   (i) in feet
  (ii) in metres.

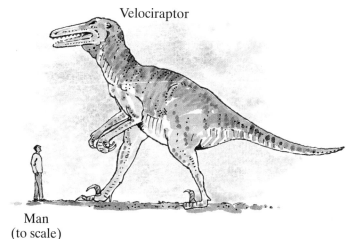

Velociraptor

Man
(to scale)

[L]

Summary of key points

1   Lengths and distances are measured in these metric
    and Imperial units:

      metric: kilometres (km), metres (m),
                     centimetres (cm), millimetres (mm)

      Imperial: miles, yards, feet, inches

2   Capacity is a measure of the amount a container can
    hold. It is measured in these units:

      metric: litres (l), centilitres (cl), millilitres (ml)

      Imperial: gallons, pints

3   Weight is measured in these units:

      metric: tonnes (t), kilograms (kg), grams (g),
                     milligrams (mg)

      Imperial: tons, hundredweight, stones, pounds,
                  ounces

4   Digital clocks have a number
    display:

5   Analogue clocks have hands:

8 Collecting and recording data

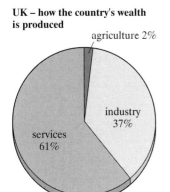

UK – how the country's wealth is produced

agriculture 2%

industry 37%

services 61%

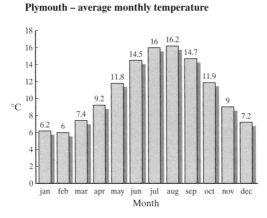

Plymouth – average monthly temperature

°C

jan 6.2 feb 6 mar 7.4 apr 9.2 may 11.8 jun 14.5 jul 16 aug 16.2 sep 14.7 oct 11.9 nov 9 dec 7.2

Month

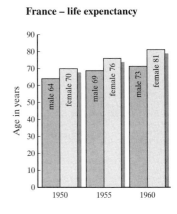

France – life expenctancy

Age in years

male 64, female 70 (1950); male 69, female 76 (1955); male 73, female 81 (1960)

You often see charts and tables like this in the press and on TV. They give you information or **data** as it is usually called. Sometimes you can use this data to make forecasts and plan for the future.

For example, the number of babies born this year helps us plan the number of school places needed in five years' time.

Statistics is the branch of mathematics concerned with:

- **collecting** and **recording** data
- **sorting** and **tabulating** that data
- presenting data visually in **charts** and **diagrams**
- making **calculations**
- **interpreting** results.

This unit shows you how to start collecting and recording data.

8.1 Ways of collecting data

You can collect data:

- using questionnaires
- by making observations and recording results
- by carrying out experiments
- from databases or records

You must be careful how you collect data. If you want to find out what people think of school dinners, don't just ask those going up for 'seconds'. They are the keen ones, so you might be led to the wrong conclusions!

8.2 Designing questions to collect data

When you are writing questions for a questionnaire:

■ **be clear what you want to find out, and what data you need.**

■ **ask short, simple questions.**

Here are some good examples:

Are you:

Male ☐   This has a clear choice
Female ☐   of **two** answers.

What age are you: Which of these do you like:

under 21 ☐   Cinema ☐
21–40 ☐   Theatre ☐
41–60 ☐   Opera ☐
over 60 ☐   Ballet ☐

These both offer **four** choices.

■ **avoid questions which are too vague, too personal, or which may influence the answer.**

Do you go swimming:

sometimes ☐   occasionally ☐   often ☐

Sometimes, occasionally and often may mean different things to different people.

Have you ever stolen anything from a shop:

Yes ☐   No ☐

Even a hardened criminal is unlikely to answer this question honestly!

Do you agree that sport is good for you:

Yes ☐   No ☐

This question suggests that the right answer is Yes. It is **biased**.

Test your questionnaire on a few people first to see if it works or needs to be improved. This is called a **pilot survey**.

Exercise 8A

1   Look at these pairs of questions. Choose whether
    Question X or Question Y is best to do the job in the
    To find out column.

	Question X	Question Y	To find out:
(a)	You like vegetables don't you?	Do you like vegetables?	if people like vegetables
(b)	How old are you?	Are you under 21, 21 to 40, 40 to 60, over 60?	the age group a person is in
(c)	Do you usually watch BBC or ITV?	Do you watch BBC?	the most popular channel
(d)	Do you use brand K?	Which soap powder do you normally use?	the most popular soap powder
(e)	Do you usually walk or ride to school?	Did you walk or ride to school this morning?	how pupils get to school
(f)	Did you enjoy your stay?	Was everything all right?	if the hotel was satisfactory
(g)	Did you see the film Henry the Fifth?	Do you like Shakespeare?	if they saw the film
(h)	Do you often have an egg for breakfast?	Do you usually have a cooked breakfast?	what sort of breakfast pupils have

Example 1

Decide if the following question is suitable for use in a
questionnaire. If not, give a reason and rewrite the question to
improve it.

> How much pocket money do you get:
>
> a little ☐   some ☐   a lot ☐

Little to some people may be *a lot* to others. It would be better
to be more precise. Also the word *some* means different
amounts to different people. A better question would be:

> How much pocket money do you get:
>
> ≥ 0 and < £2 ☐   ≥ £2 and < £4 ☐   ≥ £4 and < £6 ☐
>
> ≥ £6 and < £8 ☐   ≥ £8

Remember:
< less than
≥ greater than or equal to

Exercise 8B

1 Here are some questions that are not suitable for use in a questionnaire. For each one say why and write a more suitable question.

(a) You don't like rice pudding, do you?
Yes ☐ No ☐

(b) How well did you do in your test?
Badly ☐ Well ☐ OK ☐

(c) How many hours television do you watch?
1 ☐ 2 ☐ 3 ☐
4 ☐ 5 ☐

(d) What was the weather like?
Lousy ☐ Quite good ☐
OK ☐

(e) What type of job do you have?
Clerical ☐ Manual ☐
Other ☐

(f) Have you ever cheated in an examination?
Yes ☐ No ☐

(g) You will vote for Williams in the election won't you?
Yes ☐ No ☐

2 Draw up a questionnaire to find out what kind of holiday people had last year. (Hint: where, when, age, length, accommodation)

8.3 Collecting data by sampling

If you carry out a survey in a mixed school, but only question the first five students on each form register, you could end up asking all boys or all girls.

Ideally you should ask everyone in the school, but this is usually not practical. Instead you ask a limited number of students – a **sample**.

Make sure each student in the school has an equal chance of being picked to be part of the sample. You might question six pupils from each class, drawing their names out of a hat. This is called a **random sample**. Then questioning your sample should give a similar result to questioning the whole school.

If you do not choose a random sample your answers may be **biased**. To find out which sports a typical teenager watches you need a random sample of teenagers. Choosing a sample from teenagers at a football match will **bias** your answers – there will be more football lovers than in a random sample.

For a fair survey you may need to ask people of different ages, sexes, jobs, nationalities, and so on.

A **random sample** helps this market researcher find out what a typical person thinks without asking them all.

■ **When you carry out a survey select a random sample to avoid bias.**

Which of these methods of collecting information could be biased? Give your reasons.

Data needed:	Who to ask:
1 How people get to work	**(a)** Every fifth person near a bus stop **(b)** A group of people arriving together **(c)** A group of people during a tea break
2 If people like gardening	**(a)** People in a garden centre **(b)** Every tenth person passing in a street **(c)** People queuing for a train
3 If people think Superstore is a good shop	**(a)** People in a public library **(b)** People going into the shop **(c)** People coming out of the shop

4 Nadia wants to find out which computer games people play. She has designed a questionnaire with only boxes to tick.

> **QUESTIONNAIRE: COMPUTER GAMES**
>
> **1** Do you have a computer game at home? YES/NO
>
> **2** Tick the computer you have games for:
>
> ☐ ☐ ☐
> ZEGA   SAMURI   PC
>
> **3** Tick the type of computer game you like the best:
>
> ☐ ☐ ☐ ☐ ☐
> Arcade   Shoot-em-up   Fantasy   Factual   Educational
>
> **4** How many computer games have you bought in the last 12 months?
>
> ☐ ☐ ☐ ☐
> None   1   2   3

(a) How could you improve part 4 of the questionnaire?

(b) Nadia also wants to find out how much time people spend playing computer games each week.
Design a question that she could use. Include tick boxes for a response.   [L]

5 Write six questions you might include in a survey to decide on school uniform.

6 **(a)** Draw up a short questionnaire to find out how students in school spend their leisure time.

(b) Describe briefly how you would collect your data.

7   Laurie is designing a survey to find out about people who use a superstore near his home. One of the things he wants to know is how far people have travelled to get to the superstore.
    Decide which of these questions is best to ask. Give two reasons for your decision.
    (a) How far have you travelled to get here today?
    (b) Where do you live?
    (c) Do you live far from here?
    (d) Please show me on this map where you have travelled from.

8.4 Collecting data by observation

You could do a traffic survey by counting vehicles and recording what type they are as they pass you.

You would have to decide where, how and for how long to carry out your survey.

For example, if you did your survey during rush hour the results would be different from a survey on a Sunday.

Here is a **data capture sheet** from a traffic survey:

Traffic survey by H.Long on 5/6/96 at Main Street Ash 9.00–9.30 am.

Type of vehicle	Tally	How many
Bus	‖‖ ‖‖ ‖	12
Car	‖‖ ‖‖ ‖‖ ‖‖ ‖	22
Lorry	‖‖ ‖	7
Van	‖‖ ‖‖	10
M/cycle	‖‖ ‖‖ ‖‖ ‖	16

You record 5 in a tally chart like this:

‖‖

Exercise 8D

1   Prepare data capture sheets for surveys to find out two of the following by observation:
    (a) The colours of cars, clothes or shoes
    (b) The types and numbers of birds in a park
    (c) People using a pedestrian crossing
    (d) The approximate age groups and sexes of people entering a library or supermarket.

8.5 Collecting data by experiment

■ **When you do an experiment you can use a data capture sheet to record your results.**

Example 2

A game starts when you throw a six on a dice.

Greta throws a dice sixty times to see if it is a fair dice. Here are her results in a data capture sheet:

Score	Tally	How many
1	$\bcancel{||||}\,||||$	9
2	$\bcancel{||||}\,\bcancel{||||}\,|$	11
3	$\bcancel{||||}\,\bcancel{||||}\,||$	12
4	$\bcancel{||||}\,||||$	9
5	$\bcancel{||||}\,\bcancel{||||}$	10
6	$\bcancel{||||}\,||||$	9

The dice seems to be fair as the results for each score are about the same.

Exercise 8E

Carry out one or more of the following experiments

1   Find out how accurate people are at estimating.
    Ask people to estimate:
    (a) the length in centimetres of a piece of wood
    (b) the number of sweets in a jar
    (c) the weight in grams of a piece of metal

2   Find out whether a typical science textbook has longer words than a typical English textbook.
    ● choose two passages of about 50 words from each book.
    ● for each passage make a data collection table like this and complete it:

Number of letters in a word	Tally	How many
1		
2		
3		
4		
5		
6		
7		
8 or more		

8.6 Obtaining data from a database

■ **A database is an organized collection of information. It can be stored on paper or in a computer.**

Here is a table of data from a database of exam results:

Name	Maths		English		Science	History	French
	paper 1	paper 2	paper 1	paper 2			
Peter	34	41	53	46	57	29	43
Ahmed	73	85	60	58	63	52	46
Lucy	49	60	74	83	48	60	52
Chandra	55	38	46	40	62	45	36
Cita	61	65	50	44	71	58	52
Glenys	17	24	38	55	30	47	19

A computer database allows you to obtain information quickly and in a variety of forms, for example:

- in alphabetical order
- in numerical order
- girls' results only
- pupils scoring over 60 in one subject only . . .

Exercise 8F

1   Here is some information from a table in a gardening book.

Plant	Use	Colours	Flowering period	Where to plant
Alyssum	Edging	White, pink or purple	June–Sept	Full sun
Begonia	Small bedding	Pink, red or white	June–Sept	Any position
Convolvulus	Medium bedding	Red	July–Sept	Full sun or partial shade
Dahlia	Large bedding	Pink, red or white	July–Sept	Full sun or partial shade

(a) Which plant *must* be planted in full sun?
(b) Write down the colour of a Convolvulus.
(c) Write down the name of a pink bedding plant.   [L]

2 This database contains details of some second-hand cars.

Make	Model	Colour	Insurance group	Number of doors	Year	Price (£)
Ford	Sierra 2.0	Red	10	5	1990	3200
Ford	Escort 1.3	Blue	4	3	1992	4050
Honda	Civic 1.4	Blue	9	3	1991	5000
Renault	Clio 1.4	Silver	5	5	1992	4750
Peugeot	205 1.4GR	Red	7	5	1990	3150
Volvo	740 GL	Silver	12	4	1991	5950
Rover	1.6 LX	Green	9	4	1990	2500
Peugeot	205 1.4 XT	Silver	8	3	1992	3850
Vauxhall	Cavalier 1.6	Black	7	4	1989	3000
VW	Polo 1.3	White	6	3	1990	2300

Use the database to answer the following questions:
(a) Which is the oldest car?
(b) Which is the most expensive car?
(c) Which car has the highest insurance group?
(d) How many cars have 5 doors?
(e) Karen has £3000. Which cars could she buy?
(f) Gareth bought a silver 4-door car. What year was it?
(g) Which is the cheapest 5-door red car?
(h) How many cars are less than £3500?
(i) List the models of cars in order of price, most expensive first.
(j) Write a question of your own using at least two pieces of data.

3 Draw up a database to provide information about pupils in your class which might be useful for a new teacher.

4 This computer database has been asked to print out details
of crops which are harvested from June to October.

Crop	Form of tree	Space in metres between plants	Time in years before fully grown	Harvest time
Apple	Bush	3	3–4	Aug–Oct
Apple	Cordon	1	2–5	Aug–Oct
Apple	Standard	6	5–8	Aug–Oct
Blackberry	Fan or rod	3	2–3	Aug–Sep
Cherry	Fan	4.5	4–5	Jun–Sep
Cherry	Standard	7.5	5–7	Jun–Sep
Gooseberry	Bush	1.8	3–4	Jun–Jul
Gooseberry	Cordon	0.75	2–3	Jun–Jul
Pear	Cordon	1	3–4	Aug–Oct
Pear	Espalier	4.5	4–5	Aug–Oct
Pear	Dwarf	1	4–5	Aug–Oct
Plum	Bush	5	3–5	Aug–Oct
Plum	Fan	5	3–6	Aug–Oct

(a) Which crop has a space of 7.5 metres between plants?
(b) Which fruits can be harvested in July?
(c) Which two Cordon trees can be planted 1 metre apart?
(d) Which Fan type tree takes the longest before it is fully grown?
(e) Name two crops which grow on Standard trees.
(f) Name the crop and form of tree which is planted with a space of
4.5 metres and can be harvested in October.

Summary of key points

1 When you are writing questions for a questionnaire:
  - be clear what you want to find out and what data you need
  - ask short, simple questions
  - avoid questions which are too vague, too personal, or which may influence
    the answer.

2 When you carry out a survey select a random sample to avoid bias. This is a
sample in which everyone has an equal chance of being chosen.

3 When you do an experiment you can use a data capture sheet to record your
results.

4 A database is an organized collection of information. It can be stored on paper
or in a computer.

9 Algebra 2

9.1 Coordinates in the first quadrant

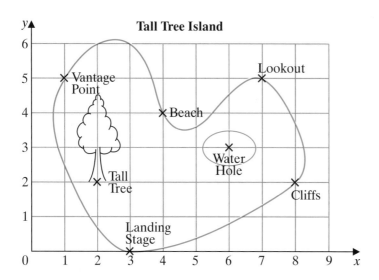

You can describe the position of a place on a grid by using two numbers.

The number of units across is put first and the number of units up is put second.

On this map 6 across, 3 up gives the position of the Water Hole. You can write this as the point (6,3). The numbers 6 and 3 are the **coordinates**.

Exercise 9A

1 Write down the names of the places on the map with these coordinates:
   (a) (8,2)   (b) (7,5)   (c) (1,5)
   (d) (3,0)   (e) (2,2)   (f) (4,4)

2 Write down the coordinates of these places on the map of Tall Tree Island:
   (a) Tall Tree   (b) Landing Stage   (c) Cliffs
   (d) Vantage Point   (e) Lookout   (f) Beach

Exercise 9B

1 On squared paper draw a coordinate grid and number it from 0 to 12 across the page and 0 to 6 up the page. Join the points in order given:

(2,3) (3,1) (10,1) (11,3) (7,3) (9,5) (6,5) (4,3) (2,3)

2 Write down the coordinates of all the points marked that make up the shape in the diagram.

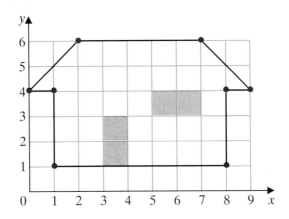

3 Write down the coordinates of all the corner points that make up this ship.

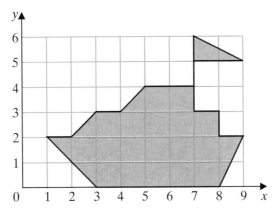

4 Draw a coordinate grid from 0 to 10 in both directions. On your grid plot the points and draw the following shapes by joining the points in order.
   (a) (1,1) (4,1) (4,4) (1,4)
   (b) (6,1) (9,1) (9,6) (6,6)
   (c) (0,6) (5,6) (0,10)
   (d) (5,7) (5,10) (8,10)

5 Draw a coordinate grid from 0 to 10 in both directions. On your grid draw a shape of your own and label the coordinates of each point.

6 Invent an island of your own and mark positions on it using a coordinate grid. List all the places with their coordinates.

9.2 Linear graphs

You can use graphs to show relationships. For example, if you buy several packets of crisps the price you pay will be related to the number of packets you buy.

Example 1

Stan sells packets of crisps at 15p each. He wants a quick way of remembering how much different amounts of packets cost.

He makes a table:

Number of packets	1	2	3	4	5	6
Cost in pence	15p	30p	45p	60p	75p	90p

Notice that the cost goes up by 15p for each extra packet. Also the cost of 3 packets is 45p and the cost of 6 packets is 90p. Double the packets means double the cost.

A pattern like the one in the table is known as a **linear relationship**. Linear relationships can be spotted very easily by drawing a graph.

Here is a graph of Stan's table.

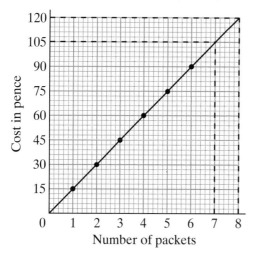

The points plotted make a straight line. This will be true for any linear relationship.

■ **A graph representing a linear relationship will always have a straight line.**

If the line of Stan's graph is made longer the cost of 7 and 8 packets can be read off. Check the dotted lines to see that the cost of 7 and 8 packets is 105p and 120p.

Example 2

Sharon charges £1 for the use of her taxi and 50p per mile after that.

You can use the information to draw up a table and then plot the points on a graph.

The table gives the charges for some journeys up to 6 miles long.

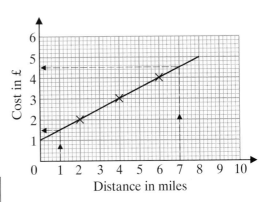

Distance in miles	0	2	4	6
Cost in £	1	2	3	4

Notice that the graph gives a straight line.

Because the relationship is linear you can use the graph to find the cost of a journey more than 6 miles, for example 7 miles, and for journeys between the values that you have worked out.

The cost of a 7 mile journey is £4.50

The cost of a 1 mile journey is £1.50

Exercise 9C

1   The table shows the cost of potatoes per kg.
    (a) Draw a graph for this table.

Weight in kg	1	2	3	4	5
Cost in pence	30	60	90	120	150

   (b) Work out how much 2.5 kg of potatoes would cost.
   (c) Extend the graph to work out the cost of 6 kg of potatoes.

2   The table shows the cost of ice lollies.
    (a) Draw a graph for the cost of ice lollies from the table.

Number of ice lollies	1	2	3	4	5
Cost in pence	25	50	75	100	125

   (b) Extend the graph and then use it work out the cost of
       (i) 8 ice lollies   (ii) 6 ice lollies

3 The table shows the number of litres of petrol left in a car's petrol tank on a journey.

Number of hours travelled	1	2	3	4	5	6	7	8
Number of litres left	55	50	45	40	35	30	25	20

    (a) Draw a graph from the information given in the table.
    (b) How many litres were in the tank at the start of the journey (after 0 hours)?
    (c) How many litres were in the tank after $5\frac{1}{2}$ hours?

4 A car uses 2 litres of petrol for every 5 km it travels.
    (a) Copy and complete the table showing how much petrol the car uses.

Distance travelled in km	0	5	10	15	20	25
Petrol used in litres	0	2	4			

    (b) Draw a graph from the information given in your table.
    (c) Work out how much petrol was used in travelling 4 km.
    (d) Work out how many kilometres were travelled after 15 litres of petrol were used.

5 A diet firm advertises that, if you follow their diet, you will lose 4 kg a week. Jim weighs 144 kg and wants to weigh 96 kg.

Copy and complete the table for Jim's expected weight under this diet if all goes to plan.

Weeks on diet	0	1	2	3	4	5	6	7	8
Jim's expected weight in kg	144	140							

    (a) Draw a graph from the information given in your table.
    (b) What would Jim expect to weigh after 10 weeks?
    (c) When does Jim expect to reach his target weight of 96 kg?

9.3 Conversion graphs

Another use of linear graphs (straight line graphs) is for converting one measurement into another measurement. These graphs are usually called **conversion graphs**.

Here is an example of a conversion graph that relates temperatures in degrees Fahrenheit (°F) to temperatures in degrees Celsius (°C).

To draw a conversion graph you need to know two pairs of values which link the two measurements you want to convert between.

In this case use the fact that

$$0\,°C = 32\,°F \text{ (the freezing point of water)}$$
and $100\,°C = 212\,°F$ (the boiling point of water)

To make a conversion graph you draw axes from 0 to 100 and label them °C and from 0 to 212 and label them °F. The two points are plotted and joined with a straight line.

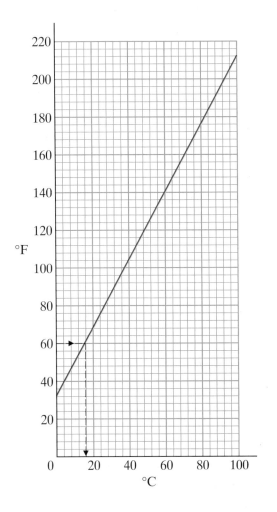

Example 3

Change 60° Fahrenheit to °Celsius.

- Draw a horizontal line from 60°F across to the straight line on the graph.
- From the line draw a vertical line down to the °C axis.
- Read off the scale.

The answer is between 15 and 16°C.

■ **A conversion graph is used to convert one measurement into another measurement.**

Exercise 9D

1   Copy the table and use the temperature conversion graph
    to complete it .

°C	5	20		28			35	80		40
°F			80		50	100			200	

2   (a) Draw a conversion graph from pounds to kilograms.
        Use the fact that 0 pounds is 0 kilograms and
        50 kilograms is 110 pounds. On your graph draw scales
        for kilograms and pounds using a scale of
        1 cm = 10 pounds and 1 cm = 10 kg.
        Plot the points (0,0) and (50,110) and join them with
        a straight line.
    (b) Copy and complete this table using your conversion
        chart to help you.

Kilograms	0			45	30	15			35	50
Pounds	0	10	20				50	14		110

3   Copy this table and then use the information in the table
    to draw a conversion graph from inches into centimetres.
    Use your graph to help you fill in the missing values.

Inches	0	1	2			9	8		12
Centimetres	0			10	15	20		25	30

4   Copy this table then use the information in the table to
    draw a conversion graph from miles into kilometres. Use
    your graph to help you fill in the missing values.

Miles	0	5		40		30		24	50
Kilometres	0		16		36		72	20		80

5   Copy this table then use the information in the table to
    draw a conversion graph from acres into hectares. Use
    your graph to help you fill in the missing values.

Hectares	0			12	15	17			3	20
Acres	0	20	30				24	45		50

9.4 Distance-time graphs

Distance-time graphs give information about journeys. We always use the horizontal scale for time and the vertical scale for distance.

Example 4

This is a graph showing a car journey.

On the graph from O to A the car travels 10 km in 10 minutes. From A to B the car travels 20 km in 10 minutes. From B to C the car does not go anywhere for 5 minutes. The journey home takes 15 minutes for the 30 km.

Suppose that the speed of the car needed to be worked out for each part of the journey.

speed = distance travelled ÷ time taken

Between O and A

speed = 10 km ÷ 10 minutes
     = 1 km per minute

There are 60 minutes in 1 hour so speed = 60 km per hour.

From the graph check that the speed:

from A to B = 120 km per hour
from B to C = 0 km per hour
from C to D = 120 km per hour

■ **Distance-time graphs are used to relate the distance travelled to the time taken, and to calculate speeds.**

Exercise 9E

1 Jane walks to the shops, does some shopping then walks home again.

A graph to show Jane's walk

(a) How many minutes did it take for Jane to walk to the shops?

(b) How far away were the shops?

(c) How many minutes did Jane spend shopping?

(d) How many minutes did it take for Jane to walk home?

(e) Work out the speed at which Jane walks to the shops. First give your answer in metres per minute, then change it to km per hour.

(f) Work out the speed at which Jane walks back from the shop. First give your answer in metres per minute, then change it to km per hour.

2 Here is a graph of David's car journey to see his aunt.

(a) Write a story of the journey explaining what happened during each part of it.

(b) Work out David's speed during each part of the journey. Give your answer in km per hour.

3 Wayne sets off from London at 08:00 and travels to a town 150 km away to meet his girl friend Tracey. He stops for a rest on the way. Once he gets to Tracey's he turns around and drives straight home because he discovers that Tracey set off for London some time ago to see Wayne.

Wayne and Tracey's journeys

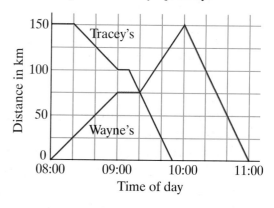

(a) Describe Wayne's journey in detail explaining after what distance he stopped on the way and for how long.

(b) Describe Tracey's journey in detail explaining after what distance she stopped on the way and for how long.

(c) At what time did Tracey and Wayne pass each other and what distance were they from London when it happened?

4 Imran has a bath. The graph shows the height of the bath water.

He starts at O by turning the hot and cold water taps on.

Between O and point A on the graph the height of water goes up to 20 cm in 5 minutes.

Explain what happens between letters AB, BC, CD DE and EF on the graph and how long each part of the process takes.

Imran's bath water

5 Gerald walks to the telephone box near his house to make a phone call. It took him 4 minutes to walk to the phone box that was 400 m away. Gerald talked on the phone for 2 minutes and he walked home in 3 minutes. Use graph paper to draw a distance-time graph for this journey.

6 Kirsti took up a trip in a hot-air balloon. The balloon rose 400 metres in the air in one hour and stayed at this height for two-and-a-half hours. The balloon then came back to earth in half-an-hour. Use graph paper to draw a distance-time graph for this balloon flight.

7 Annabel travels to school. She walks the 250 metres to the bus stop in 4 minutes, waits at the bus stop for 5 minutes then travels the remaining 1000 metres by bus. She arrives at the bus stop outside the school 15 minutes after she set off from home.
  (a) Draw a distance-time graph of the journey.
  (b) Work out the speed of the bus, first in m per min, then in km per hour.

8 Kam went shopping by car. She drove the 10 miles to the shops in 30 minutes. She stayed at the shops for 30 minutes and then started to drive home. The car then broke down after 5 minutes when she had travelled 4 miles from the shops. It took 10 minutes to repair the car and another 5 minutes to get home. Draw a distance-time graph for Kam's journey.

9.5 Graphs of simple algebraic equations

Section 9.1 shows how to plot points on a grid with positive coordinates only. You also need to be able to plot coordinates that include negative numbers:

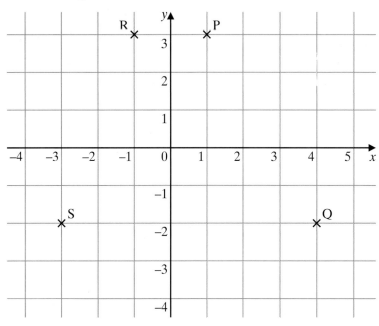

Point P is $(1,3)$.

Point R is at -1 along the x-axis and 3 up the y-axis. R is $(-1, 3)$.

Point Q is $(4,-2)$ and point S is $(-3,-2)$.

Exercise 9F

1 Write down the coordinates of all the points A to L marked on the coordinate grid.

2 Draw a coordinate grid with the horizontal axis (the x-axis) marked from -4 to $+4$ and the vertical axis (the y-axis) marked from -10 to $+10$.

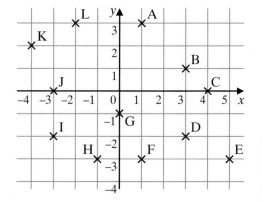

Plot the following points and join them in the order of the following list:

$(-1,6)$ $(-2,6)$ $(-4,5)$ $(-4,6)$ $(-2,7)$ $(0,8)$ $(1,7)$
$(1,-2)$ $(2,-6)$ $(1,-8)$ $(0,-9)$ $(-1,-9)$ $(-2,-8)$
$(-3,-6)$ $(-2,-5)$ $(-1,-5)$ $(0,-6)$ $(-2,-6)$ $(-1,-8)$
$(0,-8)$ $(1,-6)$ $(-1,-2)$ $(-3,0)$ $(-3,2)$ $(-1,6)$.

Using algebra to describe lines

This graph shows a linear (straight line) relationship between the numbers on the horizontal and vertical axes:
You can use algebra to describe the relationship and the line.

A grid showing the line $x = 2$

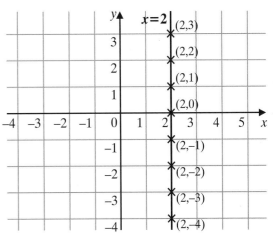

Remember: The horizontal axis is called the **x-axis** and the vertical axis is called the **y-axis**.

In a pair of numbers the x-coordinate is given first; the y-coordinate is given second:

$$(x, y)$$

For example in the point $(3, 2)$ the x-coordinate is 3 and the y-coordinate is 2.

Look for a number pattern connecting the coordinates to give the line a name. On this grid all the x-coordinates are 2 so the line is called $x = 2$

The **equation** of the line is $x = 2$

In this graph all the y-coordinates are -2 so the line is called $y = -2$

The **equation** of the line is $y = -2$

- **The equation of a line is a way of using algebra to show a relationship between x- and y-coordinates.**

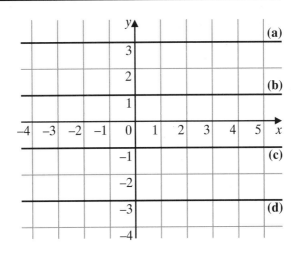

Exercise 9G

1   Write down the equations of the lines marked **(a)** to **(d)** in this diagram.

2   Write down the equations of the lines labelled **(a)** to **(d)** in this diagram.

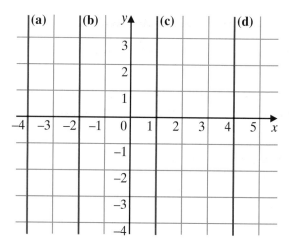

3   Draw a coordinate grid with x- and y-axes labelled from –5 to 5. On the grid draw and label the graphs of:
    (a) $x = 4$ **(b)** $x = -2$ **(c)** $x = -4$ **(d)** $x = 1$

4   Draw a coordinate grid with axes labelled from –5 to 5. On the grid draw and label the graphs of
    (a) $y = 4$ **(b)** $y = -2$ **(c)** $y = -4$ **(d)** $y = 1$

5   Draw a coordinate grid with axes labelled from –5 to 5. On the grid draw and label the graphs of
    (a) $y = 3$ **(b)** $x = -1$
    (c) Write down the coordinates of point where the two lines cross.

Example 5

Draw the graph of $y = x - 1$

Step 1: Choose some values for x, for example let $x = -2, 0$ and $+2$

Step 2: Put these values of x into the equation $y = x - 1$

if $x = -2$: $y = -2 - 1$ = -3
if $x = 0$: $y = 0 - 1$ = -1
if $x = 2$: $y = 2 - 1$ = 1

Step 3: These are three pairs of values which make the equation $y = x - 1$ true.

x	–2	0	2
y	–3	–1	1

Step 4: Plot the points $(-2, -3)$, $(0, -1)$ and $(2, 1)$ and join them to give the line.

Step 5: Label the line.

Worked examination question 1

Draw and complete a table of values for the graphs of
$y = 2x - 1$ and $y = -x + 1$.

Draw the graphs on graph paper and write down the
coordinates of the point where they cross.

Step 1
Choose three values for x.
For example

$x = -1, 0, 2$

Step 2
Put these values of x into each equation.

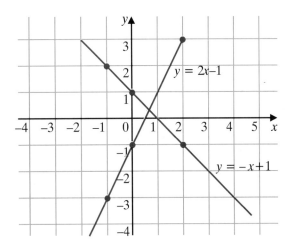

$$x = -1 \quad y = -2 - 1 \quad = -3$$
$$x = 0 \quad y = 0 - 1 \quad = -1$$
$$x = 2 \quad y = 4 - 1 \quad = 3$$

$$x = -1 \quad y = 1 + 1 \quad = 2$$
$$x = 0 \quad y = 0 + 1 \quad = 1$$
$$x = 2 \quad y = -2 + 1 \quad = -1$$

These pairs of values make
$y = 2x - 1$ true

x	−1	0	2
y	−3	−1	3

These pairs of values make
$y = -x + 1$ true

x	−1	0	2
y	2	1	−1

Plot the points $(-1, -3)$, $(0, -1)$ and $(2, 3)$ and join them with a
straight line.

Do the same for $(-1, 2)$, $(0, 1)$ and $(2, -1)$.

The lines cross at about

$$\left(\tfrac{2}{3}, \tfrac{1}{3}\right)$$

Make sure you read the coordinates accurately from your
graph.

Exercise 9H

1   On a coordinate grid with the x-axis labelled from -4 to 4
    and the y-axis labelled from -6 to 6 draw the following
    graphs.
    (a) $y = x + 2$ **(b)** $y = x + 4$ **(c)** $y = x + 1$
    (d) $y = x - 2$ **(e)** $y = x' - 4$ **(f)** $y = x - 1$

2   On a coordinate grid with the x-axis labelled from -4 to 4
    and the y-axis labelled from -10 to 10 draw the following
    graphs.
    (a) $y = x$ **(b)** $y = 2x$
    (c) $y = 3x$ **(d)** $y = \frac{1}{2}x$

3   On a coordinate grid with the x-axis labelled from -4 to 4
    and the y-axis labelled from -6 to 6 draw the following
    graphs.
    (a) $y = 2x + 1$
    (b) $y = -x - 2$
    Write down the coordinates of the point there they cross.

4   On a coordinate grid with the x-axis labelled from -4 to 4
    and the y-axis labelled from -6 to 6 draw the following
    graphs.
    (a) $y = -2x - 1$
    (b) $y = x + 2$
    Write down the coordinates of the point where they cross.

5   On a coordinate grid with the x-axis labelled from -4 to 4
    and the y-axis labelled from -10 to 10 draw the following
    graphs.
    (a) $y = x + 1$ **(b)** $y = -x - 2$
    (c) $y = 2x - 3$
    Write down the coordinates of the points where they cross
    as accurately as you can.

6   **(a)** Copy and complete the table of values for the graphs
        below

        $y = 3x - 2$ and $y = 5 - x$

x	−1	0	1	2
y				

x	−1	0	1	2
y				

   (b) Draw the graphs on graph paper and write down the
        coordinates of the point where they cross.

Using algebra to describe curves

Algebra can also be used to describe curved line graphs.

The following table shows x- and y-coordinates related by the equation $y = x^2$

Remember:

$x^2 = x$ times x

and

$-2 \times -2 = +4$

$-3 \times -3 = +9$ and so on

x	y = x²
−4	16
−3	9
−2	4
−1	1
0	0
1	1
2	4
3	9
4	16

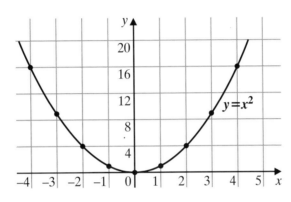

■ **Graphs of equations which have an x^2 term do not have straight lines.**

Exercise 9I

1   Copy and complete this table of values for the graph of $y = x^2 - 2$.

x	−4	−3	−2	−1	0	1	2	3	4
x²	16		4			1			
−2	−2		−2			−2			
y	14		2			−1			

Draw a coordinate grid with values for x from −4 to 4 and values of y from −2 to 15. Plot the points from the table and join them with a smooth curve.

2   Copy and complete this table of values for the graph of
$y = x^2 + 1$.

x	−4	−3	−2	−1	0	1	2	3	4
$y = x^2 + 1$	17				1			10	

Draw a coordinate grid with values for x from −4 to 4 and
values of y from 0 to 17. Plot the points from the table and
join them with a smooth curve.

3   On a coordinate grid with values for x from −3 to 3 and
values of y from −4 to 16 draw the curve of $y = x^2$ and
$y = 3x$. Write down the coordinates of *both* points where
the two lines cross.

4   On a coordinate grid with values of x from −3 to 3 and
values of y from −4 to 16 draw the curve of $y = x^2 - 2$ and $y
= 2x + 3$. Write down the coordinates of *both* points where
the two lines cross.

5   Draw a coordinate grid with values for x from −4 to 4 and
values of y from −13 to 17. On the grid draw the graphs of:
(a) $y = 3x - 1$ **(b)** $x = 5$ **(c)** $y = x^2 - 3$

Summary of key points

1   A graph representing a linear relationship always has a
straight line.

2   A conversion graph is used to convert one
measurement into another measurement.

3   Distance-time graphs are used to relate the distance
travelled to the time taken, and to calculate speeds.

4   The equation of a line is a way of using algebra to show
a relationship between x- and y-coordinates.

5   Graphs of equations which have an x^2 term do not have
straight lines.

10 Sorting and presenting data

10.1 Sorting and presenting data

Here are sixty pupils' marks out of 10 for a spelling test.

3 6 2 5 4 7 7 6 7 9 5 7 8 6 6 5 6 8 6 3 7 8 6 1 8 4 5 5 4 7 6 4 7 3 5
10 3 7 6 8 9 5 8 4 7 6 1 9 8 6 8 2 6 5 4 5 7 6 7 9

To see how well the pupils did sort them like this:

Mark	Tally	Frequency
0		0
1	||	2
2	||	2
3	||||	4
4						6
5	|||| ||||	9
6	|||| |||| |||	13
7	|||| |||| |	11
8	|||| |||	8
9	||||	4
10	|	1

This table, or tally chart, shows the frequency of each mark (how often each mark occurred). It is easier to count tally marks later on if you draw the 5th tally mark through the other four, like this:

|||| |||| |||| \|\|\|

is better than

\|\|\|\|\|\|\|\|\|\|\|\|\|\|\|

Another way of showing up any pattern in data is to draw a **bar chart**, sometimes called a bar graph.

This bar chart shows the data from the spelling test.

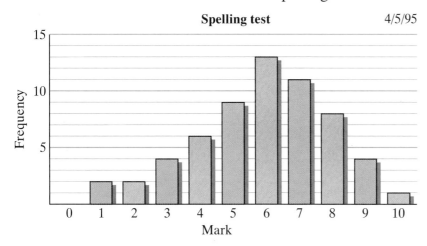

Spelling test   4/5/95

When drawing a bar chart you must make sure that:

- the horizontal and vertical axes are clearly labelled
- the chart is named and dated
- the scale is designed so that the bar chart is a sensible size.

These computer sales figures look the same until you look at the scale on the vertical axes.

For Apollo Computers Ltd the number of computers sold in a month was $4 + 2 + 6 + 8 = 20$

For Zenith Computers Ltd the number sold was $6 + 3 + 9 + 12 = 30$

■ **Tally charts and bar charts are two ways of displaying data that can be counted.**

Exercise 10A

For each of the following sets of data recorded at an island weather station, draw up:
(a) a tally and frequency chart
(b) a bar chart
to make it easier to study the data.

1 Hours of sunshine

5	6	0	1	3	1	4	7	5	6
6	2	4	3	1	0	7	10	9	11
5	4	7	6	9	9	11	12	12	7
9	10	11	10	9	7	8	4	6	5
7	8	10	8	6	3	6	8	3	3
4	1	10	9	11	7	2	6	10	7

2 Force of the wind measured on the Beaufort scale

3	1	4	4	3	5	2	6	4	2
2	2	0	1	4	2	5	3	3	4
4	3	6	7	5	4	0	1	2	3
1	5	4	3	2	2	8	10	9	7
7	8	6	5	4	3	5	2	6	7
5	5	1	2	6	4	3	4	6	5

3   Maximum temperature, in degrees Fahrenheit

64	66	66	69	67	70	68	65	67	65
63	64	63	65	64	63	66	60	65	62
69	71	69	70	69	71	71	74	72	69
74	70	70	73	70	73	69	67	68	67
66	67	65	67	66	62	67	63	68	72
69	70	72	72	71	73	70	69	67	68

Think carefully about your horizontal scale on the bar chart for this data.

10.2 Grouping data

When the range of data is wide it is usual to group it so that the charts are more compact and it is easier to spot patterns.

Here are the marks in an exam:

15	9	34	28	17	44	11	17	21	39
26	38	14	23	47	32	27	19	23	41
17	25	16	30	26	26	42	35	24	19
16	27	33	22	12	19	31	27	36	24
32	36	23	29	37	40	33	16	47	10
34	29	24	18	31	36	26	28	33	22
27	36	34	22	43	18	24	31	26	7

■   **The range is the highest mark − lowest mark.**

Check from the table that the **range** of this data is $47-7 = 40$

First group the marks in fives and make a frequency table.
Then draw a bar chart to illustrate the data.

Mark	Tally	Frequency
0–4		0
5–9	||	2
10–14	||||	4
15–19	ⵏⵏ ⵏⵏ ||	12
20–24	ⵏⵏ ⵏⵏ |	11
25–29	ⵏⵏ ⵏⵏ ||||	14
30–34	ⵏⵏ ⵏⵏ ||	12
35–39	ⵏⵏ |||	8
40–44	ⵏⵏ	5
45–49	||	2
50–		0

The intervals 0–4, 5–9 etc. are called **class intervals**.

Worked exam question 1

Thirty-five people took part in an archery competition. The points they scored are shown below.

```
18  24  19   3  24  11  25  10  25  14   9  16  26  25
21  27  13   5  26  22  12  27  20   7  28  21  20  23
22  16  12  25   7  25  19
```

(a) Work out the range of points scored.
Range is highest − lowest = 28−3
Range is 25

(b) Complete the frequency table.

Class interval	Tally	Frequency
1–5	||	2
6–10	|| ||	4
11–15	ⵀⵀ	5
16–20	ⵀⵀ ||	7
21–25	ⵀⵀ ⵀⵀ ||	12
26–30	ⵀⵀ	5
Total =		35

Exercise 10B

1 In a music contest the marks awarded were:

```
15  21  13  18  22  17   9  12   7  19
24  16  11   8  14  28  17  15  18   7
 5  17  10  26   7  16  23  14  11  20
12   6  26  16  10  19  13  29  17   8
```

(a) Using class intervals 0–4, 5–9, etc. draw up a frequency table.
(b) Illustrate your answer with a bar chart.
(c) Write down the range of marks.

2 The number of questions answered correctly in a general knowledge quiz were:

11	8	23	17	15	31	29	17	9	28
33	26	14	24	35	30	16	8	27	16
35	27	38	22	11	32	25	36	14	20
28	34	21	17	30	6	14	25	28	31
29	17	5	18	22	31	24	35	17	26

(a) Draw up a frequency table, using class intervals 0–4, 5–9, and so on.

(b) Illustrate your data with a bar chart.

(c) Give the range of correct answers.

10.3 Comparing data

You can use bar charts to compare different sets of data.

The number of patients who attended morning and evening surgeries in a doctor's practice one week are shown in the table and the following bar chart.

	Mon	Tues	Wed	Thur	Fri	Sat	Sun
Morning	145	120	96	116	125	136	27
Evening	81	65	43	55	64	28	–

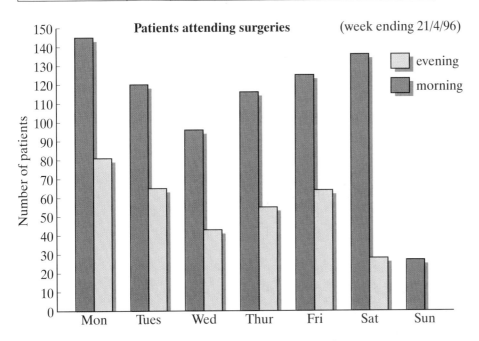

This graph is called a **dual bar chart** because it compares **two** sets of data. Often it is easier to see a pattern by looking at the chart rather than the table.

■ **A dual bar chart is used to compare two sets of data.**

Example 1

Use the table and bar chart on page 137 to answer the
following questions.

(a) Which day did most patients attend?
(b) Which day did least patients attend?
(c) On which day was there no evening surgery?
(d) On which day did 171 patients visit?
(e) How many more patients attended on Tuesday morning than
evening?

(a) Monday   (This is clearer from the bar chart.)
(b) Sunday   (This is clearer from the bar chart.)
(c) Sunday   (Use the table or the bar chart.)
(d) Thursday (Use the table for exact numbers.)
(e) 55   (Use the table.)

Exercise 10C

1   The average daily temperature, in °F, in London and
    Majorca is recorded in the table.

	Oct	Nov	Dec	Jan	Feb	Mar	Apr
London	58	50	45	42	44	50	56
Majorca	72	65	58	55	58	62	66

(a) Draw a dual bar chart to illustrate the table.
(b) Write down three things you notice from your chart.

2   The cost of holiday accommodation in Majorca per
    person, in £ sterling, per week is given in the table.

	Oct	Nov	Dec	Jan	Feb	Mar	Apr
Hotel	260	290	270	280	295	315	330
Self catering	190	150	140	110	125	150	180

(a) Draw a dual bar chart to illustrate the table. (Think
    carefully about the vertical scale you choose.)
(b) Which months have the greatest difference in price
    between hotel and self catering?
(c) What is the hotel price range?
(d) Write down three things you notice from your chart.

3   The amount of money, in pesetas, spent by Norma and
    Adrian buying presents was:

	Mon	Tues	Wed	Thur	Fri	Sat
Norma	560	0	940	120	1500	350
Adrian	320	460	150	1260	380	260

   (a) Represent this data by drawing a dual bar chart.
   (b) Write down three statements about Norma's and
       Adrian's spending.

4   Record the times you and a friend spent doing homework
    on each day during one week.
    (a) Enter the results on a table.
    (b) Draw a dual bar chart of the data.
    (c) Comment on the result.

10.4 Pictograms

■   **Pictograms are a quick, visual way of showing information
    by using symbols to represent amounts.**

For example, a school office secretary recorded the number of
Year 10 students who were late to school one week and drew a
pictogram like this:

Monday	大 大 大 大
Tuesday	大 大
Wednesday	大 大 大 大 大 大
Thursday	大 大 大
Friday	大 大 大 大 大

Each 大 represents one student.

Rashid went round a factory car-park and made a note of the
colours of the cars. His findings were:

Black	35	White	20
Red	10	Grey	15
Silver	15	Beige	2
Green	5	Other	14

He decided to use the symbol to represent 5 cars and drew this pictogram.

Car colours in car park

Exercise 10D

1   The pictogram shows how the staff at an office travel to work.

Travel

Walk	𝅺 𝅺 𝅺
Train	𝅺 𝅺 𝅺 𝅺 𝅺 𝅺 𝅺
Bus	𝅺 𝅺 𝅺
Car	𝅺 𝅺 𝅺 𝅺 𝅺
M/cycle	𝅺 𝅺
Bicycle	𝅺 𝅺
Other	𝅺

𝅺 = 10 people

(a) How many people travel by car?
(b) Which was the most popular way to travel?
(c) How many people travel by bicycle?
(d) Why was it more difficult to get an answer to part (c)?

2   Draw a pictogram to illustrate each of the tables. First decide what symbol you will use and what it will represent.
(a) This table shows the number of telephone calls to an answering service between midnight and 7:00 am during a certain week.

	Mon	Tues	Wed	Thur	Fri	Sat	Sun
Calls	24	20	32	48	28	32	12

(b) This table shows the number of cars using a car-park in a week.

	Sun	Mon	Tues	Wed	Thur	Fri	Sat
Cars	40	160	120	150	140	180	210

3 The pictograms show how many drinks were sold from two machines.

Drinks machine sales

Dining room

Coffee	
Tea	
Hot chocolate	
Soup	
Hot blackcurrant	

Staff room

Coffee	
Tea	
Hot chocolate	
Soup	
Hot blackcurrant	

Key: 🥤 10 drinks sold
      🥤 5 drinks sold

(a) (i) Which drink was most popular in the dining room?
   (ii) How many hot blackcurrants were sold in the dining room?
   (iii) How many hot chocolates were sold in the staff room?
(b) The staff room machine sold 45 teas.
   Copy and complete the pictogram.
(c) Work out the total number of drinks sold in the dining room.
(d) 64 people used the machine in the dining room.
   Work out the average number of drinks sold per person.
(e) Comment on the differences in sales from the two machines.   [L]

4 (a) Draw up a table to show the amount of time, in minutes, you spent each day last week
   (i) doing homework
   (ii) watching television.
(b) Draw a pictogram to illustrate your result.

10.5 Line graphs

The table shows the temperature, in °Centigrade in Leeds at midday during the first week in May.

May	1	2	3	4	5	6	7
Temperature (°C)	12	16	14	11	12	15	13

We could show this data on a **line graph**. Here are two ways of doing so.

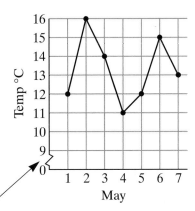

The temperature scale on this graph starts at 0 °C.

This graph gives more space on the *y*-axis to values between 10 and 16 °C. This gives a more representative line graph.

The break in the axis shows the scale goes straight from 0 to 9.

10.6 Discrete and continuous data

It is important, when drawing graphs, to know if the data is discrete or continuous.

Data which can be *counted* is called **discrete data**
For example, George has three sisters.
　　　　　Portsmouth beat Charlton 3–1.
　　　　　There are six tennis balls in the box.

Data which is *weighed* or *measured* is called **continuous data**
For example, George is 1.82 m tall.
　　　　　The athlete ran 100 metres in 10.3 seconds.
　　　　　The weight of the six tennis balls was 372.5 grams.

■　**Line graphs can be used to show continuous data.**

This table shows the number of passengers that got off a train at each stop on a line in SE London.

London Bridge (B)	Hither Green (G)	Lee (L)	Mottingham (M)
30	19	28	24

If you drew a graph like this it might give the impression that people got off the train between stations!

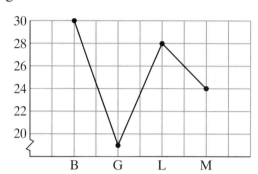

The data is *discrete* so you do not join the points.

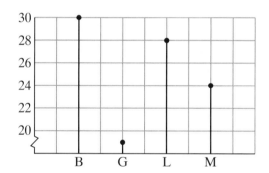

This is called a vertical line graph. This is used to display data that can be counted in a similar way to bar charts.

Exercise 10E

1   A class of 30 pupils listed their favourite hobby. The results are shown in this table.

Sport	Music	Reading	Model making	Computer games
8	5	3	2	12

Illustrate this data by drawing:
(a) a bar chart
(b) a pictogram using suitable symbols.

2 This table shows the temperatures recorded in °F one day in July.

Washington	Vancouver	Sydney	Luxor	Hong Kong	London
93	64	52	104	88	72

(a) Draw a bar chart for this data.
(b) Draw a pictogram using a suitable symbol.
(c) Which did you find easier to draw? Give your reasons.
(d) Which do you think is more accurate? Say why.

3 The graphs show the sales of bicycles during January to May.

(a) Look quickly at the graphs. Which shop appears to sell the most bicycles?
(b) How many bikes did Cycleshop sell in March?
(c) How many bicycles were sold altogether by
   (i) Cycleshop
   (ii) Bikeshop?
(d) Which shop sold more bicycles?
(e) In which month did they both sell the same number of bicycles?

4 Which of the following are discrete data and which are continuous?
(a) The number of pages in a book
(b) The weight of a bag of sweets
(c) The number of sweets in a tube of Tasties
(d) The cost of a tube of Tasties
(e) The time of a telephone call
(f) The height of a flagpole
(g) The number of peas in a pod
(h) The length of the pod
(i) The distance to the moon
(j) The number of these questions you get right
(k) The time it took you to do this exercise

5 Draw line graphs to represent each of the following:
   (a) The number of letters delivered to a guest house one week:

Mon	Tues	Wed	Thur	Fri	Sat	Sun
12	25	15	19	23	20	0

   (b) The noon temperature, in °F, in Cambridge:

July	1	2	3	4	5	6	7
Temperature	73	69	65	70	75	79	76

   Think carefully about your vertical scale.

   (c) The longest rivers in Great Britain, in km to the nearest 10 km:

River	Severn	Towy	Shannon	Tay	Thames
Length	365	100	390	190	340

6 Muriel recorded the maximum and minimum temperatures over a period of ten days. Her results are given in this table.

April 1995	4th	5th	6th	7th	8th	9th	10th	11th	12th	13th
Max (°C)	12	9	10	10	13	17	15	19	16	18
Min (°C)	5	2	4	5	6	7	5	8	6	7

   (a) On the same graph illustrate these temperatures.
   (b) Write a comment about each set of data.

7 The amount of petrol (in litres) in the storage tank at a garage was measured every hour between 7 am and 7 pm on one day. This is the shape of the line graph showing the results.

(a) When was the amount of petrol in the tank at its lowest?

(b) What do you think happened between 9 am and 10 am?

(c) What were the sales like between 1 pm and 5 pm?

(d) Give a reason for your answer to part (c).

8   The graphs show the number of petrol sales at two garages during a week.

(a) What is different about the scales?

(b) Copy and complete the table below.

Petrol sales	Wed	Thur	Fri	Sat	Sun	Mon	Tue
Morgan Cars							
Rees Motors							

(c) Draw a dual bar chart for this information.

(d) Use your chart to make three comments about the sales.

(e) On which day was the most petrol sold at each garage?

10.7 Histograms

You usually draw bar charts or line graphs to represent frequency distributions. These diagrams use the height of bars or lines to represent the frequency. If the data is continuous and is grouped as described in Section 10.2 you can use a **histogram**.

Bar chart   Histogram

You will notice that a histogram looks like a bar chart but there are no gaps between the bars in a histogram. Later you will find that when the intervals are not equal the area has to be considered.

■ **Histograms are used to display grouped data that is continuous.**

10.8 Frequency polygons

Another useful way of displaying data is a **frequency polygon** in which the midpoints of the class intervals are joined by straight lines.

The table shows the frequency distribution of the ages of members of a swimming club in 1990 and 1991.

Age	0–9	10–19	20–29	30–39	40–50	over 50
1991	5	15	21	30	19	15
1992	10	24	28	22	10	6

You can draw bar charts and join the midpoints to get frequency polygons.

■ **Frequency polygons can show the general pattern of data represented by barcharts or histograms.**

It is often easier to compare data like this by placing one polygon on top of the other:

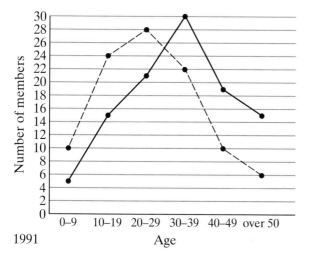

1991

Exercise 10F

1   The number of pupils late for school are given in this table.

	Mon	Tues	Wed	Thur	Fri
Week 1	6	8	14	10	12
Week 2	9	13	8	6	10

(a) Draw bar graphs of this data.
(b) Join the midpoints to make frequency polygons.
(c) Use the frequency polygons to compare the two weeks and write down three observations you have found.

2   The table shows the points scored by 75 pupils in a fitness programme held in September, January and May.

Mark	0–4	5–9	10–14	15–19	20–24
Sept	10	12	22	16	15
Jan	6	15	26	18	10
May	2	8	25	27	13

(a) Draw frequency polygons for each set of results.
(b) Make a tracing of the January and May polygons.
(c) Comment on the changes you find.

Summary of key points

1   A tally chart can be used to display data that can be counted.

2   A bar chart can be used to display data that can be counted.

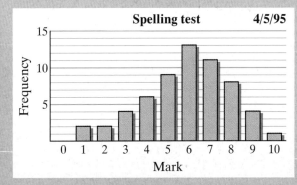

3   The Range of a set of data =
    highest value − lowest value.

4   A dual bar chart is used to compare two sets of data.

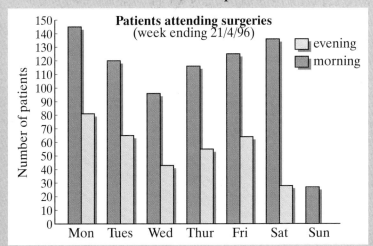

5   A pictogram can be used to illustrate data by using symbols to represent amounts.

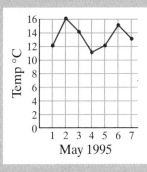

6   Line graphs can be used to display continuous data.

7   Histograms are used to display data that is continuous and which is grouped.

8   Frequency polygons can show the general pattern of data represented by bar charts or histograms.

11 Three-dimensional shapes

All the boxes and packets shown on the supermarket shelves
in the picture are 3-dimensional or 3-D. They have height,
width and depth. This unit is all about 3-D shapes.

11.1 Horizontal and vertical surfaces

In the picture at the top of the page the shelves are horizontal
surfaces. The floor and ceiling are also horizontal surfaces.

The walls and the sides of the packets are vertical surfaces.

■ **A flat surface is called a plane.**

Exercise 11A

Identify and list 5 horizontal and 5 vertical surfaces in your classroom. You can include the floor and the walls as part of your answer.

11.2 Faces, edges and vertices

■ **Surfaces of three-dimensional shapes are called faces.**

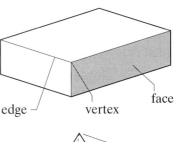

■ **The shaded surface on the box is called a *face*.**
The box has 6 faces.

■ **The line where two faces meet is called an *edge*.**
The box has 12 edges.

■ **The point where three edges meet is called a *vertex*.**
The box has 8 vertices.

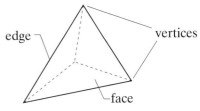

Exercise 11B

Find or make as many different 3D shapes as you can. Try to get some shapes with 4, 5, 6, 7 and 8 faces. Using straws for the edges is a quick way of getting new and unusual shapes. Count the faces, edges and vertices of your shapes and write them in a copy of this table.

Description of shape	Number of faces	Number of vertices	Number of edges

There is a rule which connects the number of faces and the number of vertices with the number of edges. Use your results to find this rule.

A **sketch** is a drawing which does not pretend to be exact. It should be good enough not to be misleading.

In sketches parallel lines are drawn parallel. Vertical lines always look vertical. Horizontal lines may go in any direction.

Exercise 11C

Draw sketches for your shapes in Exercise 11B.

11.3 Looking at shapes

The chart on this page shows pictures, sketches, names and some of the properties of some 3-D shapes.

Name and Properties	Picture	Sketch
Cube 6 square faces		
Cuboid 6 rectangular faces		
Sphere		
Square-based pyramid Square base, 4 triangular faces		
Triangular-based pyramid (Tetrahedron) 4 triangular faces		
Cone Pyramid with a circular base		
Cylinder 2 circular faces		

Stage 1
Draw a face
It is a parallelogram

Stage 2
Draw 3 parallel edges

Stage 3
Complete the cube

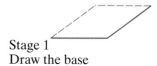

Stage 1
Draw the base

Stage 2
The top is above
the middle of the base

Stage 3
Join the top to
the other corners

Look at the picture below and make a list of as many 3-D shapes as you can. For example, the football is a sphere.

There are at least 12 3-D shapes.

11.4 Prisms

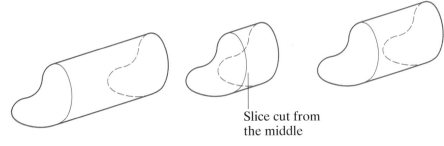

Slice cut from
the middle

The faces at either end of this shape are identical and parallel. Parallel means the faces are the same distance from each other at all points.

If the shape is cut anywhere parallel to these faces then the cut surface will be identical to the end faces. This type of shape is called a **prism**.

■ **A prism is a shape whose cross section is constant wherever it is cut.**

Some other prisms are drawn below. Where the shape of the cross section is a known 2-D shape then it is used to describe the type of prism.

Triangular prism   Hexagonal prism

Drawing a prism
These are difficult to draw. They can be made to look reasonable by drawing the front and back faces and then joining the vertices.

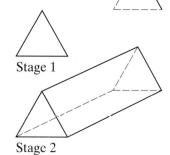

Stage 1

Stage 2

Exercise 11E

1 Which of the following shapes are prisms?

(a)   (b)   (c)

2 What name is usually given to a circular prism?

3 Write down the name of two other 3-D shapes that are also prisms.

4 Write down 5 things in your classroom which are prisms.

11.5 Nets

The box (cuboid) in the pictures has been opened out to make a 2-D shape. This 2-D shape is called the **net** of the box.

■ **A net is a 2-D shape that can be made into a 3-D shape.**

Example 1

Draw the net of this triangular prism.

The prism has three rectangular faces measuring 6 cm by 3 cm which are joined along their long sides. These faces can be drawn as:

The faces at either end of the prism are equilateral triangles with 3 cm sides. These must join to the short side of one of the rectangles. This makes the complete net.

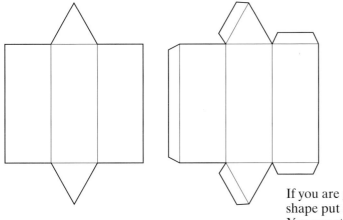

If you are going to make the shape put a tab on alternate sides. You can start with any side

You need to be able to construct accurate drawings of 2-D shapes if your nets are to fold together to make good solids. There is more about this in Unit 5 on 2-D shapes.

Exercise 11F

You need a ruler, pencil and pair of compasses for some of the questions in this exercise.

1 Sketch the nets of these solids:

(a)   (b)   (c)

2 These nets will form a 3-D solid. Draw a sketch of each solid.

(a)   (b)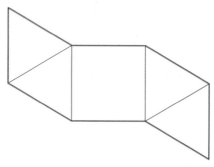

3 Which of the following are nets of a cube?

(a)   (b)   (c)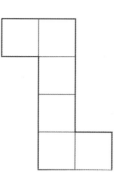

4 Which of the following are nets of a tetrahedron (triangular-based pyramid)?

(a)   (b)   (c)

5 Draw accurate nets for the triangular prism and cuboid.
You could do this on card and make the shapes.

(a) **(b)**

Exercise 11G (Mixed questions)

1 For each shape in this question write down:
   (i) the name   **(ii)** the number of edges
 (iii) the number of faces   **(iv)** the number of vertices

(a)   **(b)**   **(c)**

  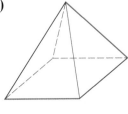

2 The base of each shape in question **1** is horizontal.
  (i) Write down the number of horizontal edges each
     shape has.
 (ii) Write down the number of vertical edges each shape
     has.

3 Which of these shapes are prisms?

(C)

(A)   **(B)**

4 Sketch the following solids and their nets:
  (a) cuboid   **(b)** cylinder   **(c)** cone
  (d) tetrahedron   **(e)** hexagonal prism

5 Sketch the solids that these nets form. Mark the measurements on your sketches.

(a)

4 cm

2 cm

(b)

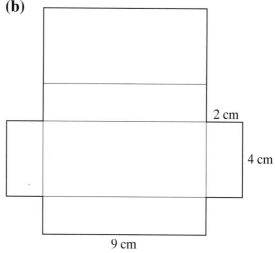

2 cm

4 cm

9 cm

6 Draw accurate nets for these solids.

(a)

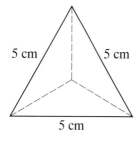

5 cm   5 cm

5 cm

(b)

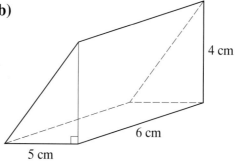

4 cm

6 cm

5 cm

7 Here is a list of the names of some shapes:

Square   Cube   Kite   Rectangle
Pyramid   Cylinder   Triangle   Circle

Use the list to help you write down the names of these shapes.

8 The diagram shows part of an accurately drawn net for a cuboid.
One face of the cuboid is missing.
The cuboid is 2 cm by 3 cm by 4 cm.
(a) Write down the size of the missing face.

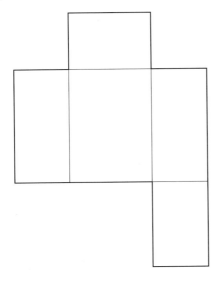

(b) Copy and complete the net by drawing in the missing face.
(c) Work out the area of the whole net.

[L]

Summary of key points

1 A flat surface is called a plane.

2 Surfaces of three-dimensional shapes are called faces.

3 The line where two faces meet is called an edge.

4 The point where three edges meet is called a vertex.

5 A prism is a shape whose cross section is the same all the way through.

6 Nets are the 2-D shapes that can be made into a 3-D shape.

12 Using and applying mathematics

In your GCSE course you will be using and applying mathematics all the time.

For your GCSE exam, using and applying mathematics is sometimes tested through coursework and sometimes through an examination. Whichever way it is tested the basic ideas are the same.

This unit uses an **investigative task** to show you how to tackle this type of work. Here is the task:

Diagonals

The diagram below shows a regular hexagon.

A diagonal of any shape is a line which joins any two of the vertices (corners) of the shape but which is not an edge of the shape.

1   Show that the regular hexagon has a total of 9 diagonals.

2   Work out the number of diagonals for a regular heptagon (seven-sided shape).

3   Draw some regular shapes of your own.
    For each shape work out the total number of diagonals.
    Investigate regular shapes to find the relationship between the number of diagonals and the number of vertices of any shape.

How investigative tasks are marked

Your work will be marked on three qualities which can be described as:

Deciding and doing   **Showing**   **Explaining**

Deciding and doing means deciding what to do and then doing it to carry out the investigation.

Showing means writing down your results so that others can understand what you have done. Tables and diagrams are good ways of showing your results.

Explaining means giving reasons for your answers.

It is important that your work contains all three qualities.

What to do in an investigation

Here is a list of things you should try to do during an investigation *and* things you should provide evidence of in your final report.

Don't worry if you don't understand it all yet. The rest of this unit will help.

If you are doing an investigative task as coursework you can refer to this list.

- Make sure you understand the problem.
- Check to see if you have worked on a similar problem. If you have, try to make use of this experience.
- Try some simple and special cases.
- Plan your work in an ordered way. Have a strategy.
- Record what you are trying to do.
- Record your observations.
- Use appropriate diagrams and forms of communication.
- Record and tabulate any findings and results.
- Predict what you think may happen and test it. This is called testing a conjecture.

For more advanced work you should try to do some or all of this list:

- Try to find and make use of any counter examples.
- Generalize, especially in symbols, if you can.
- Comment on any generalizations.
- Explain or justify your generalizations.
- Try to prove any generalizations.

The rest of this unit shows you how the task called **Diagonals** could be investigated.

Understanding the problem

You need to understand the main idea of the task:

You are being asked to investigate the number of diagonals there are in regular shapes in two dimensions.

An answer to question **1** about the regular hexagon will help to show that you understand the basic idea of the problem.

> **1**   Show that the regular hexagon has a total of 9 diagonals.

Here are the 9 diagonals drawn on the hexagon:

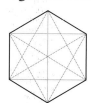

If you label the six vertices of the regular hexagon as:

then you can record the 9 diagonals as:

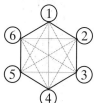

This way of recording the results for the regular hexagon may help at a later stage.

Have you worked on a similar problem?

Only you can answer this but it is quite likely that you have done similar work before.

Compare the way the diagonals of the regular hexagon are recorded:

with an array of dots like this:

You may have seen similar dot patterns when dealing with number patterns such as the triangular numbers or the square numbers. This may help later.

Question **2** helps to develop your understanding of the problem:

> **2** Work out the number of diagonals for a regular heptagon (seven-sided shape).

Here are the diagonals, the recording of them and the dot pattern:

Heptagon diagram **Recording** **Dot pattern**

Try some simple and special cases

You could just keep exploring different shapes but it is more sensible to choose an order in which to investigate them. For example: start with a triangle, square and pentagon, increasing the number of sides by one each time.

Here are the results in diagrams, the recording of them and the dot patterns:

Triangle diagram **Recording** **Dot pattern**

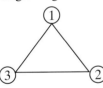

None   None

Square diagram   **Recording** **Dot pattern**

Pentagon diagram   **Recording** **Dot pattern**

Strategies

It is always worth writing a sentence or two to explain what you have done and how you have done it.

The strategy used so far has been:

Step 1 Draw the shape.
Step 2 Number the vertices.
Step 3 Join up the diagonals starting with those that go from 1; then those that go from 2 and so on.
Step 4 Make a record of the diagonals.
Step 5 Draw the dot pattern.

Once ① → ③ is drawn you do not need to draw ③ → ① in the opposite direction. This is an important part of the strategy.

Recording and tabulating observations and results

You are now at a stage where you can record the results of the investigation so far in a table:

Shape	Number of vertices	Number of diagonals
Triangle	3	0
Square	4	2
Pentagon	5	5
Hexagon	6	9
Heptagon	7	14

Forms of communication

Several forms of **communication** have been used so far: diagrams, the ① ② ③ labelling system, dot patterns and numbers and the table of results.

Now you can look for any pattern in the number of diagonals of the regular shapes.

Observations and predictions

Without the shape names the table of results looks like this:

Vertices	3	4	5	6	7
Diagonals	0	2	5	9	14

You can make many comments or **observations** about this sequence of results.

At a very basic level you might observe that the larger the number of vertices the larger the number of diagonals.

At a higher level you might observe that the numbers of diagonals follow a pattern of:

even, even, odd, odd, even

You might **predict** that for 8 vertices there would be an even number of diagonals.

Remember:
Write down any observations you try out even if they don't work.

Using differences to find patterns

One of the best ways of finding patterns about which you can make observations is the method of **differences**.

Here is the table of results so far.   Find the difference between each pair of results in the sequence   Find the difference between each pair of differences.

Vertices	Diagonals		1st difference		2nd difference
3	0				
4	2	2 – 0	2	3 – 2	1
5	5	5 – 2	3	4 – 3	1
6	9	9 – 5	4	5 – 4	1
7	14	14 – 9	5		

You might now notice that the numbers under the 1st difference column follow a very simple pattern. The numbers under the second difference column are all the same and equal to 1. This is very useful information as it *suggests* that the pattern of results can be continued as:

Vertices	Diagonals	1st difference	2nd difference
3	0		
4	2	2	1
5	5	3	1
6	9	4	1
7	14	5	1
8	20	6 14 + 6	1 5 + 1
9	27	7 20 + 7	6 + 1

Making and testing predictions

The method of differences allows you to **predict** (or **conjecture**) that the number of diagonals for a regular shape with 8 vertices is 20 and for a regular shape with 9 sides is 27.

It also tells you that if this is correct you may have found a general pattern.

You can **test** your predictions or conjectures using the diagrams, and the recording and dot pattern method used on page 163:

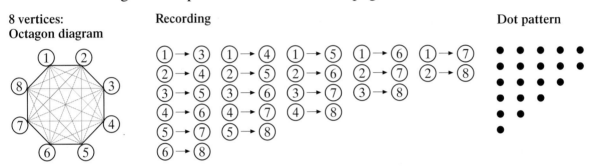

8 vertices:
Octagon diagram

Recording

Dot pattern

Counting the diagonals confirms the result of 20.

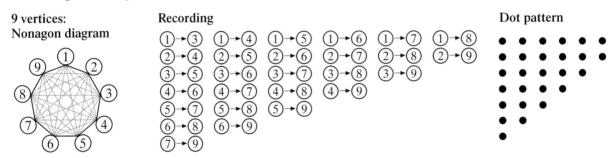

9 vertices:
Nonagon diagram

Recording

Dot pattern

Counting the diagonals confirms the result of 27.

Making and testing generalizations

When you can explain a pattern with a **general rule** for finding other numbers in the pattern you are **generalizing** or **making a generalization**.

Look at the results and the first differences again:

Vertices	3	4	5	6	7	8	9	10	11	12
Diagonals	0	2	5	9	14	20	27	35	44	54
1st difference		2	3	4	5	6	7	8	9	10

You can see that the 1st differences follow the sequence of **natural numbers** (apart from 1): 2, 3, 4, 5, 6, 7 and so on. This is a generalization. You can use it to extend the table of results like this:

Generalizing in symbols

The next stage in developing this investigation is to try to put the generalization in **symbolic** (or **algebraic**) **form**. The correct use of **symbols** is usually a very important step on the road to achieving the higher GCSE grades (C to A*).

Sometimes it is quite easy to spot a general rule, but this one is a bit harder. One of the keys here is to see that we have:

Vertices	Diagonals
3	$0 = 3 \times 0$
5	$5 = 5 \times 1$
7	$14 = 7 \times 2$
9	$27 = 9 \times 3$

which suggests that with 11 vertices the number of diagonals $= 11 \times 4 = 44$. This does work – it is a result we have already obtained.

Now we can look again at the full set of results:

Vertices	Diagonals				
3	$0 =$	3×0	$=$	$3 \times \frac{0}{2}$	
4	$2 =$	$4 \times \frac{1}{2}$	$=$	$4 \times \frac{1}{2}$	This suggests that the **general rule** is:
5	$5 =$	5×1	$=$	$5 \times \frac{2}{2}$	
6	$9 =$	$6 \times 1\frac{1}{2}$	$=$	$6 \times \frac{3}{2}$	Diagonals = Vertices ×
7	$14 =$	7×2	$=$	$7 \times \frac{4}{2}$	((Vertices − 3) ÷ 2)
8	$20 =$	$8 \times 2\frac{1}{2}$	$=$	$8 \times \frac{5}{2}$	
9	$27 =$	9×3	$=$	$9 \times \frac{6}{2}$	
10	$35 =$	$10 \times 3\frac{1}{2}$	$=$	$10 \times \frac{7}{2}$	
11	$44 =$	11×4	$=$	$11 \times \frac{8}{2}$	

Writing D for the number of diagonals and V for the number of vertices the **symbolic** or **algebraic form** of the general rule is:

$$D = V \times \frac{(V - 3)}{2}$$

or: $D = \frac{1}{2}V(V - 3)$.

Testing the generalization

You can test the general rule in one of two ways:

One way is to use a value of V and D for which you know the result, for example, choose $V = 6$, $D = 9$. Putting this in the rule gives:

$$D = \frac{1}{2}V(V - 3)$$
$$D = \frac{1}{2}6(6 - 3)$$
$$= 3(3) = 9$$

So the general rule works: when $V = 6$ it gives $D = 9$.

Another way is to test the rule for some new value of V and check the result by drawing, recording and using the dot pattern, or by extending the results table. Choose $V = 12$, for instance:

$$D = \tfrac{1}{2}(12)\,(12 - 3)$$
$$= 6 \times 9$$
$$= 54$$

You could try either extending the table of results or using the drawing, recording and dot pattern method. If you do you will find that when $V = 12$ then $D = 54$.

Hint:
Even if a test doesn't work, still record it and try to say why it failed.

This investigation does not have to stop here. You may have ideas for further work. In the Intermediate and Higher courses the same problem is developed to include the last five items on the more advanced work list at the start of this unit.

13 Measure 2

13.1 Changing metric units

Before you tackle this section you will need to be able to
multiply and divide whole numbers and decimals by 10, 100
and 1000. Check page 89 if you need to remind yourself.

■ **You need to know that:**

Length	Weight	Capacity
10 mm = 1 cm 100 cm = 1 m 1000 mm = 1 m 1000 m = 1 km	1000 mg = 1 g 1000 g = 1 kg 1000 kg = 1 tonne	100 c*l* = 1 litre 1000 m*l* = 1 litre 1000 *l* = 1 cubic metre

You need to remember:

■ **When you change from small units to large units you
divide.**

■ **When you change from large units to small units you
multiply.**

Example 1

(a) Change 2 kilometres to metres.

(b) Change 250 mm to cm.

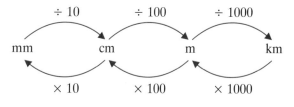

(a) Kilometres are larger units than
metres so you multiply by the number
of metres in a kilometre which is 1000.

  2 × 1000 = 2000 m

(b) Millimetres are smaller units than centimetres so you
divide by the number of millimetres in a centimetres
which is 10.

  250 ÷ 10 = 25 cm

Exercise 13A

1 Change these lengths to centimetres.
   (a) 3 m   **(b)** 30 mm   **(c)** 6 m
   (d) 12 m   **(e)** 100 mm

2 Change these lengths to millimetres.
   (a) 2 cm   **(b)** 5 cm   **(c)** 12 cm
   (d) 20 cm   **(e)** 100 cm

3 Change these lengths to metres.
   (a) 5 km   **(b)** 300 cm   **(c)** 10 km
   (d) 2000 cm   **(e)** 60 km

4 Change these weights to grams.
   (a) 5 kg   **(b)** 40 kg   **(c)** 100 kg
   (d) 250 kg   **(e)** 1000 kg

5 Change these volumes to litres.
   (a) 3000 ml   **(b)** 8000 ml   **(c)** 50 000 ml
   (d) 75 000 ml

6 Change these volumes to millilitres.
   (a) 6 l   **(b)** 40 l   **(c)** 100 l
   (d) 350 l   **(e)** 25 l

7 Change these lengths to kilometres.
   (a) 3000 m   **(b)** 7000 m   **(c)** 40 000 m
   (d) 45 000 m

8 Change these weights to tonnes.
   (a) 4000 kg   **(b)** 7000 kg   **(c)** 30 000 kg
   (d) 55 000 kg

9 Change these weights to kilograms.
   (a) 2000 g   **(b)** 3 tonnes   **(c)** 50 000 g
   (d) 12 tonnes   **(e)** 100 000 g

10 Work out the number of millimetres in 1 metre.

11 Jim's lorry weighs 8 tonnes. How many grams is this?

12 Jeremy walks 10 kilometres. How many centimetres is this?

13 Work out the number of centimetres in 1 kilometre.

14 Gerry has an average pace length of 75 cm. When she walks 3 km how many paces does she take?

15 Work out the number of millimetres in 1 kilometre.

Exercise 13B

1   Put these lines in order, smallest first.

(A) ——————————   (E)   (F)

(B) ———

(C) —————

(D) ————————————

2   Put these weights in order, largest first.
   250 g   25 g   2 kg   250 kg   3000 g

3   Put these lengths in order, smallest first.
   3 m   5 mm   20 cm   3 km   50 mm

4   Put these lengths in order, smallest first.
   75 cm   3000 mm   2 m   4000 m   4 cm

5   Put these volumes in order, smallest first.
   200 ml   5 l   600 ml   2000 ml   1 l

So far all of the answers in this section have been whole numbers.
In the following exercises you will find it easier if you use your
calculator *but* don't forget to **check if your answer is sensible**.

Example 2

(a) Change 450 g to kg.

(b) Change 2.4 l to ml.

(a) 450 ÷ 1000 = 0.45 kg

(b) 2.4 × 1000 = 2400 ml

Changing small units to
larger units so divide.
1000 g in 1 kg so ÷ 1000

Changing large units to
smaller units so multiply.
1000 ml in 1 l so × 1000

Exercise 13C

1   Change these lengths to metres.
   (a) 250 cm   (b) 50 cm   (c) 3.6 km
   (d) 75 cm   (e) 0.005 km   (f) 35 cm
   (g) 475 cm   (h) 0.6 km   (i) 0.04 km
   (j) 5 mm

2   Change these weights to grams.
   (a) 4.5 kg   (b) 0.4 kg   (c) 10.3 kg
   (d) 0.03 kg   (e) 0.005 kg

3 Change these lengths to centimetres.
   (a) 350 mm   (b) 2.5 m   (c) 5.4 m
   (d) 5 mm   (e) 0.08 m   (f) 0.8 m
   (g) 35 mm   (h) 50 mm   (i) 85 mm
   (j) 275 mm

4 Change these volumes to millilitres.
   (a) 3.5 *l*   (b) 0.5 *l*   (c) 15.4 *l*
   (d) 0.05 *l*   (e) 0.003 *l*

5 Change these lengths to millimetres.
   (a) 3.5 cm   (b) 0.7 cm   (c) 0.08 cm
   (d) 12.5 cm   (e) 0.005 m

6 Write these lengths in kilometres.
   (a) 300 m   (b) 50 m   (c) 1250 m
   (d) 75 m   (e) 375 m

7 Change these volumes to litres.
   (a) 250 m*l*   (b) 100 m*l*   (c) 50 m*l*
   (d) 3500 m*l*   (e) 1 m*l*

8 Change these weights to kilograms.
   (a) 500 g   (b) 0.3 tonnes   (c) 50 g
   (d) 5.5 tonnes   (e) 0.006 tonnes

9 Write these weights in tonnes.
   (a) 3500 kg   (b) 450 kg   (c) 50 kg
   (d) 3000 g   (e) 75 kg

10 How many 75 m*l* glasses can be filled from a bottle holding 1.5 *l* of cola?

11 How many 50 mm pieces of wood can be cut from a piece of wood of length 3 m assuming there is no waste?

12 It takes 150 g of flour to make a batch of rock cakes. How many batches of rock cakes can be made from 1.5 kg of flour?

Exercise 13D

1 Write these lengths in order, smallest first:
   (a) 25 mm, 3 cm, 2.4 cm, 50 mm, 6 cm, 57 mm
   (b) 30 cm, 0.4 m, 270 mm, 1.2 m, 500 mm, 45 cm
   (c) 2 m, 340 cm, 4000 mm, 4 m, 370 cm, 3500 mm
   (d) 5 cm, 45 mm, 36 cm, 0.3 m, 55 mm, 0.2 cm, 4 mm
   (e) 50 cm, 0.4 m, 560 mm, 0.45 m, 34 cm

2 Write these weights in order, smallest first:
   (a) 250 g, 0.3 kg, 500 g, 0.05 kg
   (b) 500 g, 350 g, 0.4 kg, 0.52 kg
   (c) 5000 g, 3000 g, 4 kg, 4.5 kg, 0.5 tonnes, 400 kg

3 Write these volumes in order, smallest first:
   (a) 300 ml, 0.4 l, 500 ml, 250 ml, 0.3 l
   (b) 500 ml, 450 ml, 0.4 l, 360 ml, 0.05 l, 45 ml

13.2 Metric and Imperial conversions

You may need to change from metric units to Imperial
units (the old style units) and vice versa. To do this it
helps to memorize these facts.

Metric	Imperial
8 km	5 miles
1 kg	2.2 pounds
25 g	1 ounce
1 l	$1\frac{3}{4}$ pints
4.5 l	1 gallon
1 m	39 inches
30 cm	1 foot
2.5 cm	1 inch

Most petrol pumps have a conversion table to show
how many litres or gallons you are buying.

Example 3

Change 10 km to miles.

8 km is approximately 5 miles
so 1 km = 5 ÷ 8 = 0.625 miles
then 10 km = 0.625 × 10 = 6.25 miles

Exercise 13E

The Evans family are going on holiday to Scotland. The family
consist of Mr and Mrs Evans and their three children, Glenys,
Eira and Gareth.

 1 Mr Evans works out the distance from their home in
    London to Scotland. He makes it 400 miles.
    What is this distance in kilometres?

2 Mrs Evans packs a 3 litre bottle of cola for the trip.
   How many pints is 3 litres?

3 The petrol tank of the family's car holds 15 gallons.
   How many litres is this?

4 Glenys estimates the weight of all the luggage as 100 kg.
   How many pounds is that?

5 Gareth puts 1 pint of water in the radiator.
   How many litres is that?

6 Mr Evans puts 30 litres of petrol in the car.
   How many gallons is that?

7 Mrs Evans puts 0.5 *l* of oil in the engine.
   How many pints is that?

8 The family stop at a service station 150 km from home.
   How many miles is that?

9 Eira buys an 800 g bar of chocolate.
   How many pounds is that?

10 When they get to Scotland there is half a bottle of cola left.
   How many pints is that?

Exercise 13F

Class 11E decide to raise money for charity by holding a cola
morning.

1 Claire cooks some rock cakes. She makes 72 cakes and
   uses 24 ounces of fat, 40 ounces of flour and 32 ounces of
   dried fruit. She only has a metric set of scales.
   How many grams of each ingredient should she use?

2 Sybil buys ten 3 *l* bottles of cola.
   How many gallons is this?

3 Henri buys 20 packets of biscuits. Each pack weighs
   1 pound.
   How many kilograms is this altogether?

4 Jonathan makes plates that are 4 inches across.
   How many centimetres is this?

5 The trays the class use are 24 inches long and 15 inches
   across.
   Change these measurements to centimetres.

6 The tables the class use are circular with a diameter of 48 inches. Will tablecloths with a 1.2 m diameter fit the tables?

7 Nilmini makes sandwiches and uses 5 one-kilogram loaves and 500 g of spread.
Change these weights to pounds.

8 At the end of the cola morning there were 5 pints of cola left.
How many litres is this?

9 In the 'guess the weight of the cake' competition the correct answer was 5 pounds. Robin said the weight was 5.1 pounds and Hazel said 2.3 kilograms.
Which of these two answers was nearer the correct one?

10 Claire sold 3.5 kilograms of cakes.
How many pounds is that?

13.3 Calculating time

■ **You need to know that:**
60 seconds = 1 minute
60 minutes = 1 hour
24 hours   = 1 day
365 days   = 1 year
366 days   = 1 leap year
3 months   = 1 quarter
12 months   = 1 year

Many people make mistakes when they are calculating with time because they forget that there are 60 minutes in an hour and not 100.

Example 4

(a) How many hours are there in 135 minutes?

(b) How many minutes are there in 3 hours?

(a) $135 \div 60 = 2.25$ hours
Many people write this as 2 hours 25 minutes but they would be *wrong*. To change the 0.25 hours to minutes you must multiply 0.25 by 60.
$0.25 \times 60 = 15$
so 135 minutes is 2 hours 15 minutes.

(b) $3 \times 60 = 180$ minutes

Why does 30 minutes and 45 minutes give 1 hour and 15 minutes?

You can't use an ordinary calculator to add time.

Exercise 13G

1 Change these times into minutes.
(a) 2 hours   (b) 5 hours
(c) 2 hours 30 minutes   (d) $5\frac{1}{2}$ hours
(e) $6\frac{1}{4}$ hours   (f) 5 hours 15 minutes

2 Change these times into hours.
(a) 180 minutes   (b) 240 minutes   (c) 75 minutes
(d) 260 minutes   (e) 325 minutes   (f) 90 minutes
(g) 3 days   (h) $5\frac{1}{2}$ days   (i) 500 minutes

3 How many seconds are there in 1 hour?

4 How many minutes are there in 1 day?

5 How many seconds are there in
(i) a year?
(ii) a leap year?

When you come to make calculations in time you have to be careful when it comes to dealing with the carry digit.

Example 5

(a) Add $2\frac{1}{2}$ hours to the time of 10:40

(b) Take 3 hours 15 minutes away from 11:10

> **Don't forget:**
> 60 minutes make 1 hour

(a)
```
  10:40
   2:30
  13:10   Not 70 since 70 minutes make 1 hour 10 minutes
    1
```

(b)
```
  11:10   You have to carry 60 minutes so 70 − 15 gives 55.
 − 3:15
   7:55
```

11:10 could be written as 10:70.

```
  11:10              10:70
 − 3:15      is     − 3:15
   7:55              7:55
```

Exercise 13H

1 Add 15 minutes to each of these times.
(a) 10:30   (b) 09:45   (c) 11:40   (d) 09:55

2 Add 50 minutes to each of these times.
(a) 09:00   (b) 10:30   (c) 11:40   (d) 08:05

3   Add 2 hours 40 minutes to each of these times.
     (a) 09:40   **(b)** 10:45   **(c)** 11:50   **(d)** 06:10

4   Add 12 hours 45 minutes to each of these times.
     (a) 02:30   **(b)** 07:15   **(c)** 12:50   **(d)** 16:45

5   Subtract 15 minutes from each of these times.
     (a) 09:55   **(b)** 11:40   **(c)** 08:10   **(d)** 09:05

6   Subtract 50 minutes from each of these times.
     (a) 08:55   **(b)** 11:40   **(c)** 10:30   **(d)** 09:00

7   Subtract 2 hours 30 minutes from each of these times.
     (a) 09:55   **(b)** 11:40   **(c)** 08:10   **(d)** 09:05

8   Subtract 12 hours 45 minutes from each of these times.
     (a) 14:50   **(b)** 17:30   **(c)** 12:00   **(d)** 08:30

13.4 Dealing with dates

You will often need to add days onto dates. This old rhyme can help:

- **30 days hath September**
  April June and November.
  All the rest have 31
  except for February alone
  which has just 28 days clear
  and 29 in each leap year.

Example 6

Jane agreed to go out with John in 10 days time.
Today is Tuesday 23rd April. When is their date?

	April					May				
Monday	1	8	15	22	29		6	13	20	27
Tuesday	2	9	16	23	30		7	14	21	28
Wednesday	3	10	17	24		1	8	15	22	29
Thursday	4	11	18	25		2	9	16	23	30
Friday	5	12	19	26		3	10	17	24	31
Saturday	6	13	20	27		4	11	18	25	
Sunday	7	14	21	28		5	12	19	26	

If you start at 23 and count 10 days on you get to Friday 3rd of May. You must of course remember that April only has 30 days.

Exercise 13I

1 Count on 10 days from the following dates.
    (a) 1st Jan   (b) 2nd March   (c) 3rd June
    (d) 5th July   (e) 10th Sept   (f) 20th May
    (g) 25th June   (h) 27th Aug

2 Count on 14 days from the following dates.
    (a) 2nd Feb   (b) 3rd March   (c) 3rd April
    (d) 7th Dec   (e) 15th Nov   (f) 18th Sept
    (g) 23rd March   (h) 25th Nov

3 Count on 30 days from the following dates.
    (a) 5th April   (b) 6th June   (c) 17th May
    (d) 1st Sept   (e) 7th June   (f) 20th May
    (g) 30th Nov   (h) 5th Dec

    Use the calendar in Example 6 to answer the following questions.

4 What day of the week and date is 5 days from the 5th April?

5 Which day and date is 5 days after the 27th April?

6 Which day and date is 7 days before 20th May?

7 What is the day and date 10 days before the 5th May?

8 Write down the day and date two weeks after the 19th April.

13.5 Timetables

Bus and train timetables are often used to test your knowledge of time in the GCSE examination.

On this timetable each train's times starts at the top and then go down the page. The time it should leave a stopping place can then be read off opposite the place name.

Example 7

Find how long it takes for the 8:15 train from Swindon to get to London (Paddington).

You first have to find the 08:15 train from Swindon. It is in the third column along. Follow that column down to the bottom and that gives the arrival time in London of 09:10.

7:10 train from Bristol arrives in London at 08:40

Bristol	07:10	07:25	07:40	07:55
Bath	07:30	07:45	08:00	08:10
Swindon	07:45	08:00	08:15	08:25
Didcot	08:05	08:20	08:35	08:45
Reading	08:15	08:30	08:45	08:55
London (Paddington)	08:40	08:55	09:10	09:20

8:15 train from Swindon

Arrives in London at 09:10

You could subtract times by doing a subtraction sum and carrying a 60. Here is another way of dealing with the problem that you may find easier:

15 minutes

08:15 to 08:30 is 15 minutes
08:30 to 09:00 is 30 minutes
09:00 to 09:10 is 10 minutes

30 minutes

Total time 15 + 30 + 10 = 55 minutes

10 minutes

Exercise 13J

Bus timetable			
Coate	07:05	07:35	08:05
Piper's Way	07:10	07:40	08:10
Old Town	07:20	07:50	08:20
Drove Road	07:25	07:55	08:25
New Town	07:30	08:00	08:30
Bus Station	07:35	08:05	08:35

Train timetable				
Bristol	07:10	07:25	07:40	07:55
Bath	07:30	07:45	08:00	08:15
Swindon	07:45	08:00	08:15	08:30
Didcot	08:05	08:20	08:35	08:50
Reading	08:15	08:30	08:45	09:00
London (Paddington)	08:40	08:55	09:10	09:25

1 At what time should the 07:35 bus from Coate arrive at Drove Road?

2 At what time should the 07:40 train from Bristol arrive at Didcot?

3 At what time should the 08:30 train from Reading start from Bristol?

4 At what time should the 07:55 bus from New Town start at Piper's Way?

5 Buses from Coate depart every half an hour.
Continue the bus timetable for the next three buses. You can assume that each bus takes the same amount of time between stops as the previous ones.

6 Trains from Bristol depart every quarter of an hour.
Continue the train timetable for the next three trains. You can assume that each train takes the same amount of time between stops as the previous ones.

7 Rashmi arrives at the train station in Bath at 07:35.
What time is the next train he could catch to London?

8 Claude arrives at the train station in Didcot at 08:25.
What time is the next train he could catch to London?

9 Cecille arrives at the train station in Swindon at 09:10.
What time is the next train she could catch to Reading?

10 Sophia arrives at the train station in Bristol at 08:00.
What time is the next train she could catch to Bath?

11 How long should it take to travel by bus from Coate to the Bus Station?

12 How long should it take to travel by bus from Pipers Way to New Town?

13 How long should it take to travel by train from Bristol to London (Paddington)?

14 How long should it take to travel by train from Swindon to Reading?

15 How long should it take to travel by train from Bath to Didcot?

16 The bus timetable is for a bus route in Swindon. It takes five minutes to walk from the bus station to the train platform. Use both timetables to work out which bus and train:
   (a) Gareth catches at Pipers Way to be in London (Paddington) at 09:00
   (b) Susan catches if she needs to be in Reading at 08:30 and she travels by bus from Coate
   (c) Mario catches if he travels by bus from Old Town and needs to be in Didcot at 08:40
   (d) Claudette catches at Drove Road to be in London Paddington by 10:00
   (e) Bridgette catches if she needs to be in Reading at 09:30 and she travels by bus from Old Town
   (f) Katrina caught if she travelled from Drove Road and arrived in Reading at 08:45

Exercise 13K

1

This signpost is on the road from Paris to Dijon.
   (a) Work out the distance, in kilometres, from Paris to Dijon along this road.
   (b) Work out the approximate distance, in miles, from the signpost to Paris.

[L]

2 Here is a timetable for Amina's school bus.

Bus stop	Time
Bus Station	08:00
Station Road	08:15
Grange Drive	08:20
Holley Ave.	08:30
Kings Road	08:40
School Road	08:45

Amina catches the bus at Grange Drive.
(a) At what time should the bus be at Grange Drive?
(b) How long should the bus take to get from Grange Drive to School Road?

[L]

3 Chippy the carpenter marks a 3 metre length of wood into three pieces.

One piece is 1.40 metres long.
Another piece is 84 centimetres long.

How long is the third piece of wood?

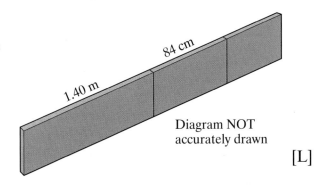

Diagram NOT accurately drawn

[L]

Summary of key points

1

Length	Weight	Capacity
10 mm = 1 cm 100 cm = 1 m 1000 mm = 1 m 1000 m = 1 km	1000 mg = 1 g 1000 g = 1 kg 1000 kg = 1 tonne	100 c*l* = 1 litre 1000 m*l* = 1 litre 1000 *l* = 1 cubic metre

2 When you change from small units to large units you divide.

3 When you change from large units to small units you multiply.

4
60 seconds	=	1 minute
60 minutes	=	1 hour
24 hours	=	1 day
365 days	=	1 year

366 days	=	1 leap year
3 months	=	1 quarter
12 months	=	1 year

5 30 days hath September,
April, June and November.
All the rest have 31
except for February
alone which has just 28 days clear
and 29 in each leap year.

14 Percentages

14.1 Understanding percentages

Every day you can see similar notices to these in the newspapers.

The symbol % and the letters pc mean 'per cent'.
These numbers are all percentages.

The words 'per cent' mean 'in every hundred'.
So 14 per cent means '14 in every hundred', written 14% for short.

14.2 Converting percentages to fractions

You can also write '14 in every hundred' as the fraction $\dfrac{14}{100}$

So the percentage 14% is equivalent to the fraction $\dfrac{14}{100}$

- **A percentage can be written as a fraction with the denominator (bottom) 100.**

Here are some more examples:

$$100\% = \frac{100}{100} \qquad 50\% = \frac{50}{100} \qquad 8\% = \frac{8}{100}$$

$$3\% = \frac{3}{100} \qquad 2\tfrac{1}{2}\% = \frac{2\tfrac{1}{2}}{100}$$

Percentages can be written as fractions and then simplified.
(For a reminder on simplifying fractions see page 55.)

Example 1

Write 40% as a fraction in its simplest form.

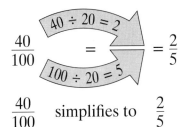

$$\frac{40}{100} = \frac{2}{5}$$

$\frac{40}{100}$ simplifies to $\frac{2}{5}$

20 is a common factor of the numerator and denominator.

Divide by the common factor.

So 40% is equal to $\frac{2}{5}$.

Example 2

Write $33\frac{1}{3}\%$ as a fraction in its simplest form.

Do this in two steps:

$$\frac{33\frac{1}{3}}{100} \xrightarrow{\times 3} = \frac{100}{300} \xrightarrow{\div 100} = \frac{1}{3}$$

Multiply by 3 to get a whole number on top.

Divide by the common factor 100.

So $33\frac{1}{3}\%$ is equivalent to $\frac{1}{3}$.

Exercise 14A

Change these percentages to fractions in their simplest form.

1 60%   2 36%   3 95%   4 17%

5 2%   6 65%   7 39%   8 18%

9 90%   10 70%   11 45%   12 $\frac{1}{2}\%$

13 $7\frac{1}{2}\%$ 14 $12\frac{1}{2}\%$ 15 40%   16 75%

17 30%   18 20%   19 15%   20 $17\frac{1}{2}\%$

14.3 Converting percentages to decimals

Percentages will also convert to decimals.

Example 3

Convert to decimals: **(a)** 39%   **(b)** 40%   **(c)** 3.7%

(a) $39\% = \frac{39}{100} = 39 \div 100 = 0.39$

(b) $40\% = \frac{40}{100} = 40 \div 100 = 0.40$ (this should be written as 0.4 to 1 decimal place)

(c) $3.7\% = \frac{3.7}{100} = 3.7 \div 100 = 0.037$

■ **To convert a percentage to a decimal divide by 100**

Exercise 14B

Convert these percentages to decimals.

1	16%	**2**	41%	**3**	99%	**4**	82%
5	7%	**6**	55%	**7**	38%	**8**	3%
9	14.2%	**10**	98.7%	**11**	3.6%	**12**	$18\frac{1}{2}\%$
13	$45\frac{1}{2}\%$	**14**	$4\frac{1}{4}\%$	**15**	19%	**16**	$12\frac{1}{2}\%$
17	1%	**18**	0.7%	**19**	$\frac{1}{2}\%$	**20**	$2\frac{1}{2}\%$

Exercise 14C

Copy and complete this table of equivalent percentages, decimals and fractions.

Percentage	Decimal	Fraction
40%	0.4	$\frac{2}{5}$
	0.61	
		$\frac{7}{10}$
35%		
$8\frac{1}{2}\%$		
	0.15	
		$\frac{3}{25}$
	0.07	
$1\frac{1}{4}\%$		
		$\frac{2}{3}$

■ **Remember these percentages and their equivalent fractions:**

$50\% = \frac{1}{2}$ $25\% = \frac{1}{4}$ $75\% = \frac{3}{4}$ $33\frac{1}{3}\% = \frac{1}{3}$ $66\frac{2}{3}\% = \frac{2}{3}$

14.4 Working out a percentage of an amount

For some percentages, you will be able to do a simple mental calculation.

Example 4

Work out 50% of £6

Convert 50% to $\frac{1}{2}$
Work out $\frac{1}{2}$ of £6 by dividing by 2
50% of £6 = £3

Not all percentages can be written as simple fractions.
The following method will work for all percentages:

■ **To work out a percentage of an amount write the percentage as a fraction with a denominator (bottom) of 100. Then multiply the fraction by the amount.**

Example 5

Work out 15% of 540 kg

$$\frac{15}{100} \times 540 \;=\; \frac{15 \times 540}{100} \;=\; \frac{8100}{100} \;=\; 81$$

So 15% of 540 kg is 81 kg.

When you work out a percentage of an amount of **money** make sure that your answer always has two figures after the decimal point.

Your calculator may have a short way of doing this with the key.

Example 6

Work out 8.57% of £685

$$\frac{8.57}{100} \times £685 = \frac{8.57 \times £685}{100} = \frac{£5870.45}{100}$$

$$= £58.7045$$

$$= £58.70 \text{ (to 2 d.p.)}$$

Exercise 14D

Work out:

1 60% of 165	**2** 45% of 920 kg	**3** 17% of £7000
4 90% of 80	**5** 6% of £420	**6** 10% of £16.80
7 17.5% of £164	**8** 30% of £264	**9** 5% of £31 240
10 0.3% of 250 tonnes	**11** 7.2% of £600	**12** 96% of 32 000
13 25% of 36 km	**14** 25% of 14.2 km	**15** 6.8% of £9840
16 4.8% of 3.6 litres		

14.5 Using percentages

In examinations percentages usually appear in the context of a real-life problem.

Example 7

Satinder earns £160 per week working at the Supermarket. She is awarded a 5% pay rise. Work out:

(a) the amount of the rise

(b) her new weekly wage.

(a) The pay rise is 5% of £160

$$\frac{5}{100} \times £160 = \frac{5 \times £160}{100} = \frac{£800}{100} = £8$$

So the amount of the rise is £8

(b) new wage = old wage + rise = £160 + £8 = £168

Example 8

At the beginning of a year the number of jobless people in a city was 5500. This number fell by 0.8% during the year.

Work out: (a) the fall in the number of jobless
(b) the number of jobless remaining.

(a) The fall is = 0.8% of 5500

$$\frac{0.8}{100} \times 5500 = \frac{0.8 \times 5500}{100} = \frac{4400}{100} = 44$$

The fall in jobless is 44.

(b) Number of jobless remaining
= Number of jobless at beginning of year – fall in jobless
= 5500 – 44 = 5456

Exercise 14E

1 Good Price Record Shop reduced the prices of all CDs and cassettes by 5%.
   Calculate: **(i)** the reduction in price **(ii)** the new price of a CD usually costing £12.

2 A furniture store reduced all normal prices by 15% for the Spring Sale.
   Work out **(i)** the reduction in price **(ii)** the Spring Sale price of:
   (a) a table normally priced at £80
   (b) a settee normally priced at £740
   (c) a TV table normally priced at £40.60

3 A school entered 150 candidates for the GCSE maths exam. The table shows the percentage of candidates gaining each grade.

Grade	A*	A	B	C	D	E	F	G
Percentage	2%	6%	12%	42%	20%	6%	8%	4%

   How many pupils gained each grade?

4 John wanted to buy a CD player and speakers costing £376. The shop keeper asked for a deposit of 30% of the price. How much deposit did John pay?

5 A new car, bought for £12 600, had lost 60% of its value after 3 years.
   (a) How much value had it lost?
   (b) What was the value of the car after 3 years?

6 Janice left £450 in her building society account for one year. The building society paid interest of $6\frac{1}{2}\%$ per year. How much interest did Janice's money earn in the year?

7 Value Added Tax (VAT) is charged at the rate of $17\frac{1}{2}\%$.
   How much VAT is there to pay on:
   (a) a telephone bill of £52.40 before VAT
   (b) a restaurant bill of £28 before VAT
   (c) a wedding reception costing £1980 before VAT
   (d) a builder's bill for repairs of £158.80 before VAT.

8 A travel company advertises a discount of 15% off all holiday prices.

   How much would it cost for:
   (a) a fly drive holiday priced at £360
   (b) an activity holiday priced at £168?

9 A sales representative is paid $6\frac{1}{2}\%$ commission on the value of all sales made.

How much commission is the representative paid on sales valued at:
(a) £1000 **(b)** £3600 **(c)** £8040?

10 An estate agency charges $2\frac{1}{2}\%$ commission on the value of houses that the agency sells.

How much commission does the agency charge for selling these houses:

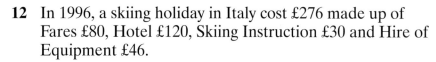

Grabbit & Runne — £68 000 — SOLD

Grabbit & Runne — £92 000 — SOLD

Grabbit & Runne — £116 000 — SOLD

11 A market trader buys knitted jumpers for £8.60 each and sports shirts for £4.80 each. She sells them for 65% more than she bought them for.

Work out the selling price of each item.

12 In 1996, a skiing holiday in Italy cost £276 made up of Fares £80, Hotel £120, Skiing Instruction £30 and Hire of Equipment £46.

By 1997, the cost of Fares had risen by 12%, Hotel costs had risen by 8%, the cost of instruction had increased by 50% and Hire of Equipment by 10%.

Work out the total cost of the holiday in 1997.

14.6 Using percentages to compare amounts

Sometimes you will need to write one amount as a percentage of another amount.

Example 9

The top mark in a test is 34 out of 40. What is this as a percentage?

To find one quantity as a percentage of another follow these steps:

Step 1 Write the two amounts as a fraction: $\frac{34}{40}$

Step 2 Convert the fraction to a decimal: $\frac{34}{40} = 34 \div 40 = 0.85$

Step 3 Multiply the decimal by 100: $0.85 \times 100 = 85$

The top mark is 85%

Example 10

What percentage of 3 kg is 240 g?

To compare the quantities the units must be the same:
3 kg is 3000 g

Step 1   Write as a fraction: $\frac{240}{3000}$
Step 2   Convert to a decimal: $240 \div 3000 = 0.08$
Step 3   Multiply by 100: $0.8 \times 100 = 8\%$

The percentage is 8%

Example 11

A jacket is reduced in price from £80 to £62

What is the percentage reduction?

The actual reduction is   £80 − £62 = £18

Step 1   Write as a fraction: $\frac{18}{80}$
Step 2   Convert to a decimal: $18 \div 80 = 0.225$
Step 3   Multiply by 100: $0.225 \times 100 = 22.5\%$

The percentage reduction is 22.5%

■   **To write an amount as a percentage of another:**
    1 write the amounts as a fraction
    2 convert the fraction to a decimal
    3 multiply the decimal by 100

Why the method works

These three numbers are **equivalent**. They represent the
same quantity written in three different forms:

percentage		fraction		decimal
85%	=	$\frac{85}{100}$	=	0.85

To convert from the decimal form to percentage form
multiply by 100: $0.85 \times 100 = 85$ or 85%

Exercise 14F

1   (a)   What percentage of £100 is £5?
    (b)   What percentage of 5 kg is 600 g?
    (c)   What percentage of £160 is £24?
    (d)   What percentage of 2l is 150 ml?
    (e)   What percentage of 3 hours is 1 hour 15 mins?
    (f)   What percentage of £4.20 is 35p?
    (g)   What percentage of £16 000 is £480?
    (h)   What percentage of 20 tonnes is 200 kg?
    (i)   What percentage of 3.6 m is 180 cm?

2 **(a)** Write £15 as a percentage of £200.
   (b) Write £600 as a percentage of £3000.
   (c) Write 15 minutes as a percentage of 1 hour 15 mins.
   (d) Write 6.3 m as a percentage of 157.5 m.
   (e) Write £5.60 as a percentage of £140.
   (f) Write 36 kg as a percentage of 900 kg.
   (g) Write 20 tonnes as a percentage of 320 tonnes.
   (h) Write 4.5 mm as a percentage of 90 cm.
   (i) Write £850 as a percentage of £4000.
   (j) Write £1575 as a percentage of £63 000.

3 Shoes in a sale are reduced in price from £60 to £42.
   What is the percentage reduction?

4 A factory employing 300 people made 18 people redundant.
   What percentage of the employees were made redundant?

5 Peter bought a new motor bike for £840 and sold it two years
   later for £378.
   By what percentage had its value fallen in the two years?

6 A stereo system, normally sold for £215, is offered for sale at
   £180.60.
   Calculate the percentage reduction in the normal price.

7 A shopworker received a wage increase from £160 per week
   to £165 per week.
   What was the percentage increase?

8 Shona deposited £450 in a bank savings account. Interest
   paid after a year increased the amount in her account to
   £478.80.
   What percentage rate of interest did the account pay?

9 Ali paid a deposit of £108 on a second-hand car costing £1350.
   What percentage of the price was the deposit?

10 The number of pupils in a school grew from 1050 to 1500.
    What was the percentage increase in the number of pupils?

Exercise 14G

1 The same sort of bike is for sale in two shops.
   Work out the price you would have to pay in each shop.

[L]

WHEELIE'S
Mountain bikes $\frac{1}{3}$ OFF
Price was £198
Price now

CHEAPER BIKES
Mountain bikes
40% OFF
BIGGEST REDUCTION
Last week's price was £239
This week's price is

2

Mega Ace Games System

Normal Price   £320

Sale Price   £272

Find the percentage reduction on the Mega Ace Games System in the sale.

[L]

3 Janet invests £50 in a building society for one year.
The interest rate is 6% per year.
(a) How much interest, in pounds, does Janet get?

Nisha invests £60 in a different building society. She gets £3 interest after one year.
(b) Work out the percentage interest rate that Nisha gets.

[L]

4 Nigel works in a service station and earns £6500 per year.
He is given a pay rise of 15%.
Ryan is a football player earning £75 000 per year. He is given a pay rise of 1.5%.
Who ends up with the biggest rise in pay?

Summary of key points

1 A percentage can be written as a fraction with the denominator (bottom) 100.

2 To convert a percentage to a decimal divide by 100.

3 Remember these percentages and their equivalent fractions:

$50\% = \frac{1}{2}$ $25\% = \frac{1}{4}$ $75\% = \frac{3}{4}$ $33\frac{1}{3}\% = \frac{1}{3}$ $66\frac{2}{3}\% = \frac{2}{3}$.

4 To work out a percentage of an amount write the percentage as a fraction with a denominator of 100. Then multiply the fraction by the amount.

5 To write an amount as a percentage of another:
   • write the amounts as a fraction
   • convert the fraction to a decimal
   • multiply the decimal by 100.

15 Algebra 3

15.1 Simple Equations

■ **In algebra letters are often used to represent numbers.**

$a + 3 = 7$ The letter a must equal 4 because 4 add 3 equals 7.

    $a = 4$

$a - 3 = 2$ a must equal 5 because 5 take away 3 equals 2.

    $a = 5$ These are examples of equations.

Exercise 15A

Find the value of the letter in these equations:

1 $a + 2 = 5$	**2** $b + 1 = 4$	**3** $c + 2 = 9$	**4** $w + 5 = 7$
5 $m + 3 = 4$	**6** $y + 5 = 5$	**7** $x - 2 = 3$	**8** $k - 4 = 1$
9 $n - 3 = 3$	**10** $h - 5 = 3$	**11** $g - 2 = 2$	**12** $f - 5 = 4$
13 $d + 2 = 7$	**14** $2 + e = 5$	**15** $4 + y = 7$	**16** $10 + x = 14$
17 $7 - m = 3$	**18** $5 - d = 2$	**19** $k + 6 = 15$	**20** $12 = y + 2$
21 $15 - t = 5$	**22** $z - 2 = 2$	**23** $z + 2 = 2$	**24** $n - 5 = 0$

In Exercise 15A you probably spotted the answers and then
wrote them down. There is another way of looking at equations.

An equation is a balancing act!

Here is a way of working out the value of the letter in an
equation that does not rely on guessing the answer.

Example 1

To find a from: $a + 6 = 9$

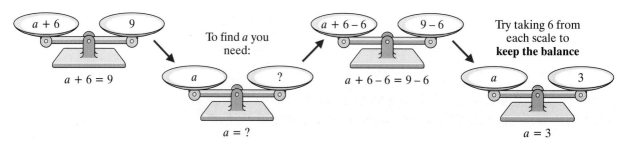

Example 2

To find k from:

$k - 7 = 13$

$k - 7 + 7 = 13 + 7$ (keeping the balance)

$k = 20$

Exercise 15B

Find the value of the letter in these equations. Use the balancing method to help you:

1 $a + 6 = 7$	**2** $y + 3 = 5$	**3** $h + 2 = 9$
4 $p - 5 = 4$	**5** $q - 3 = 7$	**6** $d - 6 = 2$
7 $x + 3 = 3$	**8** $t - 4 = 0$	**9** $r + 7 = 10$
10 $k + 2 = 3$	**11** $n + 1 = 2$	**12** $x - 2 = 3$
13 $m + 7 = 12$	**14** $y - 7 = 9$	**15** $w + 5 = 5$
16 $q - 10 = 2$	**17** $5 + p = 7$	**18** $6 + t = 6$
19 $a + 19 = 31$	**20** $21 + x = 21$	**21** $p - 15 = 23$
22 $7 = a + 3$	**23** $6 = b + 5$	**24** $10 = y + 10$

Exercise 15C

Find the value of the letter in each of these equations:

1 $a + 5 = 10$	**2** $p - 4 = 7$	**3** $q - 3 = 5$
4 $x + 7 = 15$	**5** $y + 4 = 17$	**6** $s + 12 = 15$
7 $x - 7 = 15$	**8** $y - 4 = 17$	**9** $s - 12 = 15$
10 $a + 5 = 6$	**11** $p - 5 = 6$	**12** $c + 17 = 21$
13 $5 + a = 6$	**14** $11 + p = 16$	**15** $12 + q = 12$
16 $4 = a + 2$	**17** $5 = b + 3$	**18** $12 = c - 3$
19 $10 = p + 5$	**20** $11 = y - 10$	**21** $15 = t + 10$
22 $12 = p + 12$	**23** $12 = p - 12$	**24** $p + 12 = 12$

In this next section you will learn to find the value of the letter when the letter is multiplied or divided by a number.

Example 3

$3a = 12$

$3a = 12$

This means $a \times 3 = 12$

To find $a = ?$ you need to keep the balance in the equation.

To make the equation balance you must do the same to each side.

Try: $3a \div 3 = 12 \div 3$

$a = 4$

$a = 4$

■ **To make an equation balance you must do the same to each side.**

Exercise 15D

Find the value of the letter in these equations:

1 $3a = 6$	**2** $4p = 8$	**3** $5p = 15$	**4** $6s = 18$	**5** $2k = 10$
6 $7u = 28$	**7** $2g = 14$	**8** $5k = 35$	**9** $6j = 12$	**10** $8f = 32$
11 $3r = 27$	**12** $5v = 45$	**13** $2t = 5$	**14** $4d = 48$	**15** $7t = 63$

Example 4

$\dfrac{w}{3} = 5$ (means $w \div 3 = 5$)

$\dfrac{w}{3} \times 3 = 5 \times 3$

$w = 15$

> Look for the opposite process.
> The opposite process of $\div 3$ is $\times 3$
> Multiply each side of the equation by 3

Exercise 15E

Find the value of the letter in these equations:

1 $\dfrac{a}{2} = 5$	**2** $\dfrac{b}{5} = 4$	**3** $\dfrac{s}{4} = 3$	**4** $\dfrac{c}{6} = 5$	**5** $\dfrac{t}{4} = 6$
6 $\dfrac{s}{8} = 9$	**7** $\dfrac{h}{6} = 12$	**8** $\dfrac{f}{4} = 7$	**9** $\dfrac{d}{3} = 15$	**10** $\dfrac{a}{3} = 15$
11 $\dfrac{b}{5} = 8$	**12** $\dfrac{r}{4} = 13$	**13** $\dfrac{a}{12} = 5$	**14** $\dfrac{b}{2} = 16$	**15** $\dfrac{k}{3} = 16$

Exercise 15F (Mixed questions)

1 $a + 4 = 5$ **2** $b + 3 = 6$ **3** $c + 4 = 9$

4 $p - 3 = 6$ **5** $q - 2 = 2$ **6** $d - 6 = 2$

7 $2p = 6$ **8** $4r = 8$ **9** $5t = 20$

10 $\dfrac{a}{2} = 6$ **11** $\dfrac{b}{5} = 12$ **12** $\dfrac{s}{4} = 5$

13 $4 + r = 7$ **14** $6 + e = 7$ **15** $7 + p = 7$

15.2 Equations combining operations

You have dealt with equations where you added or subtracted numbers and where you multiplied or divided numbers. You are now going to look at what happens when these are combined into one equation.

Example 5

$$\begin{aligned} 2a + 3 &= 11 \\ 2a + 3 - 3 &= 11 - 3 \qquad \text{Take 3 from each side.} \\ 2a &= 8 \\ 2a \div 2 &= 8 \div 2 \qquad \text{Divide each side by 2} \\ a &= 4 \end{aligned}$$

Example 6

$$\begin{aligned} 5p - 3 &= 7 \\ 5p - 3 + 3 &= 7 + 3 \qquad \text{Add 3 to each side.} \\ 5p &= 10 \\ 5p \div 5 &= 10 \div 5 \qquad \text{Divide each side by 5} \\ p &= 2 \end{aligned}$$

Exercise 15G

Find the value of the letter in these equations:

1 $2a + 1 = 5$ **2** $2a - 1 = 5$ **3** $3a + 2 = 8$

4 $3a - 5 = 4$ **5** $3p + 7 = 7$ **6** $3p + 7 = 13$

7 $4q + 5 = 17$ **8** $5r - 6 = 4$ **9** $6t - 12 = 18$

10 $7f - 12 = 9$ **11** $2r - 11 = 15$ **12** $10a - 5 = 5$

13 $10a + 5 = 5$ **14** $4d + 7 = 19$ **15** $5c - 2 = 18$

All the equations dealt with so far have answers that are whole numbers. Look at the following example. You can see that answers can be fractions or decimals as well.

Example 7

$$4p + 7 = 16$$
$$4p + 7 - 7 = 16 - 7 \qquad \text{Take 7 from each side.}$$
$$4p = 9$$
$$4p \div 4 = 9 \div 4 \qquad \text{Divide each side by 4}$$
$$p = 2\tfrac{1}{4}$$

Example 8

$$5q - 8 = 3$$
$$5q - 8 + 8 = 3 + 8 \qquad \text{Add 8 to each side.}$$
$$5q = 11$$
$$5q \div 5 = 11 \div 5 \qquad \text{Divide each side by 5}$$
$$q = 2.2$$

Exercise 15H

1   $2a + 3 = 6$ 2 $2a - 4 = 3$ 3 $3a + 7 = 15$ 4 $3a - 6 = 7$ 5 $5p + 7 = 15$

6   $5p - 7 = 15$ 7 $5e + 3 = 3$ 8 $4t + 3 = 9$ 9 $8j - 7 = 5$ 10 $7c - 4 = 7$

11   $8k + 3 = 5$ 12 $3d - 7 = 3$ 13 $9u + 7 = 9$ 14 $4q - 4 = 5$ 15 $7y + 6 = 15$

So far all the answers to the equations you have looked at have been positive. This is how to deal with equations when the answers are negative.

Example 9

$$2a + 7 = 1$$
$$2a + 7 - 7 = 1 - 7$$
$$2a = -6$$
$$2a \div 2 = -6 \div 2$$
$$a = -3$$

Exercise 15I

Find the value of the letter in these equations.

1   $2a + 3 = 1$ 2 $2a + 5 = 1$ 3 $2a + 9 = 1$ 4 $3a + 8 = 5$

5   $3a + 7 = 1$ 6 $5p + 12 = 2$ 7 $2s + 7 = -3$ 8 $5p - 2 = -12$

9   $4k - 5 = -9$ 10 $8h + 10 = 2$ 11 $4y + 12 = -8$ 12 $3e - 17 = 20$

13   $6t - 12 = -12$ 14 $3w + 4 = 1$ 15 $2c + 15 = 11$ 16 $13a + 9 = 9$

Exercise 15J   (Mixed questions)

Find the value of the letter in these equations:

1 $2s + 4 = 10$	**2** $5d + 3 = 18$	**3** $8m - 7 = 33$
4 $4h - 2 = 14$	**5** $4k + 7 = 43$	**6** $3y + 7 = 13$
7 $5p + 2 = 9$	**8** $4f + 4 = 17$	**9** $3s - 6 = 5$
10 $7g - 4 = 12$	**11** $4f - 5 = 12$	**12** $5k - 12 = 6$
13 $3s - 15 = 2$	**14** $6j - 3 = 19$	**15** $9b + 7 = 2$
16 $2r + 12 = 5$	**17** $5t + 15 = -12$	**18** $7y - 15 = -21$
19 $3e - 5 = -6$	**20** $4f - 7 = -2$	**21** $5g + 17 = 15$
22 $4h + 4 = 0$	**23** $3c - 5 = 0$	**24** $8s + 9 = 4$

15.3 Equations with brackets

Algebra 1 dealt with quite complicated algebraic expressions so you can use what you have learnt to solve quite complicated equations:

Example 10

$$
\begin{aligned}
3(2p + 3) &= 5 \\
3 \times 2p + 3 \times 3 &= 5 \\
6p + 9 &= 5 \\
6p + 9 - 9 &= 5 - 9 \\
6p &= -4 \\
6p \div 6 &= -4 \div 6 \\
p &= -\tfrac{4}{6} \text{ or } \tfrac{2}{3}
\end{aligned}
$$

$3(2p + 3)$

$3 \times 2p + 3 \times 3$

Remember to deal with brackets first and multiply the inside by 3

■ **In an equation with brackets remove the brackets first.**

Exercise 15K

Find the value of the letter in these equations:

1 $2(p + 4) = 10$	**2** $3(d - 2) = 9$	**3** $2(c + 5) = 16$
4 $3(b - 2) = 1$	**5** $3(g + 2) = 15$	**6** $5(g - 2) = 15$
7 $2(v + 3) = 2$	**8** $4(4 + s) = 20$	**9** $2(3d + 3) = 4$
10 $3(t - 5) = 2$	**11** $4(h - 3) = 0$	**12** $2(3h - 7) = 10$
13 $2(2s + 5) = 22$	**14** $4(2y - 3) = 16$	**15** $4(4r - 12) = 32$

Exercise 15L

Solve these equations:

1 $2(a + 2) = 6$ 2 $3(h - 4) = 12$

3 $4(g + 5) = 8$ 4 $6(f - 3) = 18$

5 $5(q + 7) = 35$ 6 $9(k - 2) = 18$

7 $5(4 + g) = 25$ 8 $4(5 + h) = 12$

9 $3(d + 2) = 3$ 10 $2(v + 7) = 3$

11 $3(s + 7) = 4$ 12 $5(2n - 3) = 20$

13 $4(4f + 5) = 6$ 14 $6(7d - 12) = 30$

15 $2(5m + 11) = 0$

If there are letters on both sides of an equation you have to deal with the problem slightly differently.

It is a good idea to always keep the letter on the side with the most; in this case the side with $5p$.

Example 11

$$5p - 2 = 3p + 6$$
$$5p - 3p - 2 = 3p - 3p + 6$$ take $3p$ from both sides
$$2p - 2 = 6$$
$$2p = 6 + 2$$ add 2 to both sides
$$2p = 8$$
$$p = 4$$ divide by 2

Exercise 15M

Find the value of the letter in these equations:

1 $2k - 3 = k + 2$ 2 $5s - 4 = 3s + 3$

3 $4p + 2 = 3p + 6$ 4 $5g + 4 = 3g + 2$

5 $7t - 4 = 4t + 7$ 6 $2k + 6 = 3k - 3$

7 $4d + 9 = 5d + 2$ 8 $5c + 8 = 7c + 2$

9 $5z + 6 = 3z + 4$ 10 $7b + 12 = 3b - 6$

11 $9p + 8 = 3p - 2$ 12 $4g + 9 = 3g + 17$

Exercise 15N

Solve the equations:

1 $5h - 5 = 4h + 7$	**2** $7t + 11 = 6t + 3$
3 $5d + 3 = 3d + 1$	**4** $6f + 9 = 4f + 3$
5 $3s + 5 = 4s - 2$	**6** $4d + 13 = 5d + 7$
7 $2a + 7 = 4a - 2$	**8** $3q + 9 = 6q - 3$
9 $4y + 4 = 7y + 6$	**10** $2e + 6 = 5e + 9$
11 $12s + 6 = 6s - 4$	**12** $5u + 9 = 3u - 2$
13 $5t - 5 = 2t - 9$	**14** $6s + 9 = 2s + 2$
15 $3q + 6 = 7q - 5$	**16** $2w + 3 = 7w + 9$
17 $8h + 4 = 3h - 4$	**18** $3s + 4 = 2s - 3$
19 $r + 2 = 5r + 6$	**20** $5a - 7 = 2a + 4$

The most complicated equations you will be asked to solve will have letters on both sides and perhaps brackets as well. Here is an example.

Example 12

$$
\begin{aligned}
4(2x - 3) &= 2(x + 3) \\
8x - 12 &= 2x + 6 \\
8x - 2x - 12 &= 2x - 2x + 6 \\
6x - 12 &= 6 \\
6x - 12 + 12 &= 6 + 12 \\
6x &= 18 \\
x &= 3
\end{aligned}
$$

The first step is to get rid of the brackets then sort out the equation in the usual way.

Exercise 15O

Find the value of the letters in these equations:

1 $4(2p + 3) = 2(p + 8)$	**2** $5(2h - 9) = 3(3h + 7)$
3 $6(5r - 7) = 4(3r + 7)$	**4** $7(2t + 6) = 3(5t + 7)$
5 $4(3g + 5) = 2(5g + 7)$	**6** $5(4d + 9) = 6(3d + 5)$
7 $8(2k - 6) = 5(3k - 7)$	**8** $7(2m + 3) = 4(5m - 3)$
9 $7(9d - 5) = 12(5d - 6)$	**10** $5(3j + 7) = 4(4j + 3)$
11 $4(8y + 3) = 6(7y + 5)$	**12** $3(6t + 7) = 5(4t + 7)$

Exercise 15P (Mixed questions)

1 $5t + 7 = 3t + 10$

2 $4g + 7 = 3g + 9$

3 $6s - 6 = 4s + 2$

4 $5q - 5 = 3q + 7$

5 $2d + 4 = 5d - 6$

6 $6k - 3 = 2k + 7$

7 $2(a + 3) = 7$

8 $5(2k - 4) = 15$

9 $5 = 2(2d + 7)$

10 $8 = 4(7p - 3)$

11 $2(3p + 2) = 5p - 7$

12 $3(5r + 2) = 12r - 7$

13 $2(6t + 2) = 3(5t - 6)$

14 $6(g + 7) = 3(4g + 2)$

15 $5(2a + 1) + 3(3a - 4) = 4(3a - 6)$

Summary of key points

1 In algebra letters are often used to represent numbers like $a = 5$.

2 To make an equation balance you must do the same to each side

$a + 4 = 7 \;\rightarrow\; a + 4 - 4 = 7 - 4 \;\rightarrow\; a = 3.$

3 In an equation with brackets remove the brackets first

$3(x + 1) = 4 \;\rightarrow\; 3x + 3 = 4.$

16 Pie charts

■ **A pie chart is a good way of displaying data when you want to show how something is shared or divided:**

. . . how Wayne spent the last 24 hours:

. . . how the land is used in the UK:

. . . how much market share different cat food brands have:

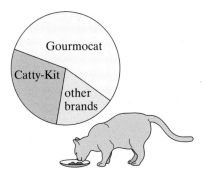

This unit shows you how to represent data on a pie chart.

16.1 Drawing a pie chart

Each slice of a pie chart is called a sector.

When you know the angle of each sector at the centre of a pie chart, here is how to draw it.

Example 1

Draw a pie chart whose angles at the centre are: 108°, 90°, 72°, 60° and 30°.

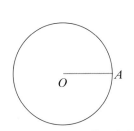

Draw a circle. Draw a line *OA* from its centre to its circumference.

Use your protractor to measure the angle 108°. Mark it and draw the line *OB*.

Place your protractor along *OB*. Measure the angle 90°, mark it and draw *OC*.

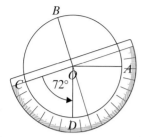

Place your protractor along *OC*. Measure the angle 72°, mark it and draw *OD*.

Place your protractor along *OD*. Measure the angle 60°, mark it and draw *OE*.

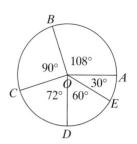

Check that the angle remaining is 30° and mark it.

16.2 Calculating the angles

Twenty students were asked on which day they would help paint the scenery for the school play. The replies were: Monday 5, Tuesday 4, Wednesday 8 and Thursday 3.

Here is the data shown on a pie chart.

The circle represents all 20 students and each section represents one of the days.

Separating the sections shows that to fit together again the shaded angles must add up to 360°: the total sum of the angles at the centre of a circle.

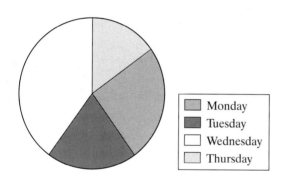

▨	Monday
▨	Tuesday
☐	Wednesday
▨	Thursday

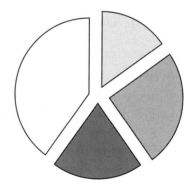

Here is how to calculate the angles of each sector:

20 students are represented by 360°

1 student is represented by $\dfrac{360}{20} = 18°$

Monday:	5 students so the angle is	$5 \times 18°$	= 90°
Tuesday:	4 students so the angle is	$4 \times 18°$	= 72°
Wednesday:	8 students so the angle is	$8 \times 18°$	= 144°
Thursday:	3 students so the angle is	$3 \times 18°$	= 54°
Check:	20 students so the angle is	$20 \times 18°$	= 360°

Another way of calculating the angles is to find what fraction of 360° the students represent:

Monday: $\dfrac{5}{20} \times 360° = 90°$

Tuesday: $\dfrac{4}{20} \times 360° = 72°$

Wednesday: $\dfrac{8}{20} \times 360° = 144°$

Thursday: $\dfrac{3}{20} \times 360° = 54°$

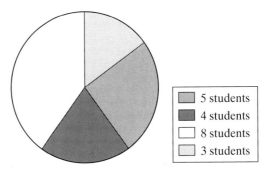

- 5 students
- 4 students
- 8 students
- 3 students

16.3 Calculating using pie charts

The same twenty students agreed to help the next week. Here is the new pie chart:

Here is how to find how many students worked each day:

20 students are represented by 360°

1 student is represented by
$\dfrac{360°}{20} = 18°$

- Monday
- Tuesday
- Wednesday
- Thursday

Monday: angle is 180° so the number of students is $\dfrac{180}{18} = 10$

Tuesday: angle is 90° so the number of students is $\dfrac{90}{18} = 5$

Wednesday: angle is 54° so the number of students is $\dfrac{54}{18} = 3$

Thursday: angle is 36° so the number of students is $\dfrac{36}{18} = 2$

Another way of finding out how many students worked each day is to find what fraction of the twenty students each angle represents.

Monday: $\dfrac{180°}{360°} \times 20 = 10$ Tuesday: $\dfrac{90°}{360°} \times 20 = 5$

Wednesday: $\dfrac{54°}{360°} \times 20 = 3$ Thursday: $\dfrac{36°}{360°} \times 20 = 2$

Exercise 16A

1   Donna wanted to draw pie charts to show examination
    entries for three classes and she calculated these angles:

	English	Maths	Science	History	Art	French
Class IIC	180	60	45	45	30	–
Class IIB	108	72	60	50	40	30
Class IIA	120	72	60	54	36	18

Draw a pie chart for each class.

2   The number of pens and pencils five students had with
    them is shown in the table.

Name	Number	Angle needed
Gwyneth	3	
Peter	8	
Wes	4	
Mario	2	
Nesta	7	

   (a) Copy and complete the table by calculating the angle
        needed to draw a pie chart.
   (b) Draw the pie chart.

3   Draw pie charts to represent the following data:
   (a) The number of A grades gained by students in Class IIB

Subject	English	Maths	French	Science	Other
Number	5	6	2	4	3

   (b) The number of pets kept by students in Class IIB

Pets	Dogs	Hamsters	Cats	Birds	Other	No pets
Number	10	5	6	4	3	8

   (c) Vehicles passing while Haji waited for the bus

Type	Car	Bus	Lorry	Van	M/Cycle
Number	24	12	10	6	8

4   A class of 30 students listed their favourite sports:

Sport	Swimming	Tennis	Football	Hockey	Athletics
Number	10	4	8	6	2

Draw a pie chart to illustrate this data.

Worked exam question

720 students were asked how they travelled to school.

The pie chart shows the results of this survey.

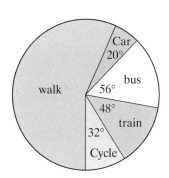

Work out:

(a) how many of the students travelled to school by bus
(b) how many students walked to school?

(a) How many travelled by bus?

360° represents 720 students

1° represents $\dfrac{720}{360}$ = 2 students

The angle of the bus sector of the pie chart is 56°, so the number of students is:

56 × 2 = 112

Here is another way of doing this:

The bus sector is 56° and the whole pie chart is 360°, so the fraction travelling by bus is: $\dfrac{56}{360}$

There are 720 students so the number of students travelling by bus is:

$\dfrac{56}{360}$ × 720 = 112

(b) First find the angle of the 'walk' sector:

360 – (20 + 56 + 48 + 32) = 360 – 156
                                        = 204°

Either each 1° represents 2 students   *or* $\dfrac{204}{360}$ × 720

        204 × 2 = 408 students   = 408 students

Exercise 16B

1   In a pilot survey Henry asked the question, 'Which main course did you choose?' His results were:

Main course	Tally	Frequency
Fish	⊞I	5
Sausages	II	2
Salad	III	3
Cheese roll	II	2

(a) How many students' results did Henry record?

(b) Henry wants to represent this information on a pie chart. How many degrees represent one person on the pie chart?

(c) Copy and complete the table:

Column 1	Column 2	Column 3	Column 4
Main course	**Frequency tally**	**Degrees per student**	**Sector angle** (Column 2 × Column 3)
Fish	5		
Sausages			
Salad			
Cheese roll			
Total			

(d) Use your answers to column 4 to draw a pie chart.

(e) Suggest a title for your pie chart.

2   The table shows the sweets served:

Rice pudding	Apple tart	Ice cream	Trifle	Fruit
2	6	16	12	4

Draw a pie chart to illustrate this data.

3   Emily also asked staff 'what drink they had at break'. She made this table.

Drink	Tea	Coffee	Milk	Water	Chocolate
Number	12	11	7	4	6

(a) Illustrate this data by drawing:
   (i)   a pictogram
   (ii) a bar chart
   (iii) a pie chart

(b) Comment on each of your charts.

4 The pie chart shows the results of another question 'Which vegetables did you have?'

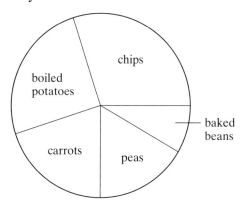

(a) Measure each angle, copy and complete the table:

Column 1	Column 2	Column 3	Column 4
Vegetable	**Sector angle**	**Degrees per vegetable**	**Number of pupils** (Column 2 ÷ Column 3)
Chips		6	
Boiled potatoes		6	
Carrots		6	
Peas		6	10
Baked beans		6	
Total			

(b) How many portions of vegetables were served?

5 Kesh takes home £120 per week. He allocates his money like this:

    Rent £30   Travel £9   Clothes £14
    Food £40   Savings £20 Spare £7

Draw a pie chart to show how he allocates his money.

6 Kesh had a £40 rise and the changes he made are shown in the pie chart.

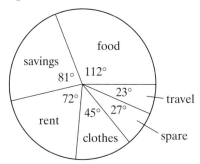

(a) Calculate show much he spent on rent, travel, clothes, food, savings and how much he had spare.
(b) Which items did not change?

7   Thirty pupils were asked to name their favourite ice
     cream. The result is shown in this pie chart.
     (a) What does the whole circle represent?
     (b) Which ice cream does the largest sector
        represent?
     (c) What does the smallest sector represent?
     (d) Use the given angles to calculate the number of
        pupils who liked strawberry ice cream.
     (e) How could you select pupils so that this was a
        random sample?

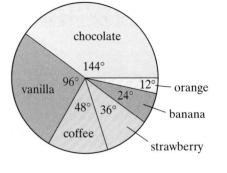

8   Sita spent £90 as in the table.
     (a) Calculate the angle of sector.
     (b) Draw a pie chart to show her spending.

Items	Amount spent	Angle of sector
Bus fares	£12	
Going out	£25	
Clothes	£30	
Records	£15	
Other	£8	
Total spending	£90	**Total angles 360°**

[L]

Summary of key points

1   You can use a pie chart to display data when you want
     to show how something is shared or divided.

2   The angles at the centre of a pie chart add up to 360°.

17 Ratio and proportion

17.1 What is a ratio?

- **A ratio is a way of showing the relationship between two numbers.**

Ratios can be used to compare costs, weights and sizes . . .

On the deck there are 2 women and 1 man, 5 cars and 2 bicycles. You can say that:

There are 5 cars and 2 bicycles on this ferry. You can say that:

> the ratio of cars to bicycles is 5 to 2. This is written as 5 : 2
> the ratio of bicycles to cars is 2 to 5, written 2 : 5
> the ratio of men to women is 1 to 2, or 1 : 2
> the ratio of women to men is 2 to 1, or 2 : 1

Ratios make it easier to work out the exact quantities needed in mixtures. Chemists making up medicines, manufacturers making chocolate biscuits, cooks baking cakes, and builders mixing cement all need to be able to make exact mixtures.

Example 1

Frank is making pastry for 5 apple pies. How much of each ingredient does he need?

I always use 4oz flour and 2oz fat to make pastry for my apple pies

> flour $4 \times 5 = 20$ ounces
> fat $2 \times 5 = 10$ ounces

This can be written as a ratio:

> The ratio of flour to fat is 4 : 2

Example 2

Vijay needs 4 mixers full of cement. How much sand, gravel and cement will he need?

    sand   15 × 4 = 60 shovels
    gravel   9 × 4 = 36 shovels
    cement   6 × 4 = 24 shovels

This can be written as a ratio:

    The ratio of sand to gravel to cement is 15 : 9 : 6

Example 3

Find the ratio of white tiles to black tiles:

There are 12 white tiles and 4 black tiles.

    The ratio of white to black is 12 : 4

This can be simplified to 3 : 1. (There is more about simplifying in the next section.)

Exercise 17A

1   Here are some tile patterns. For each one write the ratio of white tiles to black tiles:

    (a)   **(b)**

    (c)   **(d)**

2   A recipe for 6 rock cakes needs 40 g of margarine and 100 g of flour. How much margarine and flour is needed to make:
    (a) 12 rock cakes   **(b)** 18 rock cakes   **(c)** 30 rock cakes
    (d) 3 rock cakes   **(e)** 15 rock cakes.

3 A recipe for a rice cake weighing 1200 g is:
    200 g of butter   400 g of ground rice
    400 g of sugar   4 eggs (eggs weigh 50 g each)
How much of each ingredient would you use to make a
rice cake weighing:
(a) 2400 g   **(b)** 600 g   **(c)** 1800 g   **(d)** 3000 g

4 A builder uses 5 buckets of sand and 2 buckets of cement
to make concrete. How many buckets of cement will she
need if she uses:
(a) 15 buckets of sand   **(b)** 35 buckets of sand

5 The builder prepares 120 kg of mortar by mixing 20 kg of
cement with 10 kg of lime and 90 kg of sand. How much
cement, lime and sand does she use to prepare:
(a) 60 kg of mortar   **(b)** 180 kg of mortar
(c) 12 kg of mortar

6 Brass is an alloy (mixture) of zinc and
copper in the ratio 3 : 17
How much copper would you expect
to be in a brass cross which contained
120 g of zinc?

This hot rolling mill makes
mild steel – an alloy of iron
and carbon.

7 To make 25 kg of bronze you mix 6 kg of tin with 19 kg of
copper.
How much tin and copper is needed to make:
(a) 50 kg of bronze   **(b)** 250 kg of bronze
(c) 5 kg of bronze

17.2 Simplifying ratios

These ratios below are **equivalent** – the relationship between
each pair of numbers is the same:

    10 : 20
     3 : 6
     2 : 4
     1 : 2   This ratio is a **simpler form** of the ratio 10 : 20

■ **You can simplify a ratio if you can divide both its numbers
by a common factor.**

Example 4

Simplify the ratio 30 : 100

10 is a common factor of 30 and 100. Dividing both numbers by 10 gives:

$$\ldots 3 : 10 \ldots$$

30 ÷ 10   100 ÷ 10

■ **When a ratio cannot be simplified it is said to be in its lowest terms. Ratios are usually written in their lowest terms.**

Example 5

Write 40p to £1 as a ratio.

First you make the units the same so you are comparing pennies with pennies: 40p to 100p

The ratio is:

    40 : 100

Dividing both numbers by 20 gives:

    2 : 5

The ratio of 40p to £1 is 2 : 5 in its lowest terms.

Example 6

Patrick and Colleen share £35 in the ratio 3 : 4 How much does each person get?

The total number of shares is 3 + 4 = 7

Each share is worth $\frac{£35}{7}$ = £5

    Patrick gets   3 × £5 = £15

    Colleen gets 4 × £5 = £20

$$3 : 4$$

£15   £20

Exercise 17B

1 Write these ratios in their lowest terms:
   (a) 2 : 4   **(b)** 3 : 9   **(c)** 3 : 18   **(d)** 6 : 24
   (e) 8 : 24   **(f)** 16 : 24   **(g)** 10 : 2   **(h)** 28 : 4
   (i) 32 : 48   **(j)** 15 : 9

2 Write the ratios in their lowest terms. Remember that the units must be the same before you write a ratio.
   (a) 20 cm : 100 cm   **(b)** 20 cm : 1 m
   (c) 25p : £2   **(d)** £3 : 60p

3 Write these as ratios in their lowest terms:
   (a) a small loaf costing 49p and a large loaf 63p
   (b) Jeanette weighs 40 kg and Pauline weighs 44 kg
   (c) Spey school has 660 boys and 750 girls
   (d) Mr Johnson takes 1 hour to get to work by train but 2 hours by car
   (e) a salesman made 27 successful calls and 21 unsuccessful calls
   (f) a factory employs 66 craft workers, 18 clerical staff and 12 sales staff

4 £360 is divided between Sally and Nadir in the ratio 5 : 4 How much should each person receive?

5 Hermit, Mark and Gavin share £480 in the ratio 4 : 5 : 3 How much should each person receive?

6 Share 40 sweets in the ratio 2 : 5 : 1

7 Henry, Sue and Rebecca agree to look after the cake stall in the ratio 2 : 4 : 3 Rebecca looked after it for 1 hour. How long did
   (a) Henry   **(b)** Sue
   spend looking after the stall?

8 Copy and complete this table. The first one is done for you:

Quantity	Divided in the ratio		
	4 :	3 :	2
£27	£12	£9	£6
9 lbs			
36 km			
63 miles			
81 tonnes			
£144			

9 A kilo of cherries costs £1.20 and a kilo of apples cost 72p. Write these prices as a ratio in its lowest terms.

10

Mortar is made by mixing 5 parts by weight of sand with 1 part by weight of cement. How much sand is needed to make 8400 kg of mortar?

[L]

17.3 Proportion

■ **Two quantities are in proportion if their ratio stays the same as the quantities get larger or smaller.**

For example, if the ratio of teachers to students is 1 : 30 (or one per class of 30) then three classes will need a ratio of 3 : 90

Example 6

A factory employs office staff and production staff in the ratio 2 : 7   The number of office staff is increased to 10.

If the number of production staff is kept in proportion to the number of office staff, how many production staff will there be?

Here are the ratios before and after increasing the staff:

  ratio before increase: 2 : 7
  ratio after increase: 10 : ?

You need to find the number that makes these ratios **equivalent**.

Multiplying both numbers in the 'before' ratio by the same number will give an equivalent ratio. Try 5:

$$\times 5 \left(\begin{array}{c} 2 : 7 \\ 10 : 35 \end{array} \right) \times 5$$

2 : 7 and 10 : 35 are equivalent ratios.

The number of production staff after the increase is 35.

Exercise 17C

1   Calculate the missing number in these ratios:
   (a) 3 : 5 = 12 : ?   **(b)** 4 : 7 = 16 : ?   **(c)** 6 : 5 = 3 : ?
   (d) 4 : 5 = ? : 35   **(e)** 8 : 3 = ? : 15   **(f)** 7 : ? = 49 : 63

2   A telegraph pole 60 feet high casts a shadow 12 feet long.
    At the same time of day, how long is a shadow cast by:
    (a) a 90 foot pole   **(b)** a 40 foot pole   **(c)** a 25 foot pole

3   The numbers of telephone boxes made in a factory in the
    morning and in the afternoon are in the ratio 4 : 9   They
    are always completed in this ratio.
    (a) How many boxes are made in the afternoon if 60 are
        made in the morning?
    (b) How many are made in the morning if 189 are made
        in the afternoon?

4   The ratio of students going home for lunch to students
    staying at school for lunch is 3 : 5   If 273 students go
    home for lunch how many stay at school?

5   A machine can produce 1120 plastic mugs in 8 hours. At
    that rate:
    (a) how many plastic mugs will it produce in 10 hours?
    (b) how long will it take to produce 840 plastic mugs?

6   The ratio of the length of a room to its width is 5 : 4
    If the length is 6 metres, what is the width?

7   A car travels 126 miles on 18 litres of petrol.
    (a) How far will it travel on 40 litres?
    (b) How many litres will be needed to travel 540 miles?

8   Mario is paid £21.60 for working 6 hours in the
    supermarket. At that rate:
    (a) how much will he be paid for working 8 hours?
    (b) how long would it take him to earn £54?

17.4 Solving ratio and proportion problems by the unitary method

Another way of solving ratio problems is to first find the value
of **one unit** of the quantity. This is called the unitary method.

Example 8

If 6 similar CDs cost £30, how much will 8 CDs cost?

6 CDs cost £30   **Find the cost of one CD**
                                               It costs less.
1 CD costs $\dfrac{£30}{6}$

8 CDs cost $\dfrac{£30}{6} \times 8 = £40$ Eight CDs cost 8 × the
                                               cost of one CD

Example 9

If 6 men can build a shed in 3 days, how long will it take 4 men working at the same rate?

6 men take   3 days

1 man takes 3×6 days

Find how long it would take one man.
It takes longer.

$\frac{3 \times 6}{4}$ is the same as $3 \times 6 \times \frac{1}{4}$

4 men take $\frac{3 \times 6}{4} = 4\frac{1}{2}$ days.

Four men take $\frac{1}{4}$ the time taken by one man

Example 10

A factory employs office staff and production staff in the ratio 2 : 7 How many production staff are employed if there 10 office staff?

2 office staff are needed for 7 production staff

Find how many production staff are needed for one office staff.

1 office staff is needed for $\frac{7}{2}$

10 times as many production staff are needed for 10 office staff.

10 office staff are needed for $\frac{7}{2} \times 10$

The number of production staff needed is 35.

Example 11

Zoe paid £3.20 for 8 mince pies. How much would 12 mince pies cost?

8 mince pies cost   320 pence

1 mince pie costs $\frac{320}{8}$

Find how much one mince pie costs.

12 mince pies cost $\frac{320}{8} \times 12$

12 pies cost 12 × the cost of one pie.

12 mince pies cost 480 pence or £4.80

Exercise 17D

1   Ten leisure club tickets cost £48. What would 25 tickets cost?

2   Twenty daffodil bulbs cost £2.50. What would 36 bulbs cost?

3 Paul paid £7.20 for 24 Christmas cards. How much would he have to pay for 36 similar cards?

4 Camilla paid £40 for 15 CDs. How much would she have to pay for 24 CDs at the same price?

5 Vijay bought 18 postcards for £2.16 How much would he pay if he bought 27?

6 Bronwen bought 15 roses for £9. How many roses could she have bought for £12.60?

7 A train travels at 80 miles per hour. How long will it take to travel:
(a) 140 miles   **(b)** 440 miles   **(c)** 640 miles

8 A cyclist travels at an average speed of 16 km per hour. At the same rate:
(a) how far would he travel in 4 hours?
(b) how long would it take him to cycle 100 miles?

9 A wall took 6 hours for 4 men to build. At the same rate:
(a) how long would it have taken 10 men?
(b) how many men would have been needed to build it in 12 hours?

10 Eight men can build a chalet in 18 days. Working at the same rate how long would it take:
(a) 12 men   **(b)** 5 men
(c) How many men would be needed to build it in 3 days?

17.5 Scales in maps and diagrams

Ratios called **scales** are used to show the relationship between distances on the ground and distances on a map. A common scale is 1 : 50 000, this means that 1 cm on the map represents 50 000 cm on the ground.

1 : 50 000

This is part of an OS 1:50 000 scale map. 1 cm on the map represents 500 m or half a kilometre.

Example 12

Two towns are 5.2 cm apart on a map whose scale is 1 : 50 000. How far apart are the towns on the ground?

    1 cm   represents   50 000 cm
    5.2 cm represents   50 000 cm × 5.2 = 260 000 cm

The towns are 2.6 kilometres apart.

To convert from cm to m ÷ by 100
260 000 cm ÷ 100
= 2600 m

To convert from m to km ÷ by 1000
2600 m ÷ 1000
= 2.6 km

Other uses for scales

Model makers also use scales to make copies of objects, for example model aeroplanes, cars, trains, dresses or pieces of furniture. Architects use scales to draw plans of houses.

Example 13

A dolls house has a scale of 1 : 40 If the height of a room in the dolls house is 7.5 cm what would this represent in real life?

     1 cm   represents   40 cm
   7.5 cm   represents   40 × 7.5 cm = 300 cm or 3 metres

In real life the room would be 3 metres high.

Exercise 17E

1   A map has a scale of 1 : 50 000 What is the distance on the ground if the distance on the map is:
    (a) 2.5 cm   **(b)** 3.6 cm   **(c)** 5.2 cm   **(d)** 6.2 cm

2   What is the distance on the map from question **1** if the distance on the ground is:
    (a) 6 km   **(b)** 5.2 km   **(c)** 8.4 km   **(d)** 25.6 km

3   A town map has a scale of 1 : 6000
    (a) The town hall is 1500 metres from the station. How far would it be on the map?
    (b) On the map the hotel is 4.6 cm from the harbour. How far is this on the ground?
    (c) Adrian plans a walk round the town. He measures it on the map to be 36.5 cm. How far is he planning to walk?

4   A gardener draws this plan of a patio using a scale of 1 : 125

Patio

Scale 1 : 125

    (a) Measure the sides
    (b) Copy the diagram and put on the actual measurements the patio will have. Give your answer in metres.

5   A model aircraft has a scale of 1 cm represents 1.8 metres
    (a) Write this scale as a ratio.
    (b) What is the length of the model if the length of the aircraft is 42 metres?

Summary of key points

1   A ratio such as 3 : 2 is a way of showing the relationship between two numbers.

2   You can simplify a ratio if you can divide both its numbers by a common factor. For example:

divide by the common factor 2

2 : 6   and   1 : 3   are equivalent ratios.

3   When a ratio cannot be simplified it is said to be in its lowest terms. Ratios are usually written in their lowest terms.

4   Two quantities are in proportion if their ratios stay the same as the quantities get larger or smaller.

5   The unitary method is a way of solving ratio and proportion problems by finding the value of one unit of a quantity first. For example, to find the cost of 12 pies when you know the cost of 8 pies:

8 pies cost   320 pence

1 pie costs $\dfrac{320}{8}$ ——————— find the cost of one

So 12 pies cost $\dfrac{320}{8} \times 12$ —— 12 × the cost of one pie

6   A ratio called a scale is used to show the relationship between a distance on a map and the distance on the ground.   On a 1 : 50 000 scale map 1 cm represents 50 000 cm on the ground.

18 Symmetry

18.1 Reflective symmetry in 2-D shapes

The two-dimensional (2-D) picture of a butterfly below is **symmetrical**. If you could fold it in half along the dotted line each half would fit exactly on top of the other.

Line of symmetry

The dotted line is called a **line of symmetry**. One half of the shape is a mirror image of the other half.

Some shapes have more than one line of symmetry. The flags below have more than one line of symmetry.

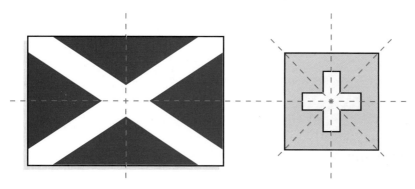

A good way to find the lines of symmetry of a shape is to draw it on tracing paper. Then you can actually fold the shape and check that each half fits exactly on top of the other. Another method is to use a mirror.

- ■ **A line of symmetry is sometimes called a mirror line.**

- ■ **A 2-D shape has a line of symmetry if the line divides the shape into two halves and one half is the mirror image of the other half.**

Example 1

Half of a symmetrical shape is shown here. The dotted line is a line of symmetry. Copy and complete the shape.

Mark the mirror images of the points (or vertices) in first...

Each point has a mirror image the same distance away from the line of symmetry, but on the other side.

... then complete the lines.

Exercise 18A

1 This question is about the following tiles.

A   B   C   D

E   F   G   H

Which shape(s) have:
(a) only one line of symmetry
(b) no lines of symmetry
(c) exactly three lines of symmetry
(d) exactly four lines of symmetry
(e) exactly two lines of symmetry?

2 Copy these shapes and draw all the lines of symmetry on each flag:

(a)

(b)

(c)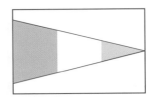

3   In each of these shapes the dotted line is a line of
    symmetry. Copy and complete each shape:

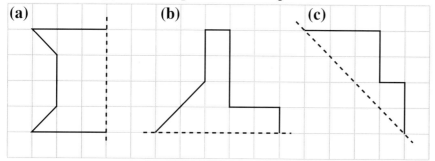

(a)   (b)   (c)

4   Use the two lines of symmetry to copy and complete each
    of these shapes. Hint: use just one line of symmetry at a
    time.

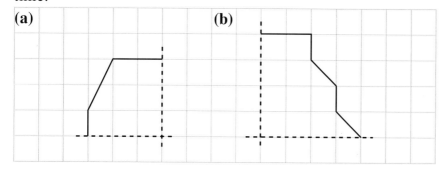

(a)   (b)

5   Write out the capital letters of the alphabet which have:
    (a) one line of symmetry
    (b) more than one line of symmetry
    (c) no lines of symmetry.

18.2 Reflective symmetry in pictures and patterns

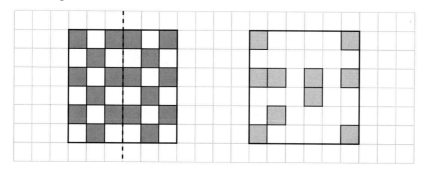

This pattern is **symmetrical**.
It can be folded in half so all
the lines and colours in each
half fit exactly on top of each
other.

This pattern is **asymmetrical**
(not symmetrical). When it is
folded in half some of the
lines and colours do not
match.

Exercise 18B

You may want to use a mirror or tracing paper in this exercise.

1   Look at these patterns:

A   B   C

D   E   F

> **Remember:**
> Asymmetrical shapes have no lines of symmetry

(a) Which patterns have only one line of symmetry?
(b) Which of these patterns are asymmetrical?
(c) Which of these patterns have two lines of symmetry?

2   Copy these patterns. Draw in all the lines of symmetry on each one.

(a)   (b)   (c)

(d)   (e)   (f)

3   In how many different ways can you arrange six squares (which must touch) to form a symmetrical pattern.

Draw your patterns. Two are done for you.

18.3 Rotational symmetry

When a square is rotated or turned through 360° it looks exactly as it did at the start on four different occasions during the rotation. Any shape that looks exactly as it did at the start at least twice during a full turn has **rotational symmetry**.

The number of times a shape looks the same during a full turn is its **order of rotational symmetry**. A square has order of rotational symmetry 4 as it looks the same 4 times during one complete turn.

A square looks the same four times during a full turn:

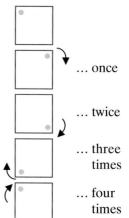

- **A 2-D shape with rotational symmetry repeats the appearance of its starting position two or more times during a full turn.**

- **The order of rotational symmetry is the number of times the original appearance is repeated in a full turn.**

Looking for rotational symmetry

Sometimes rotational symmetry can be hard to spot, so you may want to try one of the following ideas.

Either actually turn the book or paper the shape is drawn on, *or* trace the shape onto tracing paper and turn it on top of the shape in the book. Then you will be able to see when the shapes match.

Example 2

Does a kite have rotational symmetry?

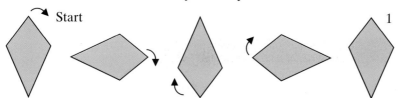

A kite only looks the same once during a complete turn, so it does not have rotational symmetry.

Example 3

Write down the order of rotational symmetry of this flag.

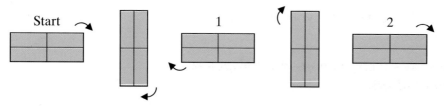

When the flag is turned through 360° it looks the same twice.

The order of rotational symmetry is 2.

Exercise 18C

You may want to use tracing paper in this exercise.

1   Write down whether or not these shapes have rotational symmetry.

(a)   (b)   (c)   (d)   (e)

2   State the order of rotational symmetry of these shapes.

(a)   (b)   (c)   (d)   (e)

18.4 The symmetry of regular polygons

A regular hexagon has 6 lines of
symmetry and rotational symmetry
of order 6.

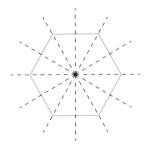

Exercise 18D

1   For each of these regular
    polygons, find:
    (a) the number of lines of
         symmetry
    (b) the order of rotational
         symmetry.

(i)   (ii)

■ **Regular polygons have the same number of lines of
   symmetry as they have sides.**

■ **The order of rotational symmetry of a regular polygon is
   the same as the number of sides.**

18.5 Symmetry in 3-dimensional shapes

■ **A plane of symmetry separates a 3-D shape into two halves which are mirror images of each other.**

plane of symmetry

Example 4

Draw diagrams to show the planes of symmetry of a cuboid.

A cuboid has 3 planes of symmetry. To show the planes of symmetry clearly, draw a diagram for each plane.

Exercise 18E

You may want to use tracing paper in this exercise.

1 Write down the number of planes of symmetry for each of the following shapes. (Some shapes may not have any.)

(a)

(b)

(c)

(d)

2 Copy or trace the following shapes and clearly mark any planes of symmetry on your drawings.

(a)

(b)

(c)

(d)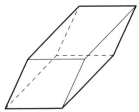

3 The drawings below show half a 3-D solid. Copy and complete each solid so that the shaded face forms a plane of symmetry.

(a)

(b)

Exercise 18F   Mixed questions

1 How many lines of symmetry does a kite have?

2 Draw a rectangle showing all the lines of symmetry.

3 Which regular polygon has five lines of symmetry?

4 Sketch a regular octagon showing its lines of symmetry.

5 What is the order of rotational symmetry of a regular octagon?

6 Which special triangle has rotational symmetry of order 3?

7   Copy or trace the shapes below. Draw all the lines of symmetry and write down the order of rotational symmetry for each shape.

(a)   (b)   (c)   (d)   (e)

8   Copy and complete the shapes below using the lines of symmetry given.

(a)   (b)

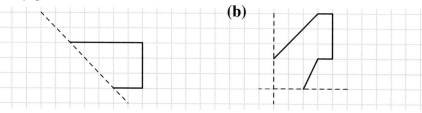

9   Using the lines of symmetry shown copy and complete the missing parts of the patterns.

(a)   (b)

10 How many planes of symmetry does each of the following shapes have?

(a)   (b)   (c)

11 Copy or trace the shapes below. Show the plane or planes of symmetry on your diagrams.

(a)   (b)

Exercise 18G

1 On a copy of each of these shapes, draw all of its lines of symmetry, if it has any.

[L]

2 These shapes each have at least one line of symmetry.
   (a) Copy these shapes and show all the lines of symmetry.
   (b) Explain how you could check whether or not a line of symmetry was correct.

[L]

3

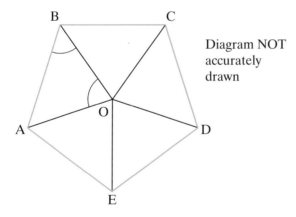

Diagram NOT accurately drawn

ABCDE is a regular pentagon.
O is the centre of the pentagon.
   (a) Write down the order of rotational symmetry of the regular pentagon.
   (b) Write down the number of lines of symmetry of triangle OCD.

[L]

4 Make a list of the designs below which have line symmetry.

(a)

Taj Mahal
floor tile

(b)

Asian carpet
design

(c)

Contemporary art

(d)

Wallpaper
patern

(e)

Tile design

[L]

5

The diagram represents a prism.
The cross section (shaded region) of
the prism is a right-angled isosceles triangle.
Draw one plane of symmetry of the prism.   [L]

Summary of key points

1 A line of symmetry is sometimes called a mirror line.

2 A 2-D shape has a line of symmetry if the line divides the shape into two halves and one half is the mirror image of the other half.

3 A 2-D shape with rotational symmetry repeats the appearance of its starting position two or more times in a full turn.

4 The order of rotational symmetry is the number of times the original appearance is repeated in a full turn.

5 Regular polygons have the same number of lines of symmetry as they have sides.

6 The order of rotational symmetry of a regular polygon is the same as the number of sides.

7 A plane of symmetry separates a 3-D shape into two halves which are mirror images of each other.

19 Measure 3

19.1 Perimeter

■ **The perimeter of a shape is the distance around the edge of the shape.**

Example 1

Find the perimeter of this rectangle.

The rectangle has two sides of length 5 cm and two sides of length 3 cm. The perimeter is:

$$5 + 3 + 5 + 3 = 16 \text{ cm}$$

Exercise 19A

1 Work out the perimeters of these shapes.

   (a) 3 cm, 2 cm   (b) 4 cm, 6 cm   (c) 2 cm, 3 cm, 4 cm   (d) 6 cm, 6 cm, 4 cm   (e) 4 cm, 3 cm, 3 cm, 2 cm, 4 cm

2 Work out the perimeters of these shapes:
   (a) a square with side 5 centimetres
   (b) a rectangle with sides 4 centimetres and 2 centimetres
   (c) an equilateral triangle with all sides 6 centimetres
   (d) an isosceles triangle with two sides of 5 cm and one of 6 cm

Example 2

Find the perimeter of this shape.

The shape is made up from a rectangle and a triangle. The rectangle is 9 cm by 6 cm and the triangle has sides 8 cm, 6 cm and 10 cm. The perimeter is:

$$6 + 9 + 10 + 8 + 9 = 42 \text{ cm}$$

Remember that the perimeter is the distance around the outside edge of the shape. It does not include lines inside the shape.

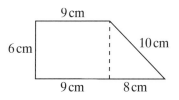

Exercise 19B

Find the perimeters of these shapes.

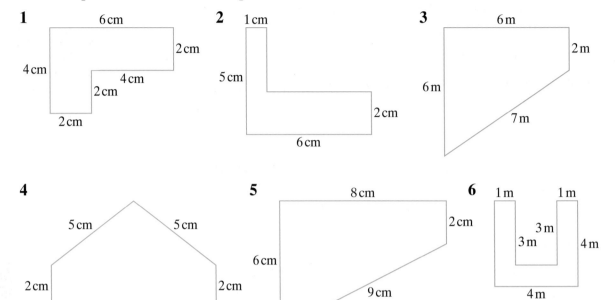

Exercise 19C

Measure these shapes and then find their perimeters.

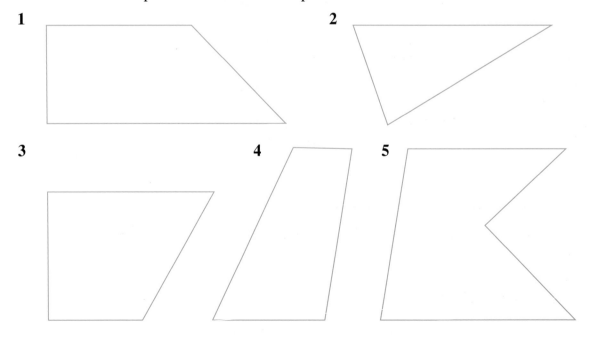

Circumference of a circle

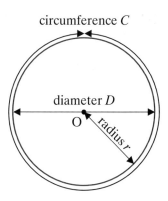

circumference C

■ **The perimeter of a circle is called the circumference.**

There is a simple formula that you need to know to work out the circumference of a circle it is:

■ $C = \pi \times D$ or $C = 2 \times \pi \times r$

where C is the circumference, D is the diameter and r is the radius of the circle. The diameter of a circle is **twice** the length of the radius.

To find the perimeter or circumference of a circle you have to multiply the diameter of the circle by a number called pi or π. This number is approximately 3.14 but you may be able to display a more accurate value on your calculator.

Example 3

Find the circumference of a circle with diameter of 5 cm.

$C = \pi \times D$
$C = 3.14 \times 5 = 15.7$ cm

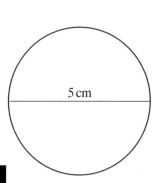

5 cm

Exercise 19D

1   Work out the circumferences of the circles with these diameters.
    (a) 2 cm   **(b)** 3 cm   **(c)** 4 cm
    (d) 10 cm   **(e)** 8 cm   **(f)** 12 cm

2   Calculate the circumferences of the circles with these diameters.
    (a) 20 cm   **(b)** 5 m   **(c)** 50 cm
    (d) 2.5 cm   **(e)** 3.6 cm   **(f)** 8.25 cm

Example 4

Find the circumference of a circle with radius 4 cm.

If the radius is 4 then the diameter is $2 \times 4 = 8$ and the circumference is:

$C = \pi \times D$
$C = 3.14 \times 8 = 25.12$ cm

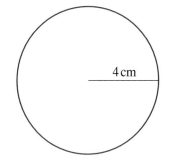

4 cm

Exercise 19E

Find the circumference of a circle with radius:

1	2 cm	**2**	3 cm	**3**	5 cm	**4**	10 cm
5	8 cm	**6**	12 cm	**7**	20 cm	**8**	5 m
9	50 cm	**10**	2.5 cm	**11**	3.6 cm	**12**	8.25 cm

Exercise 19F

Work out the circumference in each of the following cases:

1 a circle with a radius of 9 cm

2 a circle with a diameter of 9 cm

3 a circular table with a diameter of 90 cm

4 a circular fish pond whose radius is 60 cm

5 a circular paving slab of radius 15 cm

6 a circular flower bed of diameter 2.5 m

7 a circular candle of diameter 1.5 cm

8 a circular flower pot of diameter 6 inches

9 a pencil whose radius is 0.3 cm

10 a pen whose radius is 0.5 cm

Finding the diameter when you know the radius
Sometimes you know the circumference of the circle and you have to calculate the radius or diameter.

Example 5

Susie's bike wheel has a circumference of 62.8 cm. Work out the diameter of the wheel.

$$C = \pi \times D$$
so $$62.8 = 3.14 \times D$$

Dividing both sides by 3.14 gives:
$$D = 62.8 \div 3.14$$
$$D = 20 \text{ cm}$$

To find the radius divide the diameter by 2. The radius is 10 cm.

Exercise 19G

Copy this table and work out the diameter and radius of each circular shape.

	Shape	Circumference	Diameter	Radius
1	Circle	9.42 cm		
2	Circle	12.56 cm		
3	Circular table	3.14 m		
4	Circular fish pond	10 m		
5	Circular paving slab	90 cm		
6	Circular flower bed	7.5 m		
7	Circular candle	5 cm		
8	Circular flower pot	6 inches		
9	Pencil	1 cm		
10	Pen	2.5 cm		

19.2 Area

■ **The area of a shape is a measure of the amount of space it covers. Typical units of area are square centimetres (cm^2), square meters (m^2) and square kilometres (km^2).**

You can use a cm^2 grid to help you estimate the area of a shape.

Each square of a cm^2 grid has an area of one square centimetre (1 cm^2).

Example 6

Find the area of this rectangle.

This rectangle covers up 6 squares.

Each square is 1 cm by 1 cm and has an area of 1 square centimetre or 1 cm^2.

The rectangle has an area of 6 cm^2.

Exercise 19H

By counting squares find the areas of these shapes in cm².

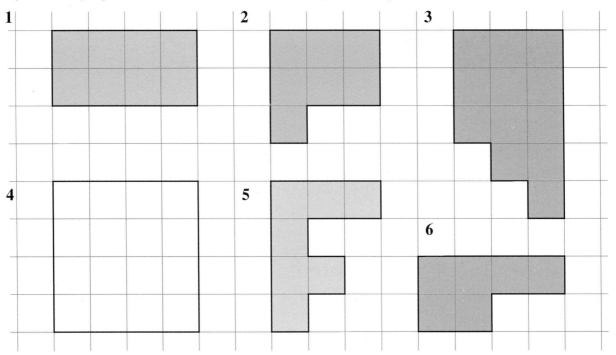

Estimating the areas of irregular shapes

Sometimes shapes do not fit exactly into whole squares. In these cases try and match up part squares to make whole ones.

It is a good idea to number the squares as you count to make sure that you don't miss a square or part of a square.

This shape has a total area of $14\frac{1}{2}$ square centimetres.

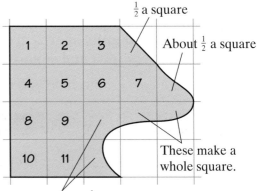

$\frac{1}{2}$ a square

About $\frac{1}{2}$ a square

These make a whole square.

These make about $1\frac{1}{2}$ squares.

Exercise 19I

Estimate the areas of these shapes in cm² by counting squares.

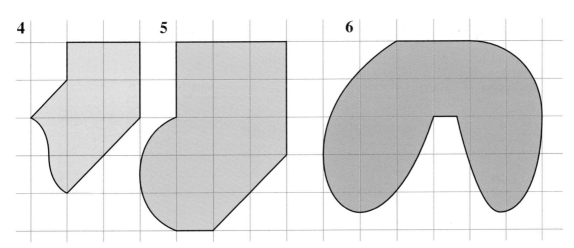

19.3 Volume

- **The volume of a 3-D shape is a measure of the amount of space it occupies. Typical units of volume are cubic centimetres (cm³) and cubic metres (m³).**

This cube has a volume of one cubic centimetre (1 cm³).

You can estimate an area using a grid of squares with area 1 cm². To estimate a volume you can use cubes of volume 1 cm³.

This cuboid is made up of 24 identical small cubes.

Each small cube is 1 cm by 1 cm by 1 cm and has a volume of 1 cm³. The cuboid has a volume of 24 cm³.

Exercise 19J

Find the volumes of these shapes in cm³ by counting cubes.

1 **2** **3**

4 **5**

19.4 Finding areas from formulae

You can find the areas of some shapes using formulae:

■ **Area of a rectangle = length × width**
$$= l \times w$$

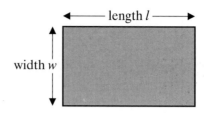

Since a square is a special type of rectangle then:

■ **Area of a square = length × length**
$$= l \times l$$
$$= l^2$$

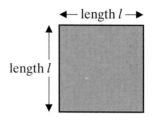

The area of a triangle is half the area of a rectangle that encloses it so:

■ **Area of a triangle = $\frac{1}{2}$ × base × vertical height**
$$= \frac{1}{2} \times b \times h$$

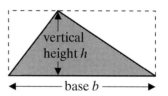

Example 7

Find the areas of these shapes.

(a)   (b)   (c)

(a) Area of rectangle $= l \times w$
$$= 4 \times 3 = 12\,\text{cm}^2$$

(b) Area of square $= l \times l$
$$= 3 \times 3 = 9\,\text{cm}^2$$

(c) Area of triangle $= \frac{1}{2} \times b \times h$
$$= \frac{1}{2} \times 4 \times 3$$
$$= \frac{1}{2} \times 12 = 6\,\text{cm}^2$$

Exercise 19K

Find the areas of these shapes.

1 **(a)** **(b)** **(c)** **(d)**

2 **(a)** **(b)** **(c)** **(d)**

3 **(a)** **(b)** **(c)** **(d)**

Area of a composite shape

You can find the area of a more complicated shape by splitting it up into simple shapes.

Example 8

Find the area of this shape.

Area of rectangle $= l \times w$
$= 8 \times 6$
$= 48 \, cm^2$

Area of triangle $= \frac{1}{2} \times b \times h$
$= \frac{1}{2} \times 5 \times 8$
$= 20 \, cm^2$

Total area $= 48 + 20 = 68 \, cm^2$

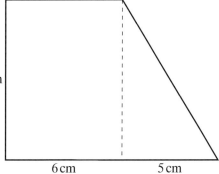

You can split this shape into a rectangle and a triangle.

Exercise 19L

Find the areas of these shapes.

1 **(a)**   **(b)**   **(c)**   **(d)**

2 **(a)**   **(b)**   **(c)**

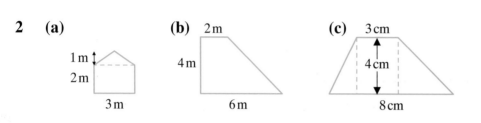

3 Copy this table and complete the columns.

	Shape	Length	Width	Area
(a)	Rectangle	5 cm	6 cm	
(b)	Rectangle	4 cm		20 cm²
(c)	Rectangle	2 cm		30 cm²
(d)	Rectangle		5 cm	40 cm²
(e)	Rectangle		12 cm	60 cm²

4 Copy this table and complete the columns.

	Shape	Base	Vertical height	Area
(a)	Triangle	10 cm	5 cm	
(b)	Triangle		12 cm	60 cm²
(c)	Triangle		5 cm	40 cm²
(d)	Triangle	4 cm		32 cm²
(e)	Triangle	16 cm		64 cm²

Area of a circle

There is a simple formula that you need to know to work out the area of a circle:

■ $A = \pi \times r^2$ **or** $\pi \times r \times r$

Where A is the area and r is the radius of the circle.

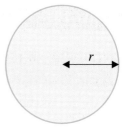

Area $(A) = \pi \times r \times r$

Example 9

Find the area of a circle with a radius of 5 cm.

$A = \pi \times r \times r$
$A = 3.14 \times 5 \times 5 = 78.5\,\text{cm}^2$

Example 10

Find the area of a circle with diameter 4 cm.

If the diameter is 4 cm then the radius is $4 \div 2 = 2$ cm and the area is:

$A = \pi \times r \times r$
$A = 3.14 \times 2 \times 2 = 12.56\,\text{cm}^2$

Remember:
The value of pi (π) is approximately 3.14. You may have a more accurate value on your calculator

Exercise 19M

1   Find the areas of the circles with these radii:
   (**a**) 2 cm   (**b**) 3 cm   (**c**) 4 cm
   (**d**) 10 cm   (**e**) 8 cm   (**f**) 12 cm

2   Work out the areas of the circles with these radii:
   (**a**) 20 cm   (**b**) 5 m   (**c**) 50 cm
   (**d**) 2.5 cm   (**e**) 3.6 cm   (**f**) 8.25 cm

3   Find the areas of the circles with these diameters:
   (**a**) 2 cm   (**b**) 3 cm   (**c**) 5 cm
   (**d**) 10 cm   (**e**) 8 cm   (**f**) 12 cm

4   Work out the areas of circles with these diameters.
   (**a**) 20 cm   (**b**) 5 m   (**c**) 50 cm
   (**d**) 2.5 cm   (**e**) 3.6 cm   (**f**) 8.25 cm

Exercise 19N

Work out the area of each of the following.

1 A circle of radius 9 cm.
2 A circle of diameter 9 cm.
3 A circular table of diameter 90 cm.
4 A circular fish pond of radius 60 cm.
5 A circular paving slab of radius 15 cm.
6 A circular flower bed of diameter 2.5 m.
7 A circular candle of diameter 1.5 cm.
8 A circular flower pot of diameter 6 inches.
9 A pencil of radius 0.3 cm.
10 A pen of radius 0.5 cm.

Finding the radius when you know the area
Sometimes you will be given the area of a circle and asked to calculate its radius or diameter.

Example 11

A circle has an area of 2826 cm^2. Work out its radius.

$$\pi \times r \times r \ \ = A$$
$$3.14 \times r \times r = 2826$$

Dividing both sides by 3.14 gives:

$$r \times r = 2826 \div 3.14$$
$$r \times r = 900$$

To find r when you know $r \times r$ take the square root of each side:

$$\sqrt{r \times r} = \sqrt{900} \text{ cm}$$
$$r = \sqrt{900} = 30 \text{ cm}$$

If you need to find the diameter then you multiply the radius by 2. The diameter is 60 cm.

Exercise 19O

1 A circle has an area of 28.26 cm^2. Find the diameter.
2 A circle has an area of 12.56 cm^2. Find the radius.
3 A circular table has an area of 3.14 m^2. Work out the diameter.
4 A circular fish pond has an area of 10 m^2. Work out the diameter.
5 A circular paving slab has an area of 90 cm^2. What is the radius?

6 A circular flower bed has an area of $7.5\,\text{m}^2$. What is the diameter?

7 A circular candle has an area of $5\,\text{cm}^2$. Work out the radius.

8 A circular flower pot has an area of 6 square inches. What is the diameter?

9 A pencil has an area of $1\,\text{cm}^2$. Work out the diameter.

10 A pen has an area of $2.5\,\text{cm}^2$. Work out the radius.

19.5 Finding volumes of cuboids from formulae

Section 19.3 shows how to find the volumes of cuboids by counting cubes. There is also a formula for finding the volume of such shapes.

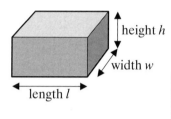

■ **Volume of a cuboid = length × width × height**
$$= l \times w \times h$$

If the shape is a cube then the length, width and height are all the same size so the formula is

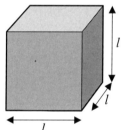

■ **Volume of a cube = length × length × length**
$$= l^3$$

Example 12

Find the volume of a cuboid with length $8\,\text{cm}$, width $6\,\text{cm}$ and height $4\,\text{cm}$.

Volume = length × width × height
$$= 8 \times 6 \times 4 = 192\,\text{cm}^3$$

Exercise 19P

Find the volumes of these cuboids.

1

2 cm
2 cm
6 cm

2

3 cm
3 cm
4 cm

3

3 cm
6 cm
6 cm

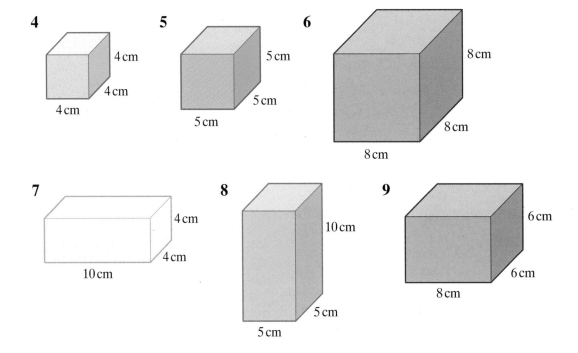

4 4 cm 4 cm 4 cm

5 5 cm 5 cm 5 cm

6 8 cm 8 cm 8 cm

7 4 cm 4 cm 10 cm

8 10 cm 5 cm 5 cm

9 6 cm 6 cm 8 cm

Exercise 19Q

Keith and Mary have bought an old house and are having some work done on it.

SEEN THE CAT ANYWHERE?

1. The lounge is a rectangle 4 m by 3 m and the carpet they buy covers it completely. The carpet costs £7.95 per square metre.
   How much does the carpet cost them?

2. The kitchen is rectangular and measures 3.4 m by 2.7 m. They have to buy a whole number of square metres of tiles to cover the floor. The tiles cost £12.50 per square metre. How much will it cost to tile the floor?

3. The bathroom walls need to be tiled to a height of 1.5 m. The tiles are all 15 cm square. The bathroom measures 3 m by 3 m. The tiles cost 65p each.
   (a) How many tiles are needed for the height?
   (b) How many tiles are needed for the length of one wall?
   (c) How many tiles are needed for all 4 walls? You can ignore the space taken up by the door.
   (d) Work out the cost of all the tiles.

4. The main bedroom measures 4 m by 3 m. Strips of wallpaper are 50 cm wide and they can get four strips out of one roll of wallpaper. Work out how many rolls of wallpaper they need to buy, ignoring doors and windows.

5   The small bedroom measures 3 m by 2 m and the walls are
    2.5 m high. The walls of this room are going to be painted
    with emulsion paint. Each tin of paint will cover $15\,m^2$.
    How many tins will they need?

6   The central heating system runs on oil. The oil tank is a
    cuboid with length 2.5 m, width 1 m and height 1.5 m.
    How many litres of oil will the tank contain? (Remember
    that $1\,l = 1000\,ml$ or $1000\,cm^3$).

7   There are 13 doors in the house. Each door measures 2 m
    by 0.9 m and has to be painted on both sides. All the doors
    are going to be painted white with two coats of paint.
    Each litre of paint covers $8\,m^2$.
    How many litres of paint will be needed?

8   All the tiles on the roof need to be replaced. Each tile
    measures 30 cm by 30 cm. Each of the two sides of the roof
    measures 10 m by 8 m. There needs to be an allowance of
    an extra 50% for overlaps.
    How many tiles are needed for the roof?

9   The lawn needs replacing and they decide to replace the
    worn-out grass with turves that measure 2 m by 0.3 m. The
    new lawn is to measure 20 m by 12 m.
    Work out how many turves they need to buy.

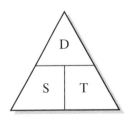

10 Keith decides to dig out the old drive which measures
    12 m by 8 m by 30 cm.
    (a) Work out the volume of rubble that Keith needs to
        dig out.
    (b) How many $4\,m^3$ skips will be needed to carry away the
        rubbish?

19.6 Compound measures: speed

Sometimes you need to work with two units at the same time. For
example, the speed of a car can be measured in miles per hour – a
measurement involving a unit of length and a unit of time.

■ **For an object moving at a constant speed:**

$$\textbf{speed} = \frac{\textbf{distance}}{\textbf{time}} \qquad \textbf{time} = \frac{\textbf{distance}}{\textbf{speed}}$$

distance = speed × time

You can use this
triangle to help you
remember the formulae.

   Typical units are miles per hour, and metres per second.

Usually the speed of a car is not constant for the whole
journey so you use the average speed:

■   **average speed** = $\dfrac{\textbf{total distance travelled}}{\textbf{total time taken}}$

Example 13

What speed does my car average if I travel 90 miles in 3 hours.

$$\text{average speed} = \frac{\text{total distance travelled}}{\text{total time taken}}$$

$$= 90 \div 3 = 30 \text{ miles per hour}$$

Example 14

How long does it take to travel 400 miles at a constant speed of 50 miles per hour?

$$\text{time} = \frac{\text{distance}}{\text{speed}}$$

$$= 400 \div 50$$

$$= 8 \text{ hours}$$

Example 15

How far can you go if you travel for 3 hours at 10 miles per hour?

$$\text{distance} = \text{speed} \times \text{time}$$

$$= 10 \times 3$$

$$= 30 \text{ miles}$$

Exercise 19R

1 Elizabeth walked for 3 hours at 4 miles per hour.
   How far did she walk?

2 Andrew drove 100 miles in 4 hours.
   At what average speed did he travel?

3 Karen drove 300 miles at an average speed of 60 miles per hour.
   How long did her journey take her?

4 David was travelling by canal boat and went 30 miles in 8 hours.
   At what average speed was he travelling?

5 Amanda rode her bike for 3 hours and travelled 21 miles.
   At what average speed was she travelling?

6 Gerry ran for 2 hours and covered 16 miles.
   At what average speed was he running?

7 Brigit swam for 3 hours and travelled 4 miles.
   At what average speed was she swimming?

8 Alfred set off from home at 8 am. He travelled 200 miles by car
   and arrived at 11 am.
   At what average speed was he travelling?

9 Jason set off for work at 07:55. He arrived at work at 08:10. If he lives 5 miles from work, at what average speed did he travel?

10 Frances was using a keep fit treadmill. She ran for 40 minutes and travelled 20 kilometres. At what average speed was she running?

Exercise 19S Mixed questions

1 Work out the perimeter of this shape.

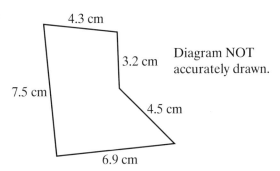

Diagram NOT accurately drawn.

[L]

2 The diagram represents an L-shaped room whose corners are all right angles.

(a) (i) Work out the value of x.

  (ii) Work out the value of y.

(b) Work out the perimeter of the shape.

(c) Work out the area of the shape.

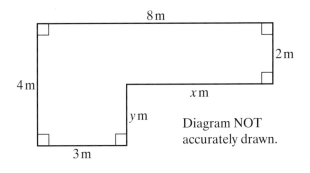

Diagram NOT accurately drawn.

[L]

3 The diagram represents the babies' pool, with paving around, at a leisure centre. The pool is rectangular, 8 m long by 5 m wide and has a depth of 0.6 m throughout.

(a) Work out the volume of the pool in m³.

The paving around the pool is 2 m wide.

(b) Work out the area of the paving.

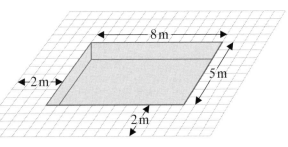

[L]

4   The diagram represents a tea packet in the shape of a
cuboid.

(a) Calculate the volume of the packet.

There are 125 grams of tea in a full packet.
Jason has to design a new packet that will contain 100
grams of tea when it is full.

(b)   (i) Work out the volume of the new packet.

   (ii) Express the weight of the tea in the new packet as
   a percentage of the weight of the tea in the
   packet shown.

[L]

5   The diagram represents a circular training track.
The diameter of the track, *AB*, is 70 metres.

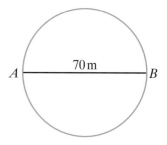

Alisa and Bryony have a race.
Alisa runs along the diameter from *A* to *B* and back again.
Bryony starts at *A* and runs all the way round the track to
A again.

Work out how much further Bryony runs than Alisa.

[L]

6

A new wire mesh fence is to be put around a circular
training ring.

The radius of the ring is 45 m.
(a) Calculate, to the nearest metre, the length of fence
   needed.
(b) Calculate, to the nearest 10 square metres, the area of
   the ring.

[L]

7

    (a) Work out the perimeter of the shape.
    (b) Work out the area of the shape.

8

    Measure and write down the perimeter of this shape.

Summary of key points

1   The perimeter of a shape is the distance around the edge of the shape.

2   The perimeter of a circle is called the circumference.

    $C = \pi \times d$ where C is the circumference, d is the diameter
    or
    $C = 2 \times \pi \times r$ and r is the radius.

3   The area of a shape is a measure of the amount of space it covers. Typical units of area are square centimetres (cm^2), square metres (m^2) and square kilometres (km^2).

4   Area formulae for 2-D shapes:

area of a rectangle $= \text{length} \times \text{width}$
$= l \times w$

area of a square $= \text{length} \times \text{length}$
$= l \times l = l^2$

area of a triangle $= \frac{1}{2} \times \text{base} \times \text{vertical height}$
$= \frac{1}{2} \times b \times h$

Area $(A) = \pi \times r \times r$

area of a circle A $= \pi \times r \times r$
$= \pi r^2$

5   The volume of a 3-D shape is a measure of the amount of space it occupies. Typical units of volume are cubic centimetres (cm^3) and cubic metres (m^3).

6   Volume formula for cuboids (3-D):

volume of a cuboid $= \text{length} \times \text{width} \times \text{height}$
$= l \times w \times h$

volume of a cube $= l \times l \times l = l^3$

7   For an object moving at a constant speed:

$$\text{speed} = \frac{\text{distance}}{\text{time}} \qquad \text{time} = \frac{\text{distance}}{\text{speed}}$$

$$\text{distance} = \text{speed} \times \text{time}$$

Typical units are miles per hour, and metres per second.

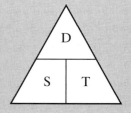

8   When an object's speed varies as it travels:

$$\text{average speed} = \frac{\text{total distance travelled}}{\text{time taken}}$$

20 Averages

The word average is often used. Think about these statements:

> Jenny is of average height
> A centre forward averages a goal a game
> Teenagers in Britain spend an average of £3 a week on hair care products

Here the word average means that something is typical, or describes something that typically happens.

In mathematics an **average** is usually a single value which is used to represent a set of data. It is in some way typical of the data and gives an idea of what the data is like.

Three different averages are commonly used:

- **the mode**   - **the median**   - **the mean**.

This unit shows you how each one is found and why it is useful.

On average a family size box contains 500 g of cereal. The weight of cereal in the box is only allowed to vary within a very small range.

20.1 The mode

■ **The mode of a set of data is the value which occurs most often.**

Example 1

The number of goals scored by a team in ten matches was:

> 1, 5, 2, 0, 4, 2, 1, 2, 2, 3

Find the mode of this data.
The score that occurred most often was 2 goals, so the mode is 2.

It is possible to have more than one mode.

Example 2

Find the mode of another team's scores:

> 3, 1, 0, 1, 4, 3, 6, 2, 1, 3

There are two modes: 1 and 3

Example 3

Find the mode of a third team's scores:

> 2, 5, 3, 4, 0, 1, 6

There is no mode since all scores occurred once only.

Exercise 20A

1 Write down the mode(s) in the following test results.
    (a) English   32, 28, 41, 17, 28, 39, 19, 28, 40
    (b) Maths   41, 29, 34, 28, 38, 41, 34, 37, 44
    (c) History   16, 27, 35, 26, 32, 27, 33, 35, 29
    (d) Science   26, 28, 36, 27, 31 24, 38, 28, 31
    (e) Art   32, 28, 30, 35, 28, 39, 32, 36, 30
    (f) What was the overall mode mark for all the data in parts **(a)** to **(e)** put together?

2 Here are some sets of test marks. Extend each set with a mark or marks so that the new set has the mode shown on the right.
    (a) 8, 5 ,9, 6, 3, 7, 4   : mode 6
    (b) 3, 7, 5, 8, 4, 3, 6, 9   : mode 5
    (c) 2, 6, 7, 8, 5, 3, 2   : mode 4
    (d) 11, 7, 15, 12, 15, 8, 9 : mode 11 and 15
    (e) 6, 3, 8, 9, 4, 6, 5   : mode 7
    (f) 8, 3, 6, 2, 7, 9, 7, 4   : mode 5 and 6

3 The bar charts below show a student's marks in different Maths and English tests given on each day of the same week.

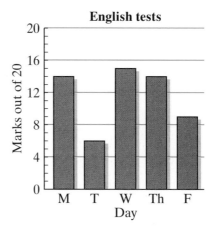

    (a) Write down a list of each of the marks.
    (b) Write down the mode for each list.

4 The table shows the number of times students were late handing in homework over a three week period.

Number of times late	0	1	2	3	4	5
Number of students	7	12	4	2	3	2

(a) Write down the mode of the 'number of times late'. (Hint: the mode will be the 'number of times late' which occurs most often.)

(b) Use your result to write a sentence about the information the mode gives.

20.2 The median

■ **The median is the middle value when the data is arranged in order of size.**

Example 4

Find the median of Brian's homework marks for:

(a) English 5, 7, 9, 4, 1, 3, 7, 4, 6
(b) History 6, 8, 3, 7, 5, 3, 7, 2

(a) Arrange the English marks in order of size:

$$1, 3, 4, 4, 5, 6, 7, 7, 9$$

The middle mark is 5. Brian has four marks higher and four marks lower.

The median is 5.

(b) Arrange the History marks in order of size:

$$2, 3, 3, 5, 6, 7, 7, 8$$

The middle mark lies between the 5 and 6

so the median is $\dfrac{5+6}{2} = 5\frac{1}{2}$

Notice that the median History mark is not a mark anyone has actually scored.

Because there is an even number of marks there is no 'middle mark' in the data.

Instead the value of a middle mark has been calculated.

Example 5

The table shows the shoe sizes of a group of students. Find the median shoe size.

Shoe size	7	$7\frac{1}{2}$	8	$8\frac{1}{2}$	9	$9\frac{1}{2}$
Number of students	2	2	5	4	3	3

To find the median you could list all the shoe sizes:

$$7, 7, 7\tfrac{1}{2}, 7\tfrac{1}{2}, 8, 8, 8, 8, 8, 8\tfrac{1}{2}, 8\tfrac{1}{2}, 8\tfrac{1}{2}, 8\tfrac{1}{2}, 9, 9, 9, 9\tfrac{1}{2}, 9\tfrac{1}{2}, 9\tfrac{1}{2}$$

and see the middle value or median is $8\tfrac{1}{2}$.

An easier way of finding the middle value is to add up the number of students. There are 19 students so the middle student is the 10th.

Starting at the left of the data table, the 10th student is in the $8\tfrac{1}{2}$ column, so the median shoe size is $8\tfrac{1}{2}$.

Exercise 20B

1 Rearrange the following marks in order and write down the median marks.
  (a) 5, 8, 3, 2, 7, 9, 6   **(b)** 15, 18, 9, 11, 17, 8, 12, 10, 9
  (c) 9, 4, 7, 3, 1, 6, 3, 8   **(d)** 8, 12, 18, 9, 14, 7, 10, 6
  (e) 9, 3, 7, 7, 2, 5, 8, 5   **(f)** 6, 14, 19, 8, 5, 16, 10, 15

2 Give examples of:
  (a) seven different marks with a median of 12
  (b) nine different marks with a median of 8
  (c) eight different marks with a median of 10
  (d) six different marks with a median of 4.5

3 What mark should Leo get in his next test to obtain the median stated?
  (a) 1, 8, 5, 2   : median 5
  (b) 8, 2, 4, 5, 3, 8, 4, 2, 9   : median 4
  (c) 7, 5, 3, 6, 8, 2, 7   : median $6\tfrac{1}{2}$
  (d) 7, 4, 3, 6, 2, 6, 8, 4   : median 5

4 The number of students getting marks in a quiz were:

Marks	0	1	2	3	4	5	6	7	8	9	10
Number of students	0	0	2	3	1	1	2	5	4	6	4

  (a) Write down the median mark
  (b) Write two statements making use of your result.

5 The chart below shows the number of parking tickets issued by a traffic officer on seven days of a week.

(a) Work out the median number of tickets issued per day.
(b) Write down the mode.

20.3 The mean

■ **The mean of a set of data is the sum of the values divided by the number of values.**

$$\text{mean} = \frac{\textbf{sum of the values}}{\textbf{number of values}}$$

Example 6

Find the mean of 3, 8, 4, 7, 7, 6, 4, 1

The sum of the values is:

$$3 + 8 + 4 + 7 + 7 + 6 + 4 + 1 = 40$$

There are 8 values, so divide 40 by 8:

$$40 \div 8 = 5$$

The mean is 5.

Example 7

The mean of three numbers is 5, the mean of four other numbers is 8. What is the mean of all seven numbers?

The sum of the three numbers is 15 $\quad(\frac{15}{3} = 5)$
The sum of the four numbers is 32 $\quad(\frac{32}{4} = 8)$

Mean of all seven numbers $= \dfrac{\text{Total sum}}{7} = \dfrac{15 + 32}{7} = \dfrac{47}{7} = 6.7$

Example 8

The mean of four numbers is 6. Three of the numbers are 4, 8 and 3. Find the value of the other number.

The sum of the four numbers is   24 $(\frac{24}{4} = 6)$

If ? is the missing number, $4 + 8 + 3 + ? = 24$
$$15 + ? = 24$$
$$? = 9$$

The other number is 9.

Exercise 20C

1   Calculate the mean for each set of data:
   (a) 12, 18, 9, 14, 8, 17   (b) 23, 15, 37, 26, 16, 21, 33, 23
   (c) 15, 25, 22, 34, 19, 20   (d) 25, 12, 31, 26, 31, 19, 30, 16
   (e) 16, 30, 15, 23, 12, 21   (f) 31, 18, 25, 33, 35, 19, 17, 24

2   Calculate the mean of:
   (a) £24, £34, £26, £18, £23
   (b) £42, £27, £36, £32, £28, £51

3   The heights of a group of students, in centimetres, are:

   158, 162, 172, 157, 161

   (a) Calculate the mean height.
   (b) Another student joins the group. His height is 159 cm.
   Calculate the new mean height.

4   Four parcels weigh in grams:

   515, 620, 542, 563

   (a) Calculate the mean weight.
   (b) A fifth parcel is added. If the new mean is 710 g,
   calculate the weight of the parcel.

5   What mark must Muriel get in her next test to obtain the
   mean given on the right:
   (a) 8, 3, 6, 7, 8, 4   : mean 7
   (b) 17, 14, 8, 11, 15, 17   : mean 14
   (c) 6, 3, 9, 7, 2, 6, 5   : mean 5.5
   (d) 23, 31, 20, 27, 32, 24 : mean 26

20.4 The range

The mean of a set of data is an average value. It does not tell you how spread out the data is.

One way of measuring the spread of a set of data is to find its **range**:

■ **The range of a set of data is the difference between the highest value and lowest value:**

Range = highest value − lowest value

Two sets of data may have the same mean but different ranges. Compare these two batsmen's scores after four innings:

Peter 0, 96, 100, 0   Mean is 49   Range is 100 − 0 = 100
Hanif 49, 51, 46, 50   Mean is 49   Range is 51 − 46 = 5

Both have the same mean or average score but Hanif has a much lower range. His scores are less spread out which shows he is a more consistent player.

Exercise 20D

1 Paul's subject marks over a period of eight weeks were:
   History: 34, 56, 45, 46, 53, 62, 39, 48
   Maths: 73, 65, 68, 56, 65, 73, 77, 58
   English: 45, 51, 57, 44, 50, 48, 43, 49
   Art: 47, 51, 36, 78, 43, 20, 39, 27
   Science: 35, 38, 42, 55, 28, 43, 61, 54

   (a) Write down the range in each subject.
   (b) In which subject do you think Paul was:
       (i) best   (ii) most consistent   (iii) least consistent
       Give reasons for your answers.

2 Copy and complete the table below, the first one is done for you.

Make	Standard	De Luxe	Price range
Ford 1.1	£7145	£7545	£400
Peugeot 1.5	£7460	£9190	
Rover 200	£9995	£13 895	
Citroen 1.9	£10 220		£3985
Volvo 1.6		£15 480	£3910
Audi 1.9	£17 693		£1821
Porche 3.6	£58 995	£93 950	
Lada 1.3		£6495	£1500
Toyota 1.3	£8040		£4727

3   The table shows the maximum and minimum
temperatures one day last year in degrees Fahrenheit.

City	Maximum	Minimum
London	64	42
Paris	69	47
Moscow	38	9
New York	72	59
Luxor	101	88

(a) Calculate the range in each city.
(b) List the cities in order, highest range first.
(c) Give a reason why someone might want to know
this range.

20.5 Using appropriate averages

The different types of averages are useful in different
situations:

The **mode** is useful when you need to know:

"Which shoe size is most common?"
"Which brand of cat food is most popular?"

The **mean** is useful for finding a 'typical' value when most of
the data is closely grouped, for example:

the height of a typical student in your class

The mean may not give a very typical value if the data is very
spread out, or if it includes a large value very different from
the rest. For example:

The Chairman of a company earns £200 000 a year and her
9 employees each earn £15 000.
Their mean pay is £33 500.

In situations like this the **median** or middle value may be more
typical. Median earnings in this company are £15 000.

The mean height of the
students in your class will
be 'typical' unless some
people are very much taller
or shorter than the rest.

Example 9

Find the mode, median and mean of these marks in a test:

1, 3, 17, 18, 19, 20, 21, 21, 24

The mode is 21.

The mean is $\frac{144}{9} = 16.$ Only two students scored less.

The median is 19. Four students were above and four below this mark.

You can see that the two very low marks lowered the result for the mean. If the students scoring 1 and 3 had scored 15 and 16 the mean would have been 19, but the mode and median would have remained the same.

Example 10

In a maths coursework assessment the scores out of 40 were:

38, 35, 35, 35, 30, 29, 28, 28, 11, 5

Find the mode, median and mean marks and the range. Comment on your results.

The mode mark is 35, the median mark is 29.5, the mean mark is 27.4 and the range is 33.

Here the median gives the best idea of a 'typical' score: half the students scored more and half less.

The mean has been distorted by the two very low scores and only 2 students have scored less.

The mode is not representative as only 1 student has scored a higher mark.

The range just tells you that there is a wide spread of marks.

Advantages and disadvantages of the three averages

	Advantages	Disadvantages
Mode	Easy to see or pick out Not influenced by extreme values	Can be more than one mode Cannot be used for further calculations
Median	Not influenced by extreme values	Actual value may not exist (Example 4, page 253)
Mean	Can easily be calculated Uses all the data Can be used for further calculation	Cannot be found graphically Extreme values can distort the result

Exercise 20E

1 Find the mode, median and mean in each of the following and make a comment about each.
   (a) The numbers of cars left in the station car-park overnight during one week were:
       12, 6, 14, 9, 13, 6, 10
   (b) The numbers of passengers boarding the train between 9am and 12am were:
       24, 17, 32, 24, 35, 32, 28
   (c) The costs of the first five tickets sold were:
       £1.15, £12.40, £3.60, £3.60, £2.95

2 The weekly wages for the station staff were:
       1 Station master   £385
       2 Ticket office clerks   £200 each
       2 Porters   £170 each
       3 Cleaners   £140 each
       2 Trainees   £85 each
   (a) Calculate the total weekly wages bill.
   (b) What is
       (i) the mode payment   (ii) the median payment
       (iii) the mean payment   (iv) the range?
   (c) Comment on your answers to part (b).

3 Find six numbers which have a mean of 5; a mode of 2 and a median of $4\frac{1}{2}$.

20.6 Averages from frequency tables

Sometimes it is convenient to collect data in a frequency table.
(There is more about this on page 000.) This frequency table
shows how many children there are in each family in a small
village:

Number of children	Tally	Frequency
0	|||	3
1	⊬⊬⊬ |||	8
2	⊬⊬⊬ |	6
3	||||	4
4	|||	3
5	|	1

You can find the mean, median and mode from a frequency table.

To find the mean, first find the total number of children:

$(0 \times 3) + (1 \times 8) + (2 \times 6) + (3 \times 4) + (4 \times 3) + (5 \times 1)$
$\quad 0 \quad + \quad 8 \quad + \quad 12 \quad + \quad 12 \quad + \quad 12 \quad + \quad 5 \quad = 49$

only one family
has 5 children

The number of families is:

$3 + 8 + 6 + 4 + 3 + 1 = 25$

The mean number of children per family is $\frac{49}{25} = 1.96$

The mode, the most frequent number of children in a family, is 1.
(Eight families had one child.)

To find the median number of children per family, find the
'middle family'. This is the 13th family when all the data is put
in order:

$$\downarrow$$
$$0\,0\,0\,1\,1\,1\,1\,1\,1\,1\,1\,2\,2\,2\,2\,2\,2\,3\,3\,3\,3\,4\,4\,4\,5$$

So the median is 2

A quicker way to find the median is to look for the 13th family
in the frequency table:

Number of children	Tally	Frequency
0	|||	3
1	⊬⊬⊬ |||	8
2	⊬⊬⊬ |	6

the first 11 families

families 12, 13, 14, 15, 16 and 17

The 13th family is one of the six that have 2 children.

Example 11

The table shows the number of grade A–C passes obtained by Class 11B.

Grades A–C	1	2	3	4	5	6	7	8
Number of students	2	4	4	7	6	4	2	1

Find (a) the mode (b) the median (c) the mean

(a) 7 students obtained 4 A–C grades so the mode is 4 passes at grades A–C.

(b) To find the median you could write out all the data in order:

Number of A–C grades

1 1 2 2 2 2 3 3 3 3 4 4 4 4 4 4 4 5 5 5 5 5 5 6 6 6 6 7 7 8
 ↑

There are 30 students so the middle of the data is between the 15th and 16th students. Both these got 4 passes so the median is 4.

(c) To find the mean you need: $\dfrac{\text{total number of passes}}{\text{number of students}}$

Total number of grades A–C is:

$$\begin{aligned}
&\ (2 \times 1) + (4 \times 2) + (4 \times 3) + (7 \times 4) + (6 \times 5) + (4 \times 6) + (2 \times 7) + (1 \times 8)\\
=&\ \ \ \ 2\ \ \ +\ \ \ 8\ \ \ +\ \ 12\ \ +\ \ 28\ \ +\ \ 30\ \ +\ \ 24\ \ +\ \ 14\ \ +\ \ \ 8\ \ = 126
\end{aligned}$$

The number of students is 30 so the mean is $\dfrac{126}{30} = 4.2$

How to find the position of the median

An easy way to find the position of the median value in a set of data is to add 1 to the number of values, then divide the result by 2.

In the families example on page 260 there are 25 families:

$\dfrac{25 + 1}{2} = 13$ so the median family is the 13th

In Example 11 there are 30 students:

$\dfrac{30 + 1}{2} = 15.5$ so the median of the data is between the 15th and 16th students

This method works whether there is an odd or even number of items of data.

Exercise 20F

1 Find the mean of:
   (a) 5, 11, 23, 16 and 20
   (b) 114, 107, 134, 96 and 49
   (c) 3.2, 1.6, 4.5, 6.3 and 2.7

2 The mean of six numbers is 12. Five of the numbers are 11, 7, 21, 14 and 9. Calculate the sixth.

3 In training Fritz ran the 100 m in 10.8, 11.1, 10.7, 10.9 and 10.8 seconds.
   (a) What was his average (mean) speed?
   (b) How fast must he run in the next race to bring his average down to 10.8 seconds?

4 Find: (i) the mode   (ii) the median of the following data:
   (a) 4, 2, 8, 8, 1, 4, 5, 8, 9
   (b) 6, 11, 5, 8, 4, 7, 3
   (c) 106, 111, 105, 108, 104, 107, 105
   (d) 3.1, 4.2, 2.6, 5.3, 3.1, 2.2, 4.6
   (e) 4, 8, 5, 2, 8, 4, 7

5 Find the mean of:
   (a) £4, £3.50, £1.36, £5.14 and £2.45
   (b) 1 hr 5 min, 3 hr 42 min, 2 hr 17 min, 5 hr 28 min
   (c) 2.1 m, 6.3 m, 5.4 m, 4.2 m, 3.6 m

6 The mean of five numbers is 7.
   If four numbers are 3, 12, 7 and 8, what is the fifth?

7 Use the information given to find the value of n in each of the following (where n is a missing number in the list):
   (a) 5, 7, 4, 1, n, 5   : the mean is 6
   (b) 3, 1, 4, 5, 4, n : the mode is 4
   (c) 1, 7, 2, 1, n, 4, 3   : the mode is 1 and 2
   (d) 2, n, 5, 7, 1, 3   : the median is $3\frac{1}{2}$
   (e) 2.6, 3.5, n, 6.2   : the mean is 4
   (f) 4, 7, 2, n, 2, 9, 6   : the median is 5

8 A stallholder bought 5 boxes of fruit at £12.40 a box and 3 boxes at £16.20.
   What was the average cost of the boxes?

9 Attendance of Class 11B for the first 10 weeks was:
   20, 23, 25, 21, 20, 24, 20, 23, 24, 20.
   Find: (a) the mean (b) the mode (c) the median

10 Rashid brought packs of cans of coke from a cash and carry to sell to friends. His sales over the first ten days were:
   4, 11, 25, 31, 31, 25, 23, 32, 31, 32
   (a) Find: (i) the mean (ii) the mode (iii) the median
   (b) Comment on your results.

11 The bar chart shows the number of cans of coke bought by Class 10C during a two-week period.

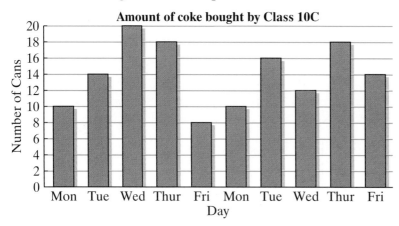

Find:
(a) the mode
(b) the median
(c) the mean number of cans bought.

12 Jez chews bubble gum until the taste has gone. He cannot decide between two different brands. He measures his chewing times on six occasions for each brand.
This table shows his chewing times in minutes.

Brand A	11	10	13	9	17	12
Brand B	11	13	12	12	14	10

The mean and range of the chewing time for Brand A are given in the next table. Calculate the mean and range of the chewing time for Brand B.

	Mean	Range
Brand A	12	8
Brand B		

Which brand should Jez decide to use, assuming they cost the same?
Give a clear explanation.

[L]

13 The numbers of students attending sports and other clubs
after school in a two-week period are given in this table.

Class	Mon	Tues	Wed	Thur	Fri	Mon	Tues	Wed	Thur	Fri
11A	22	18	20	21	12	20	18	20	21	11
11B	20	15	17	18	10	21	15	17	18	8
11C	16	19	17	16	8	17	16	16	15	7
10A	26	22	20	11	24	24	20	18	9	22
10B	19	18	21	14	17	18	20	19	11	16
10C	17	13	15	8	13	17	14	17	6	12
9A	22	20	17	16	19	21	21	13	16	20
9B	18	12	16	18	17	18	12	15	18	17
9C	23	14	18	20	18	22	14	17	20	16
9D	16	11	15	12	10	16	11	14	8	10

Find: **(i)** the mode   **(ii)** the median   **(iii)** the mean
(a) for each class
(b) for each Monday
(c) for both Thursdays together.

14 Using the table in question **13**
(a) find the range for each class
(b) find the overall range for the classes put together.

15 This table shows the number of students gaining certificates
for outstanding sporting achievement during the year.

Number of certificates	Tally	Frequency
1		4
2		9
3		8
4		10
5		6
6		3

(a) Calculate: **(i)** the mean
                   (ii) the mode
                   (iii) the median
(b) Which one of these results could be used to encourage
students to take part?
Explain your reasons for your choice.

Summary of key points

1   The mode of a set of data is the value which occurs most often.

2   The median is the middle value when the data has been arranged in order of size.

3   The mean of a set of data is the sum of the values divided by the number of values:

$$\text{mean} = \frac{\text{sum of the values}}{\text{number of values}}$$

4   The range of a set of data is the difference between the highest value and lowest value:

$$\text{range} = \text{highest value} - \text{lowest value}$$

21 Algebra 4

This unit shows you how to use word formulae and equations to help solve problems.

21.1 Using word formulae

Example 1

David works in a factory. He is paid per hour and is given an extra bonus at the end of the week. His pay can be calculated using this **word formula**:

Pay = Rate of pay × hours worked + bonus

Work out his pay when he works for 40 hours at a rate of pay of £4 and earns a bonus of £5.

Pay = £4 × 40 + £5
= £160 + £5 = £165

He earns £165

Exercise 21A

1   To work out his pay Keith uses the word formula:

Pay = Rate of pay × hours worked + bonus

Work out his pay when he works for 30 hours at a rate of pay of £4 and earns a bonus of £10.

2   To work out her pay Freda uses the word formula:

Pay = Rate of pay × hours worked + bonus

Work out her pay when she works for 35 hours at a rate of pay of £3.50 and earns a bonus of £15.

3   To work out the distance around his bicycle wheel Devon uses the formula:

Distance = 3 × diameter

Work out the distance around the wheel if the diameter is 60 cm.

4   To work out the distance around her bicycle wheel Helen uses the formula:

   Distance = 3 × diameter

   Work out the distance around the wheel if the diameter is 50 cm.

5   Use the formula:

   Cost of pens = Cost of one pen × number of pens.

   to work out the cost of 17 pens if one pen cost 25p.

Writing word formulae

Sometimes you will need to write a word formula from information you are given.

Example 2

Jill worked for 40 hours at a rate of pay of £5 an hour. How much should she get paid?

You can write a word formula to find her pay for any number of hours she works:

   Pay = Hours worked × rate of pay
       = 40 × £5
       = £200

Example 3

Rashmi buys 24 pens at 45 pence each. Work out the total cost of the pens.

Here is a suitable word formula:

   Cost = Number of pens × cost of one pen
        = 24 × 45p
        = 1080p = £10.80

■   **A word formula represents a relationship between quantities using words.**

Exercise 21B

Write down a word formula to help solve each of these problems. Use your formula to work out the answers.

1   Daniel works for 40 hours at a rate of pay of £4 an hour. How much should he get paid?

2 Helen works for 20 hours at a rate of pay of £3.25 an hour. How much should she get paid?

3 Abdul works for 30 hours at a rate of pay of £5.75 an hour. How much should he get paid?

4 Susan buys 12 pens at £1.20 each. Work out the total cost of the pens.

5 Roger buys 24 pens at 50p each. Work out the total cost of the pens.

6 Rachel buys 12 books at 28p each. Work out the total cost of the books.

7 Keith buys 15 stamps at 25p each. Work out the total cost of the stamps.

8 Andy buys 20 stamps at 19p each. Work out the total cost of the stamps.

9 Karen sold 50 cakes at 40p each. How much money does she collect?

10 Louise sold 45 loaves of bread at 92p each. How much money does she collect?

11 Mark adds together his age and the age of his sister Pauline. He gets a total of 28. If Mark is 16 how old is Pauline?

12 James loses some £1 coins from his money bag. He had £12 to start with and now only has £7. How many coins has he lost?

13 A chocolate bar machine holds 48 bars of chocolate. After 23 are sold how many are left?

14 At Anne's birthday party there were 48 cans of drink. Everybody at the party had 4 cans. How many people were at the party?

15 Naomi shared a bag of sweets equally between herself and her 6 friends. There were 56 sweets in the bag. How many sweets did the 7 people have each?

16 Norman and his 9 friends were playing football and smashed a window. The cost of repairing the window was £126. The 10 friends decide to split the cost equally between them. How much do they each have to pay?

21.2 Using algebraic formulae

Section 21.1 shows how to use word formulae. You also need to know how to use **algebraic formulae** in which quantities are represented by letters.

The next two exercises provide practice in finding the value of an algebraic expression.

Example 4

Let $a = 3; b = 2; c = 5$

Work out the value of:

(i) $a + b$ $a + b = 3 + 2 = 5$
(ii) ab $ab = a \times b = 3 \times 2 = 6$
(iii) $3c - 2a$ $3c - 2a = 3 \times c - 2 \times a$
$$= 3 \times 5 - 2 \times 3$$
$$= 15 - 6 = 9$$

Exercise 21C

In this exercise $a = 3, b = 2, c = 5$ and $d = 0$
Work out the value of:

1 $a + c$	2 $b + c$	3 $a + b + c$
4 $2a$	5 $3c$	6 $5d$
7 ac	8 ad	9 $5b + 2a$
10 $4c - 2b$	11 $5a + 2b$	12 $2a + 3b + 4c$
13 $c - a$	14 $c - 2d$	15 $ab - c$
16 $4b + 2d$	17 $3c - 2b$	18 $5a - 3c$
19 $ac - ab$	20 abc	

Exercise 21D

In this exercise $p = 2, q = 4, r = 3$ and $s = 0$
Work out the value of:

1 $3p$	2 $4q$	3 $5r$	4 $10s$
5 $p + q$	6 $q + r$	7 $r + s$	8 $p + q + r$
9 $2p + 4q$	10 $3s + 3p$	11 $5r - 2q$	12 $4r - 3q$
13 pq	14 qr	15 rs	16 pqr
17 $5q - 8p$	18 $3p - 2r$	19 $4p - 2s$	20 $3q - pr$

Example 5

The distance around the outside of a
rectangle is called the perimeter.

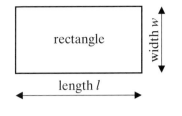

A word formula for the perimeter is:

Perimeter = 2 × length + 2 × width

If the length is represented by the letter l and the width by w
an algebraic formula for the perimeter is:

$P = 2l + 2w$

Suppose $l = 6$ and $w = 4$

$P = 2 \times 6 + 2 \times 4 = 12 + 8 = 20$

■ **An algebraic formula represents a relationship between
quantities using letters.**

Exercise 21E

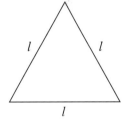

1   The formula for the perimeter of an equilateral triangle is
    $P = 3l$. Work out the value of P when:
    (a) $l = 5$ **(b)** $l = 7$ **(c)** $l = 4$ **(d)** $l = 12.4$

2   The formula for the area of a rectangle is $A = lw$. Find the
    value of A when:
    (a) $l = 6$ and $w = 4$ **(b)** $l = 5$ and $w = 3$
    (c) $l = 10$ and $w = 5.6$ **(d)** $l = 7.5$ and $w = 3.4$

3   James uses the formula $d = st$ to work out the distance
    travelled, where the time taken is t and the speed is s. Find
    the value of d when:
    (a) $s = 40$ and $t = 4$ **(b)** $s = 50$ and $t = 2.5$
    (c) $s = 70$ and $t = 3$ **(d)** $s = 15.8$ and $t = 5$

4   Ayesha uses the formula $v = u + at$ to work out velocity.
    Find the value of v when:
    (a) $u = 3, a = 2$ and $t = 5$
    (b) $u = 5, a = 10$ and $t = 3$
    (c) $u = 0, a = 10$ and $t = 6$
    (d) $u = 2.5, a = 3$ and $t = 1.5$

Remember BODMAS.
You must do at first and
then u.

5 Alex uses the formula $P = rh + b$ to work out his pay, where r is his rate of pay per hour, h is the number of hours worked, and b is his bonus. Work out the value of P when:
   (a) $r = 4, h = 12$ and $b = 5$
   (b) $r = 5, h = 40$ and $b = 10$
   (c) $r = 1.5, h = 4$ and $b = 1$
   (d) $r = 2.5, h = 6$ and $b = 2.5$

21.3 Using negative numbers

Sometimes you will need to use negative numbers in algebraic formulae.

The next four exercises provide practice in using negative numbers.

Exercise 21F

Work out:

1 $2 - 5$	**2** $-2 + 4$	**3** $-2 - 4$	**4** $3 + (-7)$
5 $-3 + 5$	**6** $-5 - 3$	**7** $2 - (-3)$	**8** $6 - (-5)$
9 $10 + (-10)$	**10** $-1 - 8$	**11** $1 - (-7)$	**12** $-4 - (-2)$

Example 6

$a = 4 \quad b = 6 \quad c = -3$

Find: (i) $a - b$ $a - b = 4 - 6 = -2$
       (ii) $c + b$ $c + b = -3 + 6 = 3$
       (iii) $a + c$ $a + c = 4 + (-3) = 4 - 3 = 1$
       (iv) $a - c$ $a - c = 4 - (-3) = 4 + 3 = 7$

Exercise 21G

In this exercise let $a = 3, b = -2, c = -5$ and $d = 0$
Work out the value of:

1 $a + b$	**2** $a + c$	**3** $b + c$	**4** $c + d$
5 $a - b$	**6** $c - a$	**7** $b - c$	**8** $c - d$
9 $b - a$	**10** $a - c$	**11** $c - b$	**12** $d - c$
13 $a + b + c$	**14** $a + b - c$	**15** $a + b - d$	**16** $d - a$
17 $a - b + c$	**18** $a - b - c$	**19** $d - a + b$	**20** $d - b + a - c$

Remember: when you
multiply two numbers
+ × + = +
+ × – = –
– × + = –
– × – = +

Exercise 21H

Work out:

1	4×-3	**2**	-2×6	**3**	10×-1	**4**	-2×-2
5	3×-7	**6**	-8×4	**7**	-6×-5	**8**	-3×-9

Example 7

$a = -5 \quad b = 3 \quad c = -3$

Find: (i) $2a$ $2a = 2 \times a = 2 \times -5 = -10$
       (ii) ab $ab = a \times b = -5 \times 3 = -15$
       (iii) ac $ac = a \times c = -5 \times -3 = 15$

Exercise 21I

In this exercise let $a = -3$, $b = 2$, $c = -5$ and $d = 0$
Work out the value of:

1	$a + c$	**2**	$b + c$	**3**	$a + b + c$	**4**	$2a$
5	$3c$	**6**	$5d$	**7**	ac	**8**	ad
9	$5b + 2a$	**10**	$4c - 2b$	**11**	$5a + 2b$	**12**	$2a + 3b + 4c$
13	$c - a$	**14**	$c - 2d$	**15**	$ab - c$	**16**	$4b + 2d$
17	$3c - 2b$	**18**	$5a - 3c$	**19**	$ac - ab$	**20**	abc

Negative numbers in algebraic formulae

Example 8

The formula $v = u + at$ is used in Maths and Science to work out velocities.

Work out the value of v when $u = 5$, $a = -2$ and $t = 10$.

$v = u + at$
$v = 5 + -2 \times 10$
$v = 5 + -20$
$v = -15$

Exercise 21J

1 Using the formula $v = u + at$ to work out velocity, find the value of v when:
   (a) $u = 3, a = -2, t = 5$ **(b)** $u = -5, a = 10, t = 3$
   (c) $u = 0, a = -10, t = 6$ **(d)** $u = -2.5, a = -3, t = 1.5$

2 Using the formula $P = a(b - c)$, find the value of P when:
   (a) $a = 2, b = 3, c = 3$ **(b)** $a = 2, b = 3, c = -3$
   (c) $a = 3, b = -2, c = 3$ **(d)** $a = 3, b = -2, c = -3$

3 Using the formula $r = st + (t - s)$, find the value of r when:
   (a) $s = 2, t = -3$ **(b)** $s = 3, t = -2$
   (c) $s = -2, t = 3$ **(d)** $s = -2, t = -3$
   (e) $s = 4, t = 2$ **(f)** $s = 5, t = -4$

21.4 Using algebraic equations

You can solve some problems using **algebraic equations**. Though they can look similar an equation is different from a formula:

formulae can be used to calculate a result:

Pay = rate of pay × hours worked

> You could put **any** values into these parts of the formula and get a result for the amount of pay.

equations may be true for one value or several values but are not generally true for any value:

$3x = 6$

> This equation is **only** true when $x = 2$.
> $x = 2$ is called a solution of the equation.

■ **An algebraic equation can be used to help find an unknown quantity.**

Example 9

The perimeter of this rectangle is 30 cm.
The length is x cm and the width is 4 cm.
Work out the value of the length.

$$x + x + 4 + 4 = 30$$
$$2x + 8 = 30$$
$$2x + 8 - 8 = 30 - 8 \quad \text{(Subtract 8 from each side)}$$
$$2x = 22$$
$$x = 11$$

The length x is 11 cm.

Example 10

Suzanne thought of a number, multiplied it by 4 then took away 3. The answer was 13. What was the number she thought of?

Call the number n. Suzanne can make the following equation:

$$4 \times n - 3 = 13$$
$$4n - 3 = 13$$
$$4n - 3 + 3 = 13 + 3 \quad \text{(Add 3 to each side)}$$
$$4n = 16$$
$$n = 4$$

The number was 4.

Exercise 21K

Use the information in these diagrams to find the values of the letters:

1 **(a)**

(b)

(c)

(d)

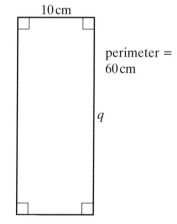

2 The perimeter of this isosceles triangle is 30 cm. Work out the lengths of the sides marked y.

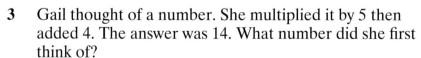

3 Gail thought of a number. She multiplied it by 5 then added 4. The answer was 14. What number did she first think of?

4 Andrew thought of a number. He multiplied it by 6 then took away 15. The answer was 27. What number did Andrew first think of?

5   Darren started a new book and read x pages of the book for each of the first four days. On the fifth day he read 12 pages and finished the book. The book had 100 pages. Work out the value of x.

6   Julia thought of a number, took 5 away from it, then multiplied the answer by 6 to get a final answer of 30. What number did Julia first think of?

7   There were 25 chocolates in a box. Four friends had an equal number of chocolates and this left 9 chocolates in the box. How many chocolates did each of the friends have?

8   Trevor thought of a number, added 7 to it and then multiplied the answer by 5. This gave an answer of 55. What number did Trevor first think of?

9   Sigourney thought of a number, took 12 away from it and then divided her answer by 3 to get a final answer of 4. What number did Sigourney first think of?

Summary of key points

1   A word formula represents a relationship between quantities using words:

      Pay = Rate of pay × hours worked

2   An algebraic formula represents a relationship between quantities using letters. For example, the perimeter of a rectangle is related to its length l and width w by:

      $P = 2l + 2w$

3   An algebraic equation can be used to help find an unknown quantity.

22 Transformations

Karen decided to rearrange the furniture in her bedroom.

First she moved her stereo further along the wall by sliding it.

Then she turned her bed a quarter turn.

This slide is a **translation**.

This turn is a **rotation**.

The mirror was now in a position where she could see her own **reflection** close up without the bed being in the way.

The photograph on the stereo was rather small, so she had an **enlargement** made of this.

Reflections, rotations, translations and enlargements are all **transformations**. To help distinguish between the 'before' and 'after' positions of a shape they have special names: The starting shape is called the **object** and the finishing position of the shape is called the **image**.

22.1 Translation

The rook in these pictures has moved 4 squares forward.

The knight has moved
2 squares forward and
1 square to the right.

■ **Sliding movements like this are called translations.**

Here are some examples:

Example 1

Draw the image of *ABCD* after a translation of 3 squares to
the right and 1 square up.

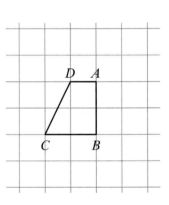

In a translation all the points of the shape have to move exactly
the same amount. The vertices are all going to be displaced
3 squares to the right and 1 square up.

Translate each vertex.

Join up the vertices.

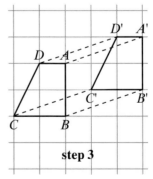

Vertices are corner
points.

You could check
that this is right by
making the shape
out of card or paper
and sliding it from
object to image.

Exercise 22A

1 Draw each shape on squared paper and translate it by the amount shown.

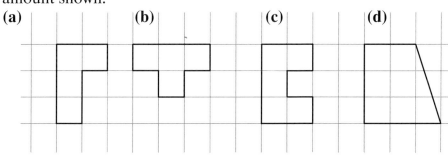

(a)   (b)   (c)   (d)

     2 squares right   3 squares up   4 squares down   1 square left

2 Draw these shapes on squared paper and their images after translating by the amount shown.

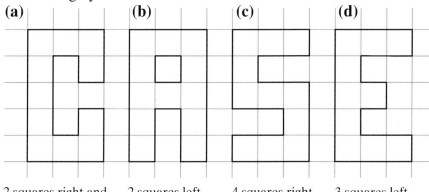

(a)   (b)   (c)   (d)

2 squares right and 3 squares up   2 squares left and 4 squares down   4 squares right and 1 square down   3 squares left and 4 squares up

3 Perform the four translations of question **2** on this shape.

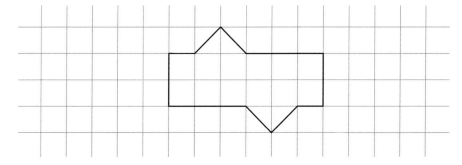

4 Describe the translation for each object-image pair.

(a)   **(b)**   **(c)**

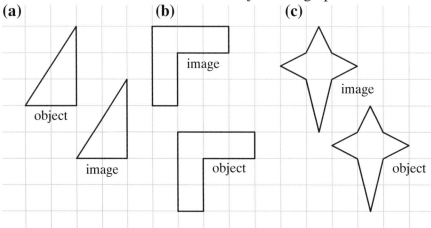

22.2 Rotation

■ **Images of a shape which are formed by turning are called rotations of the shape.**

Object and image are congruent.

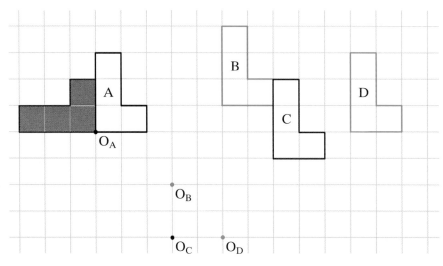

The shaded shape rotated around point OA becomes A.

The shaded shape rotated around point OB becomes B.

The shaded shape is the object. All the others are images and they are all $\frac{1}{4}$ turns but they are not the same rotation.

The point about which the turning occurs is important.

■ **The point about which the turning occurs is called the centre of rotation.**

Example 2

Draw the image of each shape after it has been rotated $\frac{1}{4}$ turn using the point O as centre.

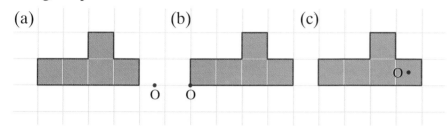

(a)　　　　　(b)　　　　　(c)

Tracing paper makes this task much easier. Once the tracing has been done fix the centre of rotation with a pencil so that point of the tracing paper does not move. The tracing paper can then be rotated (turned) $\frac{1}{4}$ turn.

With a little practice this is quite easy to do.

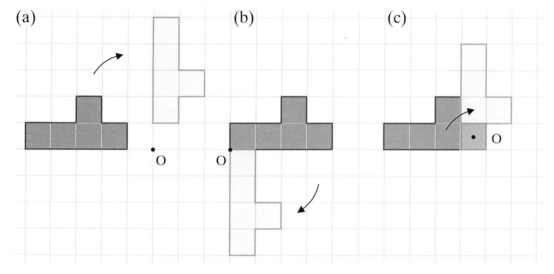

(a)　　　　　(b)　　　　　(c)

Notice that each line of the object has turned $\frac{1}{4}$ turn. This is obvious on this shape which is drawn on grid lines but would be true for diagonal lines as well.

Exercise 22B

1　Draw separate images for each shape after a rotation of 90° clockwise about each of the centres marked.

(a)　　　　　(b)　　　　　(c)

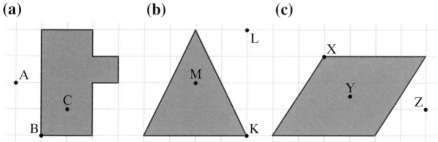

2   Copy these shapes and perform $\frac{1}{2}$ turns using the centres marked.

(a)   **(b)**   **(c)**

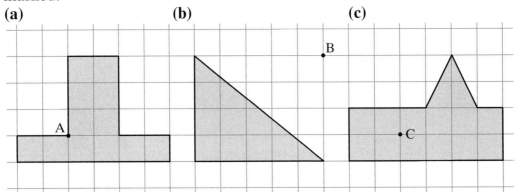

3   Each picture shows an object and its image. Copy each picture and write down how much the object has been rotated and the direction of the rotation. Try to identify the centre of the rotation.

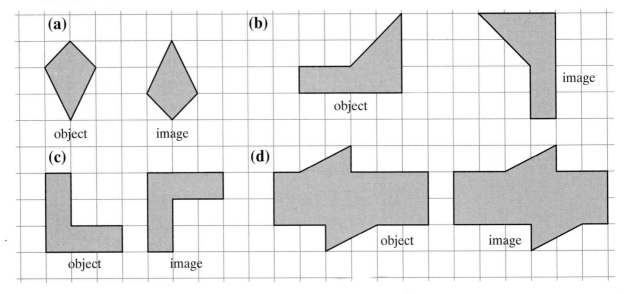

22.3 Reflection

When you next look in a mirror check to see that your image appears to be as far behind the mirror as you are in front. You can test this by moving nearer and further away from the mirror.

■   **Mathematical reflections have images which are the same distance behind the mirror line as the object is in front.**

Example 3

Reflect shape A in the mirror line drawn.

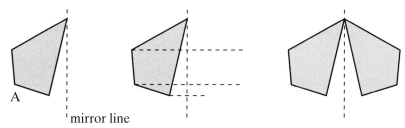

mirror line

Step 1: Identify the image points. These are the same distance on the other side measured at right angles.

Step 2: Join up the points.

■ **Mirror lines are two-way. The mirror line may go through the object requiring reflections to go both ways.**

Here is a reflection which is two-way.

object and mirror line

object with image points

object with image

Example 4

Reflect the shape in the sloping mirror line.

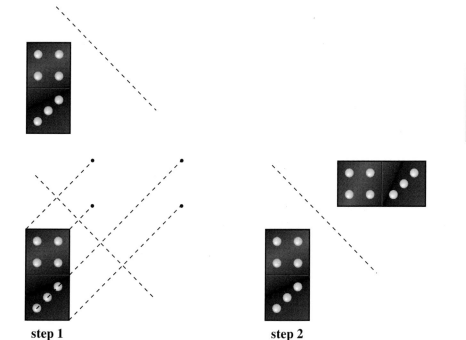

step 1

step 2

> When the mirror line is sloping it is a good idea to turn the paper until the mirror line is vertical.
>
> This way it is easier to find the images of the vertices.

Exercise 22C

1   Copy each shape onto squared paper and draw the image
    after reflection using the dotted line as the mirror line.

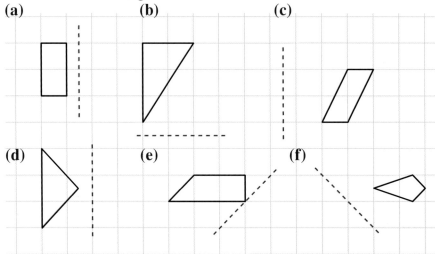

(a)   (b)   (c)

(d)   (e)   (f)

2   Each diagram shows an object with its image. Copy the
    diagrams onto squared paper and draw in the mirror line.

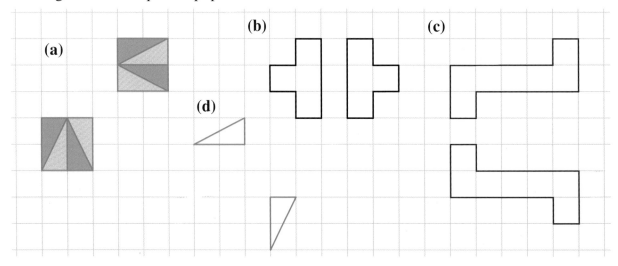

(a)   (b)   (c)

(d)

22.4 Enlargement

■   **In an enlargement all angles stay the same and lengths
    are changed in the same proportion.**

■   **The scale factor is the multiplier for lengths.**

■   **The centre of enlargement determines the final position of
    the enlarged figure.**

Example 5

Enlarge the shape *ABCD* by a scale factor of 2 using *A* as the centre of enlargement.

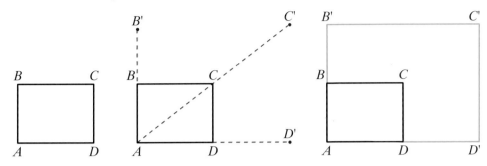

Point *A* is the centre and is fixed.

All other points move 2 times as far away.

A'D' = 2*AD*   *A'C'* = 2*AC*   *A'B'* = 2*AB*

A' is at *A*.

A'D' is the image of *AD*.

Example 6

Enlarge shape *EFGHJ* by a scale factor of 2 with the centre *C* marked inside the shape.

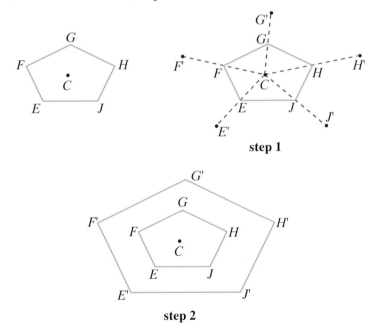

step 1

step 2

Again, all points move to image positions which are 2 times as far away from the fixed centre.

Example 7

In this example the centre O is outside the shape.

The scale factor is still 2.

Again, all points have their images twice as far away from the fixed centre as the object point.

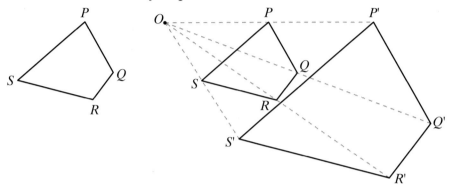

■ **In an enlargement image lines are parallel to their corresponding object lines.**

If the shape is drawn on a grid you can see if the lines which go along the grid lines are the right length by counting. Be sure to use the lengths.

You can check sloping lines by regarding them as a combination of sideways movement and up/down movement.

Example 8

Enlarge shape *KLMN* by a scale factor of 2 and with the centre of enlargement at the origin.

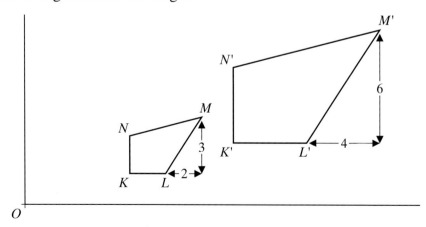

LM is 2 across and 3 up.

The image *L'M'* will be 4 across and 6 up.

MN is 4 left and 1 down.

The image *M'N'* will be 8 left and 2 down.

Exercise 22D

In this exercise each question has a scale factor and three possible centres of enlargement. Copy each diagram and draw the three enlargements either on the same diagram or on separate diagrams.

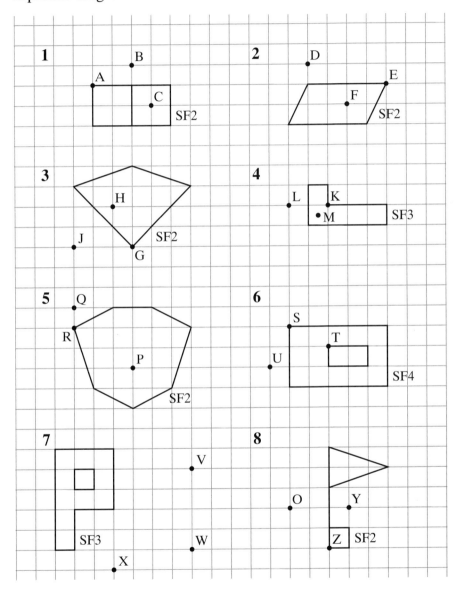

Exercise 22E

1 On a copy of the grid, enlarge the shaded shape by a scale factor of 3.
Start your enlargement at point B.

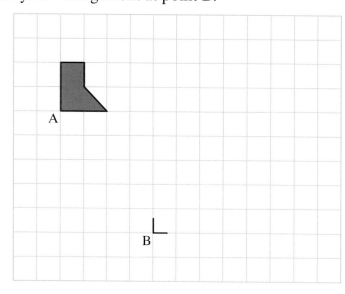

[L]

2 Copy and reflect each of the shapes in the mirror lines given.

(a)

(b)

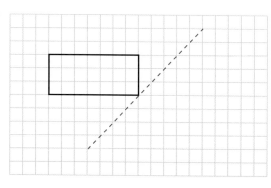

[L]

3 One drawing is an enlargement of the other.
   (a) Find the centre of enlargement and label this point C.
   (b) State the scale factor of the enlargement.

[L]

4 Make copies of the figures to answer the questions.
   (a) Reflect the shape A in the mirror line.

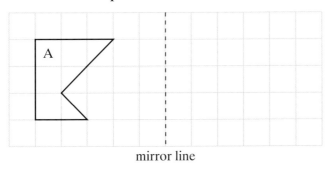

mirror line

   Label the reflection B.

   (b) Describe the transformation which maps the triangle
   C onto the triangle D.

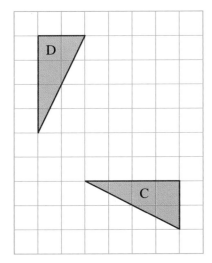

[L]

Summary of key points

1   Sliding movements are called translations.

2   Images of a shape which are formed by turning are called rotations of the shape.

3   The point about which the turning occurs is called the centre of rotation.

4   Mathematical reflections have images which are the same distance behind the mirror line as the object is in front.

5   Mirror lines are two-way. The mirror line may go through the object requiring reflections to go both ways.

6   In an enlargement all angles stay the same and lengths are changed in the same proportion.

7   The scale factor is the multiplier for the lengths in an enlargement.

8   The centre of enlargement determines the final position of the enlarged figure.

9   In an enlargement, image lines are parallel to their corresponding object lines.

23 Probability

This morning there is a **chance** of heavy rain with the **possibility** of thunder. In the afternoon the rain will die away and it is likely that the sun will break through the clouds, **probably** towards evening

Weather forecasts are made by studying weather data and using a branch of mathematics called probability.

Probability uses numbers to represent how likely or unlikely it is that an event such as 'a thunderstorm' will happen.

Probability is used by governments, scientists, economists, medical researchers and many other people to **predict** what is likely to happen in the future by studying what has already happened.

23.1 The probability scale

■ **An event which is certain to happen has a probability of 1.**
For example, the probability that night will follow day is 1.

■ **An event which cannot happen has a probability of 0.**
For example, the probability that you will grow to be 5 metres tall is 0.

All probabilities *must* have a value greater than or equal to 0 and less than or equal to 1.

This can be shown on a **probability scale**:

Exercise 23A

1 Draw a 0 to 1 probability scale and mark on it the probability that:
   (a) it will rain tomorrow
   (b) the sea will disappear
   (c) Boxing Day follows Christmas Day
   (d) you will buy a new pair of shoes soon
   (e) you will have homework tonight
   (f) the sun will not rise next week
   (g) a member of the class will be late tomorrow
   (h) if you toss a coin it will be tail uppermost
   (i) you will see a TV star on your way home.

2 Give two examples where you think the event is:
   (a) impossible   (b) unlikely
   (c) about an even chance   (d) likely
   (e) certain

23.2 Using numbers to represent probabilities

In Exercise 23A you may have found it difficult to know where to put some of the statements on the probability scale. It becomes easier if the probability is given a value.

When you toss a coin there are two possible outcomes: either a head or tail. One of these outcomes is tossing a head.

The probability P of tossing a head can be written:

Probability of a head $P(H) = \dfrac{\text{number of successful outcomes}}{\text{total number of possible outcomes}}$

$= \dfrac{1 \text{ outcome (head)}}{2 \text{ possible outcomes (head or tail)}} = \dfrac{1}{2}$

Another way of writing this is:

$P(\text{head}) = \frac{1}{2}$

Probabilities can be written as fractions, decimals or percentages.

$P(\text{head}) \quad = \frac{1}{2}$
$\qquad\qquad = 0.5$
$\qquad\qquad = 50\%$

■ **The probability that something will happen is:**

$$\text{Probability} = \frac{\textbf{number of successful outcomes}}{\textbf{total number of possible outcomes}}$$

assuming that the outcomes are all equally likely.

Probability is a measure of *how likely* it is that something will happen on a scale 0 to 1. If you toss a coin 10 times that does not mean you will get *exactly* 5 heads, but if you toss a coin 500 times it is *likely* that you will get about 250 heads.

If getting a head is a *success* then getting a tail is a *failure*.

Example 1

Find the probability of getting a 6 when a fair dice is rolled.

Probability P(6) $= \dfrac{\text{number of successful outcomes}}{\text{total number of possible outcomes}} = \dfrac{1}{6}$

This is the number of successful outcomes.

There are six possible outcomes: 1, 2, 3, 4, 5, 6.

The word *fair* is used because each number has an equal chance of turning up: the outcomes are *equally likely*.

1   A fair six-sided dice is rolled.
    What is the probability of getting:
    (a) a 4   **(b)** a 1 or 2
    (c) an odd number   **(d)** an even number
    (e) a 5 or 6   **(f)** 3 or more
    (g) less than 5   **(h)** a prime number
    (i) more than 6   **(j)** $2\frac{1}{2}$?

2   A card is selected from a pack of 52 cards.
    What is the probability it will be:
    (a) an ace   **(b)** the ace of spades
    (c) a black card   **(d)** a 5 or 6
    (e) smaller than a 4   **(f)** a picture card
    (g) a 3, 4 or 5   **(h)** a diamond
    (i) a club or spade   **(j)** any card other than a club?

3   A token is taken from a bag containing 6 red and 5 blue tokens.
    What is the probability that the token will be:
    (a) a blue   **(b)** a red
    (c) a yellow   **(d)** a red or blue?

23.3 Certain and impossible events

In question 3 of the previous exercise it is *impossible* to pick a yellow token. It is *certain* that you will pick either a red or blue token because they are the only colours available.

If you write these probabilities as fractions you find:

P(yellow) which is *impossible* is $\frac{0}{11}$ which is 0.

P(red or blue) which is *certain* is $\frac{11}{11}$ which is 1.

■ **The probability of an event happening is always greater than or equal to 0 (impossible) and less than or equal to 1 (certain). This can be written:**

$$0 \leq \text{Probability} \leq 1$$

Remember:
$a < 5$ a is less than 5
$a \leq 5$ a is less than or equal to 5

$5 > a$ 5 is greater than a
$5 \geq a$ 5 is greater than or equal to a

Exercise 23C

1 Write down the probability of the following:
   (a) You will grow to be 5 metres tall.
   (b) Christmas Day is the 25th December.
   (c) It will rain tomorrow.
   (d) You will live to be 150 years old.
   (e) You will die.
   (f) If you toss a coin it will be a tail.
   (g) If you roll a dice it will be an odd number.

2 Write three statements for each of the following. The first one is done for you:
   (a) a probability of 0
       'A baby will be born with false teeth' has a probability of 0.
   (b) a probability of 1
   (c) a probability of about $\frac{1}{2}$
   (d) a probability of about $\frac{3}{4}$

3   Here are the nets of two differently numbered dice:

Dice A

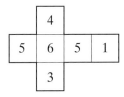
Dice B

If both dice are rolled what is the probability that using
(i) Dice A   **(ii)** Dice B   that you will get:
(a) a 6   **(b)**   a 5
(c) a score of 4 or more   **(d)**   a 2
(e) an even number   **(f)**   an odd number
(g) a prime number   **(h)**   a square number?

4   A bowl of fruit contains 3 apples, 4 bananas, 2 pears and 1
orange. Norma takes one piece of fruit without looking.
Write **(i)** as a fraction **(ii)** as a decimal and **(iii)** as a
percentage, the probability that she takes:
(a) an apple   **(b)** a banana
(c) a pear   **(d)** an orange.
The first one is started for you.
(a) P(apple) is   **(i)** $\frac{3}{10}$ **(ii)** 0.3   **(iii)** 30%

5   A hundred raffle tickets are sold. Gary buys 8 tickets,
Susan 5 tickets and Raman 12 tickets. What is the
probability that the first prize will be won by:
(a) one of these three   **(b)** Gary
(c) Susan   **(d)** somebody other than Raman?
Write each answer in three ways: as a fraction, a decimal,
and a percentage.

23.4 The probability that something will *not* happen

The probability of rolling a 6 on a fair dice is $P(6) = \frac{1}{6}$,

The probability of *not* getting a 6 is:

$$P(\text{not a 6}) = \frac{5}{6}$$

There are 5 ways of
not getting 6: 1, 2, 3, 4, 5

The six possible
outcomes are still:
1, 2, 3, 4, 5, 6

Notice that: $P(6) \qquad\quad = \quad \frac{1}{6}$

$P(\text{not a 6}) = \quad \frac{5}{6} \quad = \quad 1 - \frac{1}{6} \quad = 1 - P(6)$

■ **If the probability of an event happening is *p* then the probability of it *not* happening is 1 − *p*.**

1   (a) The probability it will rain tomorrow is $\frac{1}{3}$.
         What is the probability it will not rain?
    (b) The probability that it will snow on Christmas day is 0.2.
         What is the probability it will not snow on Christmas day?
    (c) The probability that Rovers will get to the next round of a competition is 30%.
         What is the probability that they will not get to the next round?

2   Susan rolls a fair six-sided dice. What is the probability that she will:
    (a) get a 2   (b) *not* get a 2
    (c) get 3 or more   (d) *not* get 3 or more
    (e) *not* get an even number?

23.5 Finding an estimated probability by experimenting

Sometimes you will need to estimate the probability that an event will happen. For example, you can estimate the probability of getting a head when you toss a coin by carrying out a trial:

Toss it several times and keep a record of:

• the number of successful trials (heads)
• the total number of trials (how many tosses altogether)

■ **The estimated probability that an event will happen in a game or experiment is:**

Estimated probability = $\dfrac{\textbf{number of successful trials}}{\textbf{total number of trials}}$

The estimated probability may be different from the theoretical probability.

Example 2

If you toss a coin 20 times and get 12 heads and 8 tails the **estimated probability** of getting a head is: $\dfrac{12}{20} = \dfrac{3}{5}$

The **theoretical probability** is: $\dfrac{10}{20} = \dfrac{1}{2}$

From the experiment it would seem that you are more likely to get a head than a tail. Next time you do the same experiment you may well get a different result but the theoretical probability is *always* $\frac{1}{2}$.

If the estimated probability of Adrian winning a tennis match is $\frac{3}{4}$ then if he plays 24 matches he would expect to win 18 times.

So:
$\frac{3}{4} \times 18 = 24$

Exercise 23E

1 (a) Roll a dice 36 times and record your results in a frequency table like this. Work out the probability of rolling each number from your results.

Number	Tally	Frequency	Probability
1			$\overline{36}$
2			$\overline{36}$
3			$\overline{36}$
4			$\overline{36}$
5			$\overline{36}$
6			$\overline{36}$
		Total	$\overline{36}$

Use the table to answer these questions:
(b) What is the probability of rolling (i) a three (ii) a five?
(c) What is the probability of rolling an even number?
(d) What was the total of all the probabilities?
(e) Explain your result to part (d).

2 Roll a dice another 36 times and complete a table as in question **1**.
Compare your results with the previous question and make comments.

3 Combine your results for questions **1** and **2** in a table and comment on the probabilities you obtain.

4 Roll two dice 36 times, add the total spots on the uppermost faces and record your results in the table like this:

Number	Tally	Frequency	Probability
2			
3			
4			
5			
12			

Total 8

(a) What is the probability of a score being:
  (i) even   (ii) greater than 8
  (iii) a square number   (iv) 12
  (v) 7   (vi) 3
  (vii) 11   (viii) 1?
(b) What is the total of the probabilities?
(c) What is the probability that you will not score 12?

5 Roll two dice a further 36 times and complete a table as in question **4**.
Compare the results with those in question **4**.

6 Combine your results for questions **4** and **5** in a table and make comments on your results.

7 Using your frequency column data from question **6** draw a bar chart to show your result.
(a) Which number occurred the most times?
(b) Which number occurred the least?
(c) Write two sentences about the shape of your chart.
(d) Which of these numbers are most likely to occur:
  (i) 12 (ii) 6 (iii) 2?
(e) Why did the number 1 not occur?

23.6 Using a sample space diagram to find theoretical probabilities

If you roll a red dice and a blue dice what are all the outcomes? If the red dice shows 1 the blue dice could show 1, 2, 3, 4, 5 or 6. You can record these outcomes as ordered pairs putting the red result first, then the blue result like this:

red dice 1

(1, 1) (1, 2) (1, 3) (1, 4) (1, 5) (1, 6)

blue dice 6

If the red dice showed 2 first the outcomes could be:

(2, 1) (2, 2) (2, 3) (2, 4) (2, 5) (2, 6)

You can represent all the outcomes on a **sample space diagram**:

```
     6 ⊣ (1,6)  (2,6)  (3,6)  (4,6)  (5,6)  (6,6)

     5 ⊣ (1,5)  (2,5)  (3,5)  (4,5)  (5,5)  (6,5)

     4 ⊣ (1,4)  (2,4)  (3,4)  (4,4)  (5,4)  (6,4)
Red dice
     3 ⊣ (1,3)  (2,3)  (3,3)  (4,3)  (5,3)  (6,3)

     2 ⊣ (1,2)  (2,2)  (3,2)  (4,2)  (5,2)  (6,2)

     1 ⊣ (1,1)  (2,1)  (3,1)  (4,1)  (5,1)  (6,1)
        └──┬─────┬─────┬─────┬─────┬─────┬──
           1     2     3     4     5     6
                      Blue dice
```

The sample space diagram shows that there are 36 possible outcomes.

■ **You can represent all possible outcomes on a sample space diagram.**

Example 3

Use a sample space diagram to find the probability of getting a total score of 7 when two dice are rolled.

```
     6 ⊣ (1,6)  (2,6)  (3,6)  (4,6)  (5,6)  (6,6)

     5 ⊣ (1,5)  (2,5)  (3,5)  (4,5)  (5,5)  (6,5)

     4 ⊣ (1,4)  (2,4)  (3,4)  (4,4)  (5,4)  (6,4)
Red dice
     3 ⊣ (1,3)  (2,3)  (3,3)  (4,3)  (5,3)  (6,3)

     2 ⊣ (1,2)  (2,2)  (3,2)  (4,2)  (5,2)  (6,2)

     1 ⊣ (1,1)  (2,1)  (3,1)  (4,1)  (5,1)  (6,1)
        └──┬─────┬─────┬─────┬─────┬─────┬──
           1     2     3     4     5     6
                      Blue dice
```

There are 6 ways of scoring 7:

(1, 6) (2, 5) (3, 4)
(4, 3) (5, 2) (6, 1)

There are 36 possible outcomes so:

$$P(\text{scoring } 7) = \tfrac{6}{36}$$

Exercise 23F

1   Use the sample space diagram in Example 3 to find the probability of:
    (a) a total score of (i) 5 (ii) 9 (iii) 12
    (b) **not** rolling a score of (i) more than 4 (ii) less than 10
    (c) rolling a 2 on one of the dice
    (d) rolling a double
    (e) rolling a double 6.

2   This sample space diagram shows the outcomes when the ace, king, queen, jack, and ten from both the spades and hearts suits are placed in two separate piles and one card is taken from each pile:

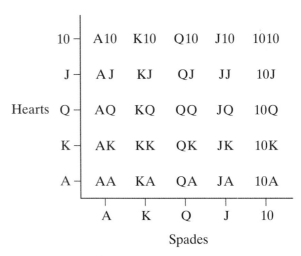

Find the probability that:
    (a) both cards will be kings
    (b) both of the cards could be either an Ace or a King
    (c) both cards will be a pair
    (d) at least one card will be an ace
    (e) neither card will be a 10
    (f) neither card will be a king or jack
    (g) one card will be a spade
    (h) both cards will be hearts.

23.7 Using tree diagrams to find probabilities

This bag contains a red disc and a blue disc. If you take one out and then another, these outcomes are possible:

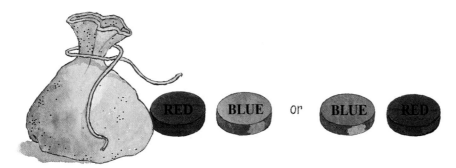

If you have two discs of each colour in the bag then these outcomes are possible:

red, red   or   red, blue   or   blue, red   or   blue, blue

One way of showing all the possible outcomes is to draw a **tree diagram**:

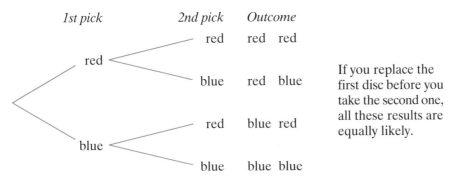

1st pick   *2nd pick*   *Outcome*

red
    red   red   red
    blue   red   blue

blue
    red   blue   red
    blue   blue   blue

If you replace the first disc before you take the second one, all these results are equally likely.

There are four outcomes so the **theoretical probability** of obtaining red, red is $\frac{1}{4}$.

■ **Sample tree diagrams can be used to help solve probability problems.**

Example 4

You have three discs: one red, one blue and one green. Pick one without looking, record its colour and replace it, then take a second disc. The nine different possible outcomes are:

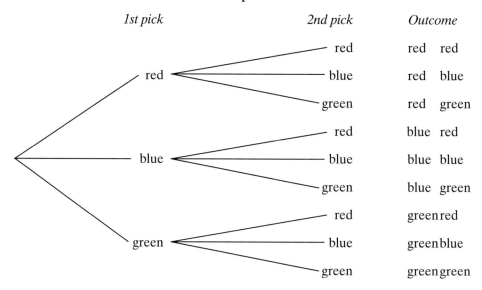

1st pick	2nd pick	Outcome

What is the probability of:
(a) picking red, red
(b) picking two colours the same
(c) one of the colours picked being red
(d) not picking a green?

If you replace the disc after the first pick, then pick again, there are 9 possible outcomes. Each outcome has an equal chance of occurring so the probability of:
(a) red, red is $\frac{1}{9}$
(b) two colours the same is $\frac{3}{9}$
(c) one of the colours being red is $\frac{5}{9}$
(d) not picking a green is $\frac{4}{9}$

Exercise 23G

1 Write out all the possible outcomes for each of the following:
    (a) tossing a coin twice
    (b) tossing a coin three times
    (c) obtaining an odd or even number when a dice is rolled twice
    (d) when a coin is tossed and a dice is rolled
    (e) when a coin is tossed twice and a dice is thrown once.

2 Work out the number of possible outcomes:
   (a) when a dice is thrown twice
   (b) when a coin is tossed four times
   (c) when three discs are taken from a bag containing 2 red discs, 2 blue discs and one yellow disc, one at a time.

3 Four discs: red, green, yellow and blue are placed in a bag. One disc is taken at random, its colour recorded and then replaced. A second disc is then taken.
   Draw a sample space diagram to show all the possible outcomes.

4 **(a)** Copy and complete this table to show the possible outcomes when a red dice and a blue dice are rolled:

Total score	Ordered pairs	Theoretical probability
2	(1,1)	$\frac{1}{36}$
3	(1,2) (2,1)	$\frac{2}{36}$
4	(1,3) (2,2) (3,1)	$\frac{3}{36}$
5		
6		
7		
11		
12		

   (b) Which was the most likely score?
   (c) What is the sum of all the probabilities? Explain your answer.

5 **(a)** Copy and complete this tree diagram to show all the possible outcomes if a family has two children:

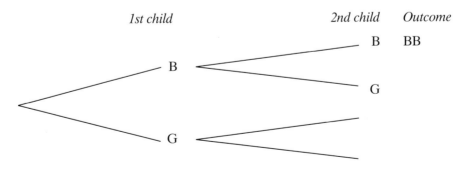

   (b) If the outcomes are equally likely what is the probability there will be one child of each sex?

6   Draw a tree diagram to show all the possible outcomes if a family has three children.

Example 5

A match can be won, drawn or lost. One week a school is to play two matches. List all the possible outcomes.

If the outcomes are equally likely calculate the probability that:

(a) both matches are won
(b) one match is drawn
(c) *at least* one match is drawn
(d) no match is lost
(e) both matches are *not* lost.

(a) P(both matches are won) There are 9 outcomes so
$$P(WW) = \tfrac{1}{9}$$

(b) P(one match is drawn) P(WD or DW or DL or
$$LD) = \tfrac{4}{9}$$

(c) P(at least one match is drawn) P(WD or DW or DL or LD
or DD) $= \tfrac{5}{9}$

(d) P(no match is lost) P(WW or WD or DW or
$$DD) = \tfrac{4}{9}$$

(e) P(both matches are *not* lost) P(all except LL) $= 1 - \tfrac{1}{9} = \tfrac{8}{9}$

Sometimes probability questions include phrases such as 'twice as likely'.

For example if Sarah is twice as likely to win her game of squash as to lose it you can show this on a tree diagram like this:

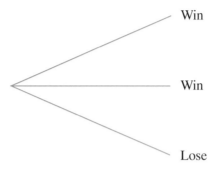

Win

Win

Lose

Exercise 23H

1   Edward is twice as likely to win a game as he is to lose it. A match cannot be a draw. A match consists of three games.
   (a) Draw a tree diagram to show all the possible outcomes of two matches.
   (b) What is the probability he:
      (i) wins both matches
      (ii) loses both matches?

2   Nicola is twice as likely to turn right at a T-junction as turn left.
   List all the possible outcomes after she has passed two junctions.

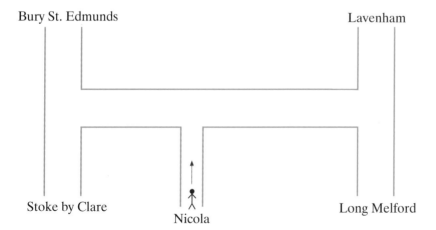

3 Carl is twice as likely to win than lose. The tree diagram shows all the possible outcomes after two games:

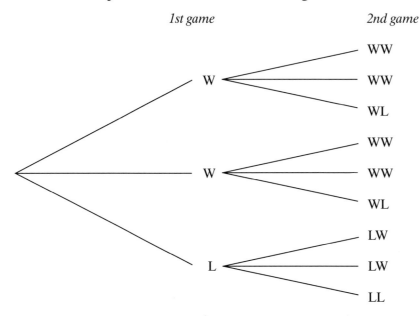

1st game   *2nd game*

WW
WW
WL
WW
WW
WL
LW
LW
LL

The tree diagram shows how the four outcomes can be achieved in nine different ways.

(a) How many possible outcomes are there?
(b) What is the probability he will win both games?
(c) What is the probability he will lose just one game?
(d) What is the probability he will lose both games?

4 Hamish is three times as likely to play on his computer (C) as he is to watch television (T) when he gets home from school. He does not do both.
(a) Draw a diagram to represent this.
(b) List all the possible outcomes for Hamish for two days.
(c) What is the probability he watches television on both days?

5 Nick is twice as likely to be early as he is to be late.
(a) Draw a tree diagram to show all the possible outcomes after three days.
(b) What is the probability he is:
  (i) early on all three days
  (ii) late on all three days
  (iii) late on any two of the days
  (iv) late on only one of the days?

23.8 Using two-way tables to find probabilities

Another way to show possible outcomes is to use a two-way table. You can do this even if you do not know all the outcomes.

Example 6

This table shows some information of how staff got to school. None of them came by car.

	Walk	Bus	Cycle	Total
Monday	4	p	3	12
Tuesday	7	q	u	t
Total	r	9	s	25

(a) Fill in the missing numbers. The boxes are labelled to help you.

(b) What is the probability that one of these members of staff:
   (i)   walked to school on Monday
  (ii) cycled on Tuesday
 (iii) came by bus?

(a) Monday: $4 + p + 3 = 12$
                so the number who travelled by bus p is 5.

    Tuesday: The total who travelled by bus is $5 + q = 9$
                so the number who travelled by bus q is 4.

The total r who walked is $4 + 7 = 11$.

The total who walk + bus + cycle is 25
                         $11 + 9 + s = 25$

so the total s who cycle is 5.

The total t for Tuesday is $25 - 12 = 13$

The number u who cycle on Tuesday is $13 - (7 + 4) = 2$

The completed table is:

	Walk	Bus	Cycle	Total
Monday	4	5	3	12
Tuesday	7	4	2	13
Total	11	9	5	25

(b) (i) 4 walked out of a total of 12 arriving at school so the probability is $\frac{4}{12} = \frac{1}{3}$.
   (ii) 2 cycled out of 13 so probability is $\frac{2}{13}$
 (iii) A total of 9 bus journeys over the two days so probability is $\frac{9}{25}$.

Exercise 23I

1 The number of clients interviewed by Jackie and Sam about their holiday is shown in this table:

	Monday	Tuesday	Total
Jackie	25	35	
Sam			
Total	55		100

(a) How many people did Jackie question?
(b) How many people did Sam question on Monday?
(c) How many people were questioned on Tuesday?
(d) Copy and complete the table.
(e) If a person is chosen at random what is the probability that they were questioned by:
  (i) Jackie on Monday
  (ii) Sam on Tuesday   (iii) Jackie
  (iv) Sam on Monday or Jackie on Tuesday

A **random** selection is one in which each person has the same chance of being chosen.

2 Jackie and Sam asked the 100 clients how they travelled to France and in which month they travelled. Some of the information is recorded in this table:

	Air	Le Shuttle	Boat	Total
July	8		10	20
August	15	5		50
September		8		
Total	30			100

(a) Copy and complete the table.
(b) What is the probability that a client selected at random travelled:
    (i) in July   (ii) in August or September (iii) by air
   (iv) by boat   (v) by Le Shuttle in August (vi) by boat in August
  (vii) not by air (viii) not by boat in July.

3 The same 100 people were asked if they had their holiday in France, went on to Italy or went elsewhere. Some details are given in this table:

	France	Italy	Elsewhere	Total
July		10	4	20
August	18		8	
September		16		30
Total	28	50		

(a) Copy and complete the table.

(b) What is the probability that Carole:

    (i) went to Italy   **(ii)** went to France

   (iii) went in July   **(iv)** did not go to Italy

    (v) went elsewhere in August   **(vi)** went to France in September

  (vii) went to Italy in September.

4 The same 100 people were also asked in what type of accommodation they stayed. Part of the information is given in this table:

	Hotel	Caravan	Camping	Other	Total
July	11	4	3		
August		14		6	
September		7	4	3	30
Total	49		15	11	100

(a) Copy and complete the table.

(b) What is the probability a person selected at random:

    (i) went camping in August   **(ii)** stayed in a caravan in July

   (iii) stayed in a hotel   **(iv)** did not stay in a hotel

    (v) stayed in a caravan   **(vi)** used other accommodation

  (vii) went camping in August.

■ **Two-way tables can be used to help solve probability problems.**

Summary of key points

1   An event which is certain to happen has a probability of 1.

2   An event which cannot happen has a probability of 0.

3   The probability that an event will happen is:

$$\text{Probability} = \frac{\text{number of successful outcomes}}{\text{total number of possible outcomes}}$$

assuming all outcomes are equally likely.

4   The probability of an event happening is always greater than or equal to 0 (impossible) and less than or equal to 1 (certain). This can be written:

$$0 \leq \text{Probability} \leq 1$$

5   If the probability of an event happening is p then the probability of it not happening is $1 - p$.

6   The estimated probability that an event will happen in a game or experiment is:

$$\text{Estimated probability} = \frac{\text{number of successful trials}}{\text{total number of trials}}$$

7   Sample space diagrams, tree diagrams and two-way tables can be used to help solve probability problems.

24 Calculators and computers

This unit shows you some ways of using scientific calculators, graphical calculators and computers to help you solve mathematical problems.

The examples will work on Casio calculators and most computers. Your teacher will tell you if you need to change any of the instructions.

24.1 How well do you know your calculator?

Examples 1 to 7 apply only to scientific calculators.

You can use your calculator to help you with fractions, decimals, percentages and money problems. Try these examples:

Example 1   Fractions and decimals

Work out $\frac{2}{5} + 1\frac{1}{4}$

Press the keys   [2] [ab/c] [5] [+] [1] [ab/c] [1] [ab/c] [4] [=]

Answer: $1\frac{13}{20}$

> **Converting to fractions or decimals**
>
> Press [SHIFT] [ab/c] (%) to convert your answer to an improper (top-heavy) fraction.
>
> Press [ab/c] again to convert the answer to a decimal.

Example 2   Fractions and money

Work out $\frac{3}{8}$ of £6

Press the keys   [3] [ab/c] [8] [×] [6] [=]

Press [ab/c] again to get £2.25

Example 3   Percentages

Work out 20% of 6 metres.

Press   [6] [×] [2] [0] [SHIFT] [=] (%) [=]

Answer: 1.2 metres

Example 4   Percentage increase or decrease

Reduce £18 by 10%

Press   [1] [8] [×] [1] [0] [SHIFT] [=] (%) [−]

The calculator display is 16.2
The answer is £16.20

You can make your calculator show pounds and pence correctly by using *Fix 2*

This will always display two decimal places. Don't forget to return your calculator to *normal* mode after doing this.

Example 5   Constant calculations

Work out   £2.80 × 1.2
          £8.90 × 1.2
          £7.65 × 1.2

Find out what happens when you press
any of the keys +, −, × or ÷ *twice*

Press   `1` `·` `2` `×` `×` `2` `·` `8` `0` `=`
                      `8` `·` `9` `0` `=`
                      `7` `·` `6` `5` `=`

Answers: £3.36, £10.68, £9.18

Example 6   Brackets

Work out $\dfrac{7 + 12 + 5}{3}$

Press   `(` `7` `+` `1` `2` `+` `5` `)` `÷` `3` `=`

Answer: 8

Example 7   Memory calculations

Find the total cost of the following items, and calculate the
change from £10

      2 at £1.15,   3 at 98p,   and 1 at £1.79

Press   `2` `×` `1` `·` `1` `5` `=` `Min`
          `3` `×` `0` `·` `9` `8` `=` `M+`
              `1` `·` `7` `9` `=` `M+`
                      `MR`

The total is £7.03

Now press   `1` `0` `−` `MR` `=`

The change is £2.97

24.2   Using memories to represent formulae

Examples and exercises
in Sections 24.2 to 24.6
apply only to graphical
calculators.

Look at this problem:

Find the area and perimeter of a rectangle 9.83 cm by 5.21 cm
using the calculator memories.

Use the A memory

Use the L memory
to represent this

Length

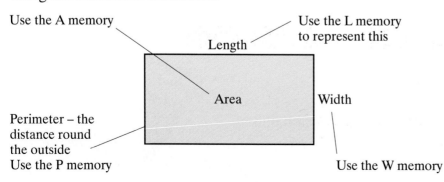

Area

Width

Perimeter – the
distance round
the outside
Use the P memory

Use the W memory

Example 8

Use memories L, W, A and P to calculate the area and perimeter of a rectangle 9.83 cm by 5.21 cm.

It is useful, but not essential, to store each answer in a memory for future use like this:

(a) Store the number 9.83 in memory L.
Press the keys   9   ·   8   3   →   L   EXE

(b) Store the number 5.21 in memory W.
Press the keys   5   ·   2   1   →   W   EXE

(c) Multiply memories L and W and store the answer in memory A.
Press the keys   L   W   →   A   EXE

(d) Calculate the perimeter and store it in memory P.
Press the keys   2   L   +   2   W   →   P   EXE

Now try pressing the keys   L   W   EXE

This produces the same result for the area but the answer is not stored in a memory.

Remember to press the ALFA key before each memory.

```
9.83→L
           9.83
5.21→W
           5.21
LW→A
        51.2143
2L+2W→P
          30.08
```

Example 9

Use the memories set up in Example 8.

(a) To find the area of a rectangle again, press:
  (i)   L   W   EXE   (ii)   W   L   EXE
  (iii)   L   ×   W   EXE   (iv)   W   ×   L   EXE

(b) To find the perimeter of a rectangle, press:
  (i)   2   L   +   2   W   EXE
  (ii)   2   ×   L   +   2   ×   W   EXE
  (iii)   2   (L   +   W   )   EXE
  (iv)   2   ×   (L   +   W   )   EXE

(a) All four answers are the same.

(b) All four answers are the same.

Entering formulae
Formulae are typed exactly as you would write them. Multiplication signs are not required between letters or before brackets.

Exercise 24A

1   Calculate the area A and perimeter P of a rectangle 73 cm by 49 cm using any of the methods described above. Write down the sequence of keys as you press them.

2   Calculate the area A and circumference C of a circle whose radius R is 12 cm. You should store the value 12 in memory R, then use the formulae

$$\pi R^2 \to A$$
and $2\pi R \to C$

To get π you might have to press SHIFT first.
To get R^2 you might have to press
ALFA R SHIFT x^2

3   Calculate the area A of a triangle whose base B is 15 cm and whose height H is 9 cm, using the formula

$$(BH) \div 2 \to A$$

4   Calculate the volume V of a rectangular box whose length L is 120 cm, width W is 60 cm and height H is 20 cm using the formula

$$LWH \to V$$

24.3 Saving formulae so you can use them again

If you want to use the same formula *several times*, you should *save* it as a **program**.

Then you can use it again with different numbers.

Select the WRT mode on the calculator, and choose a program number, say Prog 3.

Now type $\pi\ R^2 \to A$

Select the RUN mode on the calculator and then press

Find out how to *write*, *run* and *clear* programs on your graphical calculator.

```
10→R
           10.
Prog 3
       314.1592654
11→R
           11.
Prog 3
       380.1327111
12→R
           12.
Prog 3
       452.3893421
```

You can improve this program by adding more lines which tell you what to do:

```
"RADIUS"
? → R ——————
π R² → A
```
? is used to input a number which is then stored in memory R

To run this new program, press Prog 3 EXE

When the ? appears press

Notice that EXE is pressed twice.

The first EXE enters the radius and Prog 3 produces the area.

The second EXE runs the program again.

You can do the same thing by writing a computer program in BASIC:

```
10  PRINT "RADIUS"
20  INPUT R
30  LET A = PI * R ^ 2
40  PRINT A
50  END
```

```
RUN
RADIUS
?
10
314.1592654
RUN
```

Exercise 24B

1   Write a program for your graphical calculator or computer which will calculate the volume V of a cube whose sides are of length L.
Use your program to find the volumes of cubes whose sides are 5 cm, 6 cm and 7 cm.

2   Write a program for your graphical calculator or computer which will convert a temperature in degrees Fahrenheit (°F) to degrees Celsius (°C) using the formula
$C = (F - 32) \times \frac{5}{9}$
Use your program to convert 86° F, 50° F, 68° F to degrees Celsius.

24.4 Solving problems by trial and improvement

Look at this problem.

Find the radius of a circle whose area is 100 cm².

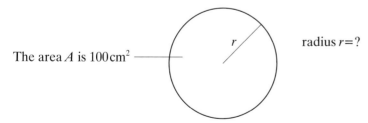

The area A is 100 cm²

r

radius $r = ?$

Sometimes you can solve problems like this by guessing a solution and trying it out. You can find the radius by guessing it and trying it in the formula $A = \pi r^2$

You can improve your guess and try again until you get a good enough answer.

This method of solving problems is called **trial and improvement**.

You can use your calculator or computer to help you do this.

Example 10

Use a trial and improvement method to find the radius of a circle whose area is $100\,\text{cm}^2$.

Your answer should be accurate to 2 dp.

Method:
Guess a value for R
Calculate πR^2
Compare your answer with 100
Decide whether your chosen value for R was too big or too small.
Make a better choice for R and repeat the process until you achieve the accuracy you need.

If at first you don't succeed,
try,
try,
and try again!

Solution:

Type ? → R : πR^2 EXE

You *must* include the colon : or replace it by SHIFT EXE

Notice that EXE is pressed twice.

When the ? appears, enter your first guess. Suppose this is $R = 10$ cm.

Type 1 0 EXE EXE

The first EXE enters the radius and the area is calculated.

The answer, 314.159 265 4 is too big, so now try a smaller value for R

The second EXE repeats the process and another ? appears

Type			keys		giving	result	
Type 5			EXE EXE		giving	78.539 816 34	too small
Type 7			EXE EXE		giving	153.938 04	too big
Type 6			EXE EXE		giving	113.097 335 5	too big
Type 5 . 5			EXE EXE		giving	95.033 177 77	too small
Type 5 . 7 5			EXE EXE		giving	103.868 907 1	too big
Type 5 . 6 5			EXE EXE		giving	100.287 491 5	too big
Type 5 . 6 4			EXE EXE		giving	99.932 805 67	too small
Type 5 . 6 4 2			EXE EXE		giving	100.003 692 6	too big

You can now see that the radius R lies between 5.64 cm and 5.642 cm, so:

$$R = 5.64 \text{ cm to 2 d.p.}$$

You can do the same thing by writing a computer program in BASIC:

```
10 INPUT R
20 PRINT PI * R ^ 2
30 GOTO 10
40 END
```

```
RUN
?
5
78.53981634
?
7
153.93804
?
```

Try it using the numbers 5, 7, 6, 5.5, 5.75 and so on until you decide when to stop.

Exercise 24C

1 Use a trial and improvement method to find the length L of the side of a cube whose volume V is $100\,\text{cm}^3$.
The formula is $V = L^3$.
Hint: Find out how to enter L^3 (L raised to the power 3) on your graphical calculator.
Your answer should be accurate to 2 dp.

2 Use $? \rightarrow F : (F - 32) \times 5 \div 9$ to convert a temperature of $22°\,\text{C}$ to Fahrenheit (°F) by trial and improvement. Stop at 1 dp accuracy.

24.5 Using the [Ans] and [EXE] keys to produce number sequences

You can use these keys together to generate number sequences. For example:

Press [1] [EXE]

Press [Ans] [+] [1] [EXE] [EXE] [EXE] ... keep pressing [EXE]

The calculator appears to be 'counting'.

Each time [EXE] is pressed, 'Ans + 1' is calculated, where Ans is the *last displayed answer*.

Example 11

[Ans] recalls the most recent answer.

(a) Use the Ans and EXE keys to produce the Even Numbers, starting with 2.

(b) Show how the Ans and EXE keys can be used to produce the sequence 2, 6, 18, 54, ...

(a) [2] [EXE] [Ans] [+] [2] [EXE] [EXE] [EXE] . . .

(b) [2] [EXE] [Ans] [×] [2] [EXE] [EXE] [EXE] . . .

[EXE] performs (or repeats) the most recent calculation(s).

Exercise 24D

Write down the key presses, including and , which will generate the following sequences:

1   1, 3, 5, 7, 9, . . .

2   5, 10, 15, 20, 25, . . .

3   2, 4, 8, 16, 32, . . .

4   3, 9, 27, 81, 243, . . .

5   10, 9, 8, 7, 6, . . .

6   16, 8, 4, 2, 1, . . .

7   200, 20, 2, 0.2, 0.02, . . .

8   −5, −7, −9, −11, −13, . . .

24.6 Drawing graphs on your calculator

Choose the default ranges for x and y by pressing

[Range] [INIT] [Range]

On some calculators you may need to press

[Range] [SHIFT] [MCR] [Range]

Clear the graphics screen by pressing [SHIFT] [Cls]

Have a look at the graphics screen by pressing [G↔T] .

Both axes are marked off in intervals of 1.

Find out how to set the ranges of x and y to your own chosen values.

Example 12

Draw the graphs of $y = x + 1$ and $y = x - 1$

Press the [Graph] key, then press [X] [+] [1] [EXE]

If your calculator has a key marked [x, θ, T] press it to get [X] .

You will see graph $y = x + 1$

The first graph is drawn. To see the second graph, press the

[Graph] key again and press [X] [−] [1] [EXE]

Notice that the second graph is drawn on the same axes as the first without erasing the first. It is superimposed. This will continue to happen with further graphs until you *clear the graphics screen*.

Clear the screen by pressing [SHIFT] [Cls] .

Example 13

Draw the graphs of $y = 2x + c$ for several different values of c in the range -4 to 4.

Type `"C"  :  ?  → C :  Graph Y = 2X + C` EXE

When the ? appears, enter your values for c

Press: — 4 EXE (wait until the graph is drawn)

EXE — 2 EXE (wait until the graph is drawn)

EXE 0 EXE (wait until the graph is drawn)

EXE 2 EXE (wait until the graph is drawn)

EXE 4 EXE (wait until the graph is drawn)

Clear the screen to finish.

Exercise 24E

In each question draw all the graphs on the same axes and write down what you see.

Clear the screen before starting the next question.

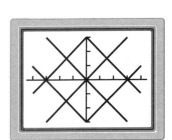

1 $y = x$, $y = x + 3$, $y = x - 3$,
    $y = -x$, $y = -x + 3$, $y = -x - 3$

2 $y = x$, $y = 2x$, $y = 3x$,
    $y = -x$, $y = -2x$, $y = -3x$

3 $y = x^2$, $y = x^2 + 1$, $y = x^2 - 1$,
    $y = -x^2$, $y = -x^2 + 1$, $y = -x^2 - 1$

24.7 Investigating number sequences with a spreadsheet

> Examples and exercises in Sections 24.7 to 24.9 apply only to spreadsheets.

You can generate many number sequences on the same spreadsheet and compare them.

Find out how to enter numbers and formulae in the cells of your spreadsheet.

Find out how to copy a formula from one cell to other cells.

Example 14

Generate the whole numbers from 1 to 10 in column A.

Put the number 1 in cell A1.
Put the formula A1 + 1 in cell A2.
Copy the formula in A2 down column A as far as A10.

Example 15

Generate the even numbers in column B.

Put the number 2 in cell B1.
Put the formula B1 + 2 in cell B2.
Copy the formula in B2 down column B as far as B10.

Example 16

Generate the odd numbers in column C.

Put the number 1 in cell C1.
Put the formula C1 + 2 in cell C2.
Copy the formula in C2 down column C as far as C10.

Formula A2=A1+1	Formula B2=B1+2	Formula C2=C1+2	
	A	B	C	D
1	1	2	1	
2	2	4	3	
3	3	6	5	
4	4	8	7	
5	5	10	9	
6	6	12	11	
7	7	14	13	
8	8	16	15	
9	9	18	17	
10	10	20	19	

Example 17

Generate the triangular numbers in column D.

Put the number 1 in cell D1.
Put the formula D1 + A2 in cell D2.
Copy the formula in D2 down column D as far as D10.

Example 18

Add consecutive odd numbers and put the answers in column E.

Put the formula C1 + C2 in cell E2.
Copy the formula in E2 down column E as far as E10.

You should now be able to see that the numbers in column E are multiples of 4.

Seventh odd number

Eighth odd number

Example 19

Add consecutive triangular numbers and put the answers in column F.

Put the formula D1 + D2 in cell F2.
Copy the formula in F2 down column F as far as F10.

What is the name of the sequence of numbers in column F?

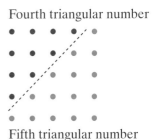

Fourth triangular number

Fifth triangular number

	A	B	C	Formula D2=D1+A2 D	Formula E2=C1+C2 E	Formula F2=D1+D2 F	G
1	1	2	1	1			
2	2	4	3	3	4	4	
3	3	6	5	6	8	9	
4	4	8	7	10	12	16	
5	5	10	9	15	16	25	
6	6	12	11	21	20	36	
7	7	14	13	28	24	49	
8	8	16	15	36	28	64	
9	9	18	17	45	32	81	
10	10	20	19	55	36	100	

24.8 Problem solving with a spreadsheet

Look at this problem:

A farmer has 200 metres of fencing. He wants to use all the fencing to enclose a rectangular area of his field for his animals to graze. Find the length and width of the rectangle which gives his animals the maximum grazing area.

You can solve problems like this on a computer by using a spreadsheet.

Example 20

Think of all the rectangles you can draw whose perimeters are 200 metres. For example, some could be long and thin; others short and wide.

Use a spreadsheet to find the length L and width W of the rectangle which has the maximum area. (There is more about this in Section 24.2.)

The perimeter of each rectangle is 200 metres, so

$$2L + 2W = 200$$

You can divide by 2 to make this equation simpler

$$L + W = 100$$

Use your spreadsheet to try lots of values for L from $L = 0$ to $L = 100$ metres.

Increase L by 10 metres each time. For each value of L calculate a value for W using

$$W = 100 - L$$

Then multiply the values of L and W to get the area of each rectangle.

Make sure your spreadsheet has at least 12 rows and 3 columns. Use column A for the length, column B for the width and column C for the area of each rectangle.

	Formula A3=A2+10	(W=100−L) Formula B2=100−A2	(A=L×W) Formula C2=A2×B2	
	A	B	C	D
1	L	W	LW	
2	0	100	0	
3	10	90	900	
4	20	80	1600	
5	30	70	2100	
6	40	60	2400	
7	50	50	2500	
8	60	40	2400	
9	70	30	2100	
10	80	20	1600	
11	90	10	900	
12	100	0	0	

You can now find the maximum value for the area in column C quite easily.

Find out how your spreadsheet produces graphs.

Drawing graphs of the data in the spreadsheet can give you a better understanding of how the area changes as the lengths and widths of the rectangles change.

Rectangles can be long and thin or short and wide, but the rectangle with the biggest area is SQUARE!

Area increases then decreases
The maximum area is 2500 m²

Length increases from 0 m to 100 m

24.9 Trial and improvement on a spreadsheet

Example 21

The width of a rectangle is 2 cm less than the length. Use a trial and improvement method to find the length when the area of the rectangle is 30 cm². Your answer should be accurate to 2 dp.

Area = 30 cm² Width W
$W = L - 2$

Length L

Use L for the length and W for the width of the rectangle.

Put the length in column A, the width in column B and the area of the rectangle in column C.

Make sure your spreadsheet has at least 12 rows and 3 columns.

Use your spreadsheet to try lots of values for L.

For each value of L calculate a value for W using: $W = L - 2$

Then multiply each value of L by the corresponding value of W to find the area of each rectangle.

> This is much easier than it looks.
> Remember that the computer is doing all the really hard work.

Now you can look for the two areas which are nearest to 30 cm².

Use these answers to try new values for L and repeat the process until you achieve the accuracy you need.

Values of L from 0 to 10 in steps of 1

	A	B	C
1	L	W	LW
2	0	−2	0
3	1	−1	−1
4	2	0	0
5	3	1	3
6	4	2	8
7	5	3	15
8	6	4	24	too small
9	7	5	35	too big
10	8	6	48
11	9	7	63
12	10	8	80

Values: A2=0
Formulae: A3=A2 + 1
B2=A2 − 2
C2=A2 × B2

Values of L from 6 to 7 in steps of 0.1

	A	B	C
1	L	W	LW
2	6	4	24
3	6.1	4.1	25.01
4	6.2	4.2	26.04
5	6.3	4.3	27.09
6	6.4	4.4	28.16
7	6.5	4.5	29.25	too small
8	6.6	4.6	30.36	too big
9	6.7	4.7	31.49
10	6.8	4.8	32.64
11	6.9	4.9	33.81
12	7	5	35

Values: A2=6
Formulae: A3=A2 + 0.1
B2=A2 − 2
C2=A2 × B2

Values of L from 6.5 to 6.6 in steps of 0.01

	A	B	C
1	L	W	LW
2	6.5	4.5	29.25
3	6.51	4.51	29.360
4	6.52	4.52	29.470
5	6.53	4.53	29.580
6	6.54	4.54	29.691
7	6.55	4.55	29.802
8	6.56	4.56	29.913	too small
9	6.57	4.57	30.024	too big
10	6.58	4.58	30.136
11	6.59	4.59	30.248
12	6.6	4.6	30.36

Values: A2=6.5
Formulae: A3=A2 + 0.01
B2=A2 − 2
C2=A2 × B2

Values of L from 6.56 to 6.57 in steps of 0.001

	A	B	C
1	L	W	LW
2	6.56	4.56	29.913
3	6.561	4.561	29.924
4	6.562	4.562	29.935
5	6.563	4.563	29.946
6	6.564	4.564	29.958
7	6.565	4.565	29.969
8	6.566	4.566	29.980
9	6.567	4.567	29.991	too small
10	6.568	4.568	30.002	too big
11	6.569	4.569	30.013
12	6.57	4.57	30.024

Values: A2=6.56
Formulae: A3=A2 + 0.001
B2=A2 − 2
C2=A2 × B2

You can now see that the length L lies between 6.567 cm and 6.568 cm.

So $L = 6.57$ cm correct to 2 dp.

Examination practice paper

1 There were 3604 people watching Accrington Stanley
playing football last Saturday.
(a) Write this number in words.
(b) Write this number to the nearest hundred.

2 Work out the value of:
(a) $3a + b$ when $a = 4$ and $b = 5$
(b) cd when $c = 2$ and $d = 7$

3 (a) Write down the name of
these shapes:

(b) Draw in any lines of
symmetry that the shapes
may have.

(c) Write down any order of
rotational symmetry that
the shapes may have.

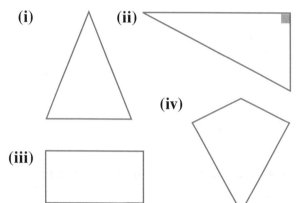

(i)   (ii)

(iv)

(iii)

4 Jenny and Simon threw a dice 30 times and obtained the
following scores:

5, 6, 1, 4, 3, 6, 3, 5, 3, 2, 4, 6, 5, 4, 3,
3, 2, 1, 3, 4, 6, 4, 6, 2, 1, 4, 5, 6, 3, 4

(a) Design a suitable table and use it to work out the
frequency of each score.
(b) Draw a bar graph to show your results.
(c) Work out the:
   (i) modal score
  (ii) mean score
 (iii) range.

5 In the local elections the following votes were cast.

George Evans 3641, Shenna Read 5643, Precious Davies 4904, Sybil Jones 3667

Arrange the votes cast in order, largest first.

6 Write down the value of
   (a) 4^3
   (b) $\sqrt{25}$

7 **(a)** Write down the two missing numbers in this number pattern.

          $3, 8, 13, \ldots, \ldots, 28$
   (b) Write down in words the rule that you used to work out your answers.
   (c) Work out the 20th member of the pattern.
   (d) Write down the algebraic rule to give the nth term of the pattern.

8 Here is a sketch of triangle ABC.
   (a) Draw a full size accurate drawing of the triangle.
   (b) Measure the size of angle B.
   (c) By taking suitable measurements from your drawing work out its:
     (i) perimeter
     (ii) area.

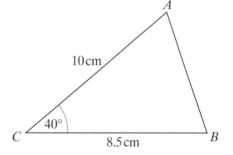

9 Jasmine has a bag containing 12 beads. 5 of them are white, 4 are black and the rest are red. If one bead is taken from the bag write down the probability that it will be:
   (a) white
   (b) not black
   (c) blue.

10 Work out the area of this shape by counting squares.

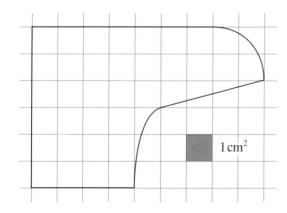

11 A coin and a dice are thrown at the same time. Make a list of all the possible outcomes of the event.

12 In this question do *not* use a calculator but show *all* of your working.
   (a) Simon buys 24 packets of stamps, each of which contains 144 stamps. How many stamps does he have in total?
   (b) The shopkeeper has a box with 600 stamps in it. He makes packets of stamps that each contain 36 stamps from the stamps in the box. How many packets of stamps can he make?

13 Solve these equations to find the value of the letter.
   (a) $2a + 3 = 9$
   (b) $4(2s - 5) = 7$
   (c) $2(3c + 4) = 5(2c - 7)$

14 Henri has the choice of buying the same training shoes in 3 different shops. Work out the cost of the shoes in each shop and give the name of the shop with the best buy.

Ben's shoes	Shoe Box	Sale o' Shoes
£30 with **25%** off	**£20** with **$17\frac{1}{2}\%$** VAT to be added	**£34** with **$\frac{1}{3}$** off

15 **(a)** Complete these tables for the lines
   $y = 2x - 1$ and $y = x^2 - 3$

	−3	−2	−1	0	1	2	3
$y = 2x - 1$	−7		−3		1		5

	−3	−2	−1	0	1	2	3
$y = x^2 - 3$	6		−2	−3			6

   (b) Use the tables to draw the graphs of the two lines. Use an x-axis labelled from −3 to +3 using a scale of 2 cm for one unit and a y-axis labelled from −8 to +6 using a scale of 1 cm for one unit.

16 Boris travelled 200 miles at an average speed of 50 miles per hour.
   (a) How long did the journey take him?

He completed the return journey in 4 hours 30 minutes.

   (b) At what average speed did he travel on the return journey?
   (c) How many kilometres was the whole journey?

17 On a copy of the probability line below mark the probability of the following events happening:
   (a) it snows in London in August, with an S
   (b) a coin when thrown comes down heads, with a C
   (c) you have been born, with a B.

0                              $\frac{1}{2}$ 1

18

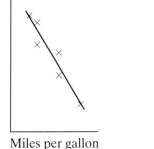

Graph A	Graph B	Graph C
Miles per gallon	Miles per gallon	Miles per gallon

   (a) For each of the three graphs write down the types of correlation they show.

The 3 scatter graphs connect the number of miles travelled on one gallon of petrol with 3 different measurements.

   (b) Write down possible measures for the vertical axes in Graphs A, B and C.

19 The diameter of each of the wheels on this rickshaw is 45 cm.

Work out the circumference of each wheel.

Formulae sheet: Foundation tier

Area of triangle $= \frac{1}{2} \times$ base $\times$ height

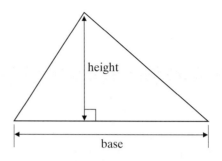

Circumference of circle $= \pi \times$ diameter

$= 2 \times \pi \times$ radius

Area of circle $= \pi \times (\text{radius})^2$

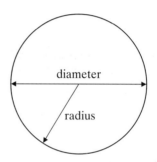

Volume of cuboid $=$ length $\times$ width $\times$ height

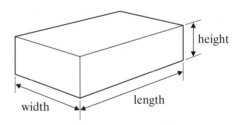

Answers

Unit 1 Number

Exercise 1A

1

	Ten thousands	Thousands	Hundreds	Tens	Units
(a)		4	x	x	x
(b)				3	x
(c)	x	x	1	x	x
(d)			x	x	9
(e)		x	x	0	x
(f)	x	x	4	x	x
(g)			7	7	7
(h)		6	x	x	6

Exercise 1B

1 (a) Thirty six (b) Ninety five (c) Five hundred and ninety eight
(d) Two hundred and forty six (e) Five thousand six hundred
and twenty three (f) One thousand two hundred and fifty one
2 (a) Seven hundred and nine (b) Eight hundred and ninety
(c) Six thousand and fifty four (d) Nine thousand two hundred
and one (e) Twenty six thousand and seven (f) Forty thousand
two hundred (g) Thirty two thousand (h) Seventy thousand
and ninety (i) Thirteen thousand four hundred and six
3 (a) Thirty thousand five hundred and thirteen
Nine million nine hundred and ten thousand
(b) Two thousand five hundred and seventy six
Four hundred and three thousand
(c) Five hundred and four thousand seven hundred and eighty two
Thirty seven million nine hundred thousand
(d) Ninety two thousand and eighty two
Nine million nine hundred and thirteen thousand
(e) Five hundred and forty seven thousand and twenty six
Fifty four million two hundred thousand
4 (a) France   (b) France
Spain   Spain
Portugal   Portugal
Belgium   Belgium
Luxembourg   Luxembourg
5 (a) 69   1010   2306   (b) 45 270   83 663   80 774
(c) 294 000   682 000   2 600 000   3 990 000
6 (a) 1984   (b) 1961   (c) 1982   (d) 1984
7 (a) 63   (b) 708   (c) 7000   (d) 18 600
(e) 75 000   (f) 809 000   (g) 4 000 000   (h) 1 001 000
(i) 9020   (j) 40 600
8 Ford Fiesta   9 010   Rover 623   19 435
Volks Polo   9 110   Ford Granada   20 270
Vaux Astra   10 530   Jaguar Sport   30 479
Cit Xantia   17 065   Marcos Mantera   31 007
Volvo 940   17 815   Merc Benz   31 394
9 (a) 7   23   56   93   234   469   614
(b) Four hundred and sixty nine

Exercise 1C

1 43   2 80   3 331   4 270   5 45   6 96
7 84   8 216   9 401   10 416

Exercise 1D

1 1003   2 3166   3 305   4 12
5 (a) 19   (b) 17   (c) 36
6 (a) 88   (b) 59   (c) 133
7 (a) £21 898   (b) £22 960   (c) £17 874

Exercise 1E

1 1080   2 4494   3 456   4 4558   5 2268
6 (a) 1500 m   (b) 2800 m   (c) 18 000 m   56 000 m
7 36   108   216
8 (a) 204 miles   (b) 2040 miles   (c) 10 608 miles

Exercise 1F

1 (a) 21   (b) 15   (c) 40   (d) 20   (e) 14
2 £480   3 (a) 10   (b) 30   (c) 36
4 (a) 7   (b) 13   (c) 36
5 (a) 12   (b) 41   (c) 80

Exercise 1G

1 33   2 368   3 2016   4 49
5 (a) 3 (b) 2   (c) 8   (d) 12
6 (a) 90   (b) 19
7 (a) 561   (b) 23   (c) 6   (d) 1683
8 (a) 576   (b) 458

Exercise 1H

1 (a) 60   (b) 60   (c) 190   (d) 190   (e) 990
(f) 2410
2 (a) 300   (b) 700   (c) 2400   (d) 3100   (e) 8800
(f) 29 500
3 (a) 2000   (b) 36 000   (c) 29 000   (d) 322 000
(e) 717 000   (f) 2 247 000
4 (a) 1030   1020   900   960   990   820
(b) 83 700   80 800   67 000   65 900   53 300   45 300
(c) 30   30   20   30   40   30

5

Area	Population
132 000	9 800 000
301 000	57 400 000
34 000	14 300 000
357 000	80 200 000
70 000	3 500 000

6 (a) 150 to nearest fifty   (b) 300 to nearest hundred
(c) 6300 to nearest hundred   (d) 35 000 to nearest thousand
(e) £45 000 000 to nearest million pounds
(f) 13 300 to nearest hundred

Exercise 1I

1 (a) $\dfrac{60 \times 60}{30} = 120$ (b) $\dfrac{200 \times 300}{150} = 400$
(c) $\dfrac{10 \times 30 \times 100}{300} = 100$ (d) $\dfrac{2000}{10 \times 100} = 2$
(e) $\dfrac{500}{10 \times 50} = 1$ (f) $\dfrac{100 \times 90}{20 \times 30} = 15$

2 (a) 378.35294 $\dfrac{200 \times 100}{50} = 400$
(b) 22.155242 $\dfrac{10 \times 1000}{500} = 20$
(c) 107.91304 $\dfrac{140 \times 50}{70} = 100$
(d) 9.2592593 $\dfrac{1000}{10 \times 10} = 10$
(e) 5.6772083 $\dfrac{5200}{130 \times 10} = 4$
(f) 6.3631905 $\dfrac{900 \times 80}{40 \times 300} = 6$

3 (a) $50 \times 100 = 5000$ (b) Bigger – numbers both rounded up.
4 $1350 \div 50 = 27$ 5 $900 \times 400 \div 1000 = 360$. Answer wrong
6 $16 \times 2 \times 195 = 30 \times 200 = 6000$ 7 $120 \times 40 \times 50 = 240\,000$

Exercise 1J

1 2 18 1110 536 500 000 2 537 811 225
3 17 19 23 29 31 37 41
4 (a) 450 (b) 71 (c) 71

Exercise 1K

1 (a) 3 or 9 (b) 2, 3, 4, 6, 8, 12 or 24 (c) 2, 4, 8, 16 or 32
(d) 5, 11 or 55 (e) 2, 3, 4, 6, 9, 12, 18, 27 or 54
(f) 5, 25, 125 or 625
2 1, 2, 3, 4, 6, 12
3 (a) 1, 2, 4, 8, 16, 32 (b) 1, 2, 4, 5, 8, 10, 20, 25, 40, 50, 100, 200
(c) 1, 2, 4, 5, 10, 17, 20, 34, 68, 85, 170, 340
(d) 1, 2, 4, 5, 10, 20, 25, 40, 50, 100, 200, 250, 500, 1000
4 9, 18, 27 . . . 5 99
6 (a) 54, 60, 66 etc. (b) 1020, 1040, 1060 etc
(c) 105, 120, 135 etc.
7 (a) 16, 24, 32 etc. (b) 150, 300, 450 etc.
(c) 3, 15, 27 e.g.
8
10	20	30	40	50
60	70	80	90	100
110	120	130	140	150
160	170	180	190	200
210	220	230	240	250
(f) 180

Exercise 1L

1 (a) 16, 25, 36 (b) 100, 400, 900 (c) 81, 144, 196
(d) 64, 125, 216 (e) 312, 1000, 8000 (f) 64, 125, 216
2
①	2	3	④	5	6	7	8̶	⑨	10
11	12	13	14	15	⑯	17	18	19	20
21	22	23	24	㉕	26	2̶7̶	28	29	30
31	32	33	34	35	㊱	37	38	39	40
41	42	43	44	45	46	47	48	㊾	50
51	52	53	54	55	56	57	58	59	60
61	62	63	6̶4̶	65	66	67	68	69	70
71	72	73	74	75	76	77	78	79	80
㊱81	82	83	84	85	86	87	88	89	90
91	92	93	94	95	96	97	98	99	⑩⑩
(d) 1 and 64

Exercise 1M

1 (a) 5, –10 (b) 0, –13 (c) 13, –15 (d) –2, –21
2 (a) 0, –1 (b) –2, –5 (c) –5, –9 (d) –7, –12
(e) –15, –24 (f) –1, 2
3 (a) 7 (b) –3 (c) –1 (d) –5 (e) –6 (f) 3
(g) 0 (h) –7 (i) –5 (j) 0
4 (a) –40 (b) –70 (c) 30 (d) –30 (e) –160
(f) 270 (g) –30 (h) 0 (i) 120 (j) 0
5 (a) Minsk (b) Minsk (c) Tripoli
6 18°C 7 6°C

Unit 2 Algebra 1

Exercise 2A

1 $a + 3$ 2 $x + 4$ 3 $x + 7$ 4 $b - 2$ 5 $c - 3$
6 $q - p$ 7 $x + y$ 8 $a + 4$ 9 $3b - 6$

Exercise 2B

1 $6a$ 2 $4p$ 3 $5b$ 4 $6q$ 5 $2c$ 6 $3n$ 7 $5w$
8 $5y$ 9 $7z$ 10 $7a$ 11 $5b$ 12 $8p$
13 $a + a + a + a$ 14 $p + p$ 15 $p + p + p + p + p$
16 $a + a + a + a + a + a + a$ 17 $y + y$ 18 $q + q + q + q$
19 $c + c + c$ 20 $d + d + d + d + d$
21 $a + a + a + a + a + a + a + a + a + a$
22 $h + h + h + h + h$ 23 $g + g + g + g + g + g$
24 $z + z + z + z$

Exercise 2C

1 $6a$ 2 $7b$ 3 $7c$ 4 $2d$ 5 $4e$ 6 $4f$ 7 $7a$
8 $8a$ 9 $12c$ 10 $14g$ 11 $4g$ 12 $3s$ 13 $14q$
14 $18p$ 15 $6p$

Exercise 2D

1 $7a + 6b$ 2 $9m + 7n$ 3 $p + 5q$ 4 $16e + 6c$
5 $2y + 12p$ 6 $4a + 13g$ 7 $9k + q$ 8 $d + 10f$
9 $3h + 10$ 10 $5f + 2e$ 11 $4g + 7n$ 12 $4 + 2g$
13 $14a$ 14 $5b$ 15 $4c$ 16 $5d$ 17 $7a + b$
18 $6c + 8b$ 19 $p + 1$ 20 $14y + 4z$ 21 $17a$
22 0 23 $7s$ 24 a

Exercise 2E

1 $p \times q$ 2 $r \times s \times t$ 3 $2 \times e \times f$ 4 $5 \times a \times b \times c$
5 $7 \times k \times l \times m$ 6 $9 \times a \times b$ 7 $15 \times a \times b \times c$
8 $3 \times p \times q \times r$ 9 $16 \times s \times t$ 10 $6 \times y \times z$
11 $8 \times d \times e \times f \times g$ 12 $20 \times a \times b \times c \times d$ 13 pq
14 efg 15 rst 16 $2ef$ 17 $2cd$ 18 hds 19 $2sf$
20 $3def$ 21 $4pq$ 22 $3hj$ 23 $5kv$ 24 $12rst$

Exercise 2F

1 $8ab$ 2 $15cd$ 3 $12pq$ 4 $20st$ 5 $30fg$
6 $28pq$ 7 $36mn$ 8 $24abc$ 9 $24rst$ 10 $20pq$
11 $12ab$ 12 $40pqr$ 13 $12st$ 14 $28pt$ 15 $45ce$
16 $64gqr$ 17 $48dr$ 18 $60st$ 19 $30ty$ 20 $40rst$

Exercise 2G

1 (a) b^3 (b) p^2 (c) r^7 (d) s^5 (e) q^4 (f) c^5
2 (a) a^4 (b) s^3 (c) t^6 (d) v^3 (e) f^5 (f) y^5
3 (a) $a \times a \times a$ (b) $a \times a \times a \times a$ (c) $d \times d$
(d) $e \times e \times e \times e \times e$ (e) $f \times f \times f \times f$
(f) $p \times p \times p \times p \times p$ (g) $a \times a \times a \times a \times a \times a \times a$
(h) $s \times s$ (i) $k \times k \times k \times k \times k \times k$ (j) $n \times n \times n$
(k) $n \times n \times n \times n \times n \times n \times n$
(l) $a \times a \times a \times a \times a \times a \times a \times a \times a \times a \times a$
4 (a) a^5 (b) c^6 (c) d^2 (d) e^3 (e) f^7
5 (a) 9 (b) 8 (c) 16 (d) 625 (e) 32
(f) 64 (g) 16 (h) 128 (i) 216 (j) 125
(k) 25 (l) 100 000

Exercise 2H

1 (a) 9 (b) 1 (c) 25 (d) 13 (e) 21 (f) 15
(g) 6 (h) 4 (i) 8 (j) 5 (k) 6 (l) 2
(m) 1 (n) 5 (o) 4
2 (a) $4 + 5 = 9$ (b) $4 \times 5 = 20$ (c) $(2 + 3) \times 4 = 20$
(d) $(3 - 2) \times 5 = 5$ (e) $(5 - 2) \times 3 = 9$ (f) $5 \times 2 \times 3 = 30$
(g) $5 \times 4 + 5 + 2 = 27$ (h) $5 \times 4 + 5 - 2 = 23$

Exercise 2I

1. $2p + 2q$ 2. $3c + 3d$ 3. $5y - 5n$ 4. $3t + 3u$
5. $14p + 7q$ 6. $6a - 4b$ 7. $8a + 4b$ 8. $3a - 6b$
9. $12r - 15s$ 10. $10a - 70b$ 11. $24s + 16t$
12. $30p + 20q - 10r$ 13. $36a + 48b$ 14. $28s - 35t$
15. $15a - 12b + 6c$

Exercise 2J

1. $5a + 5b$ 2. $11a + 6b$ 3. $18a - b$ 4. $7p + 7p$
5. $26a + 2c$ 6. $18p$ 7. $44t + s$ 8. $2d + 33e$
9. $7z + 9b$ 10. $8a + 11b + c$ 11. $17a - b$ 12. $12p + 4q$
13. $22a$ 14. $5g + 24h$ 15. $21a + 5b + 10c$

Exercise 2K

1. (a) 5 (b) 17 (c) 10 (d) 4 (e) 4 (f) 4
   (g) 0 (h) 14
2. (a) $-p - q$ (b) $-p + q$ (c) $-a - b - c$ (d) $-a - b + c$
   (e) $-r - s$ (f) $-r + s$ (g) $-p - q + r$ (h) $-p + q - r$

Exercise 2L

1. $3a + 2b$ 2. $4p + q$ 3. $3a - 7$ 4. $y - 4z$
5. $7r + 10s$ 6. 7 7. $6s + 7t$ 8. $6a - 11b$ 9. $5n$
10. $12h - 23k$ 11. c 12. $a - 5b$

Exercise 2M

1. $3a + 4b$ 2. $4p + 3q$ 3. $3a + 17$ 4. $y - 2z$
5. $7r + 14s$ 6. 23 7. $6s + 23t$ 8. $6a + 19b$ 9. $7n$
10. $12h - 7k$ 11. $c + 12d$ 12. $a + 5b$

Exercise 2N

1. $5a$ 2. a^6 3. $6p$ 4. p^5 5. $11p$ 6. $7k$
7. $11s$ 8. $13t$ 9. $-2d$ 10. $-3j$ 11. $2a + 2b$
12. $15p - 5q$ 13. $4s + 8t$ 14. $36p - 8p + 20r$
15. $23m + 13n$ 16. $18s + 2t$ 17. $12a - 23b$ 18. $4p + 11d$
19. $9a - 2b$ 20. $4b$ 21. $11t - 3s$ 22. $5p - 12q$ 23. $5n$
24. $25a - 22b$ 25. $-a - 7b$

Exercise 2O

1. 12, 15; +3 2. 25, 30; +5 3. 5, 6; +1 4. 35, 42; +7
5. 18, 24; +6 6. 40, 50; +10 7. 13, 15; +2
8. 16, 19; +3 9. 23, 28; +5 10. 17, 21; +4

Exercise 2P

1. 9, 6; –3 2. 12, 8; –4 3. 15, 10; –5 4. 21, 14; –7
5. 13, 10; –3 6. 17, 12; –5 7. 13, 11; –2 8. 13, 9; –4
9. 18, 13; –5 10. 17, 10; –7

Exercise 2Q

1. 27, 81; × 3 2. 64; × 4 3. 5, 625; × 5
4. 1000, 10 000; × 10 5. 24, 48; × 2 6. 54, 162; × 3
7. 128, 512; × 4 8. 2000, 20 000; × 10 9. 250; × 5
10. 375; × 5

Exercise 2R

1. 16, 2; ÷ 2 2. 16; ÷ 4 3. 1000, 100; ÷ 10 4. 25; ÷ 5
5. 12, 6; ÷ 2 6. 18, 6; ÷ 3 7. 32, 8; ÷ 4 8. 200, 20; ÷ 10
9. 10; ÷ 5 10. 15; ÷ 5

Exercise 2S

1. add 2, 11 2. add 4, 21 3. cube numbers, 1296 4. ?
5. add 3, 17 6. add 4, 23 7. add two previous numbers, 26
8. add two previous numbers, 39 9. add 2, 15 10. add 3, 19
11. add 5, 27 12. add 5, 28

Exercise 2T

1. $3n$, 60 2. $5n$, 100 3. n, 20 4. $7n$, 140
5. $6(n - 1)$, 114 6. $10n$, 200 7. $2n + 3$, 43 8. $3n + 1$, 61
9. $5n - 2$, 98 10. $4n - 3$, 77

Unit 3 Angles and turning

Exercise 3A

1. (a), (b), (c) and (f).
2. (a) South (b) North (c) West (d) West.
3. (a) North-West (b) North-East (c) South-East.
4. (a) $\frac{1}{4}$ turn (b) $\frac{1}{2}$ turn (c) $\frac{1}{4}$ turn.

Exercise 3B

1. a = acute 2. b = right 3. c = obtuse
4. d = right, e = acute
5. f = obtuse, g = acute, h = obtuse, i = acute
6. j = obtuse, k = acute.
7. 50° 8. 145° 9. 40° 10. 135° 11. 85° 12. 90°.

Exercise 3C

1.   2.

3.   4.

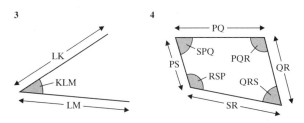

Exercise 3D

1 $ABC = 50°$ 2 $EFG = 134°$
3 $SPQ = 142°, PQR = 65°, QRS = 98°, RSP = 55°$
4 $ZXY = 62°, XYZ = 80°, YZX = 38°$
5 $ABC = 49°, BCA = 84°, CAB = 47°$
6 $RST = 124°, STU = 59°, TUR = 121°, URS = 56°$
7 $RPQ = 105°, PQR = 45°, QRP = 30°$
8 $ZXY = 47°, XYZ = 53°, YZX = 80°$

Exercise 3F

1 $a = 85°$ 2 $b = 102°$ 3 $c = 46°$ 4 $d = 99°$
5 $e = 60°$ 6 $f = 45°$

Exercise 3G

1 $a = 90°$ 2 $b = 120°, c = 60°, d = 60°$ 3 $e = 38°$
4 $f = 261°$ 5 $g = 33°, h = 147°, i = 147°$
6 $j = 132°, k = 48°, i = 48°$ 7 $m = 135°$
8 $n = 60°, p = 60°, q = 120°$ 9 $r = 36°.$

Exercise 3H

1 $a = 30°$ 2 $b = 70°$ 3 $c = 97°$ 4 $e = 25°$
5 $f = 74°$ 6 $g = 66°$ 7 $h = 40°$ 8 $i = 85°$ 9 $j = 60°$

Exercise 3I

1 A/B C/E D/F G/H I/J K/L

Unit 4 Fractions

Exercise 4A

1 $\frac{1}{2}, \frac{1}{2}; \frac{1}{4}, \frac{3}{4}; \frac{2}{5}, \frac{3}{5}; \frac{3}{10}, \frac{7}{10}; \frac{5}{8}, \frac{3}{8}; \frac{4}{9}, \frac{5}{9}$

2 (a) (b)

(c)   (d)

3 (a)   (b)   (c)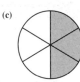

Exercise 4B

1 (a) $\frac{15}{28}$ (b) $\frac{13}{28}$ 2 (a) 75 (b) $\frac{28}{75}$ (c) $\frac{47}{75}$
3 (a) $\frac{37}{51}$ (b) $\frac{10}{51}$ (c) $\frac{4}{51}$ 4 (a) $\frac{198}{217}$ (b) $\frac{19}{217}$
5 (a) 16 (b) $\frac{7}{16}$ (c) $\frac{3}{16}$ (d) $\frac{5}{16}$ (e) $\frac{1}{16}$
6 (a) 17 (b) $\frac{5}{17}$ (c) $\frac{6}{17}$ (d) $\frac{4}{17}$ (e) $\frac{2}{17}$
7 (a) $\frac{6}{11}$ (b) $\frac{4}{11}$ (c) $\frac{1}{11}$

Exercise 4C

1 (a) $2\frac{1}{2}$ (b) $1\frac{3}{4}$ (c) $1\frac{2}{7}$ (d) $1\frac{3}{8}$ (e) $1\frac{1}{8}$
(f) $3\frac{1}{5}$ (g) $2\frac{3}{10}$ (h) $4\frac{4}{5}$ (i) $2\frac{2}{7}$ (j) $2\frac{2}{5}$
(k) $6\frac{2}{3}$ (l) $1\frac{1}{9}$ (m) $9\frac{3}{4}$ (n) $5\frac{2}{5}$ (p) $2\frac{8}{9}$
(q) $1\frac{7}{10}$
2 (a) $\frac{3}{2}$ (b) $\frac{11}{2}$ (c) $\frac{11}{4}$ (d) $\frac{5}{3}$ (e) $\frac{13}{4}$ (f) $\frac{22}{5}$
(g) $\frac{37}{10}$ (h) $\frac{26}{5}$ (i) $\frac{31}{4}$ (j) $\frac{9}{4}$ (k) $\frac{19}{10}$ (l) $\frac{28}{3}$
(m) $\frac{17}{6}$ (n) $\frac{43}{8}$ (p) $\frac{29}{8}$ (q) $\frac{109}{100}$

Exercise 4D

1 (a) $\frac{2}{3}$ (b) $\frac{1}{2}$ (c) $\frac{1}{2}$ (d) $\frac{1}{3}$ (e) $\frac{2}{5}$ (f) $\frac{2}{3}$
(g) $\frac{2}{3}$ (h) $\frac{3}{4}$ (i) $\frac{7}{11}$ (j) $\frac{6}{7}$ (k) $\frac{3}{4}$ (l) $\frac{5}{6}$
2 (a) $\frac{2}{4}, \frac{1}{2}; \frac{2}{8}, \frac{1}{4}; \frac{4}{10}, \frac{2}{5}; \frac{3}{12}, \frac{1}{4}; \frac{3}{9}, \frac{1}{3}; \frac{6}{16}, \frac{3}{8}$
3 (a) $\frac{2}{7}$ (b) $\frac{5}{7}$ 4 (a) $\frac{2}{7}$ (b) $\frac{1}{2}$ (c) $\frac{3}{14}$
5 (a) $\frac{8}{15}$ (b) $\frac{1}{6}$ (c) $\frac{1}{5}$ (d) $\frac{1}{10}$

Exercise 4E

1 (a) 35 (b) £26 (c) 24 kg (d) 64 (e) £21
(f) 45p (g) £1.70 (h) 63p (i) £2.80
2 (a) 34 (b) 51
3 (a) $130\,000$ (b) $30\,000$ (c) $40\,000$ 4 46
5 £74.40 6 375 kg
7 140 ham, 224 salad, 70 tuna, 126 cheese
8 (a) 305 (b) 427 (c) 2318
9 (a) 320 (b) 120 (c) 40

Exercise 4F

1 (a) $\frac{1}{2}, \frac{5}{10}, \frac{50}{100}, \frac{4}{8}, \frac{6}{12}, \frac{3}{6}$ (b) $\frac{2}{3}, \frac{4}{6}, \frac{6}{9}, \frac{40}{60}, \frac{60}{90}, \frac{20}{30}$
(c) $\frac{7}{10}, \frac{14}{20}, \frac{35}{50}, \frac{70}{100}, \frac{1400}{2000}, \frac{28}{40}$
(d) $\frac{3}{4}, \frac{12}{16}, \frac{15}{20}, \frac{21}{28}, \frac{300}{400}, \frac{90}{120}$
(e) $\frac{1}{8}, \frac{3}{24}, \frac{4}{32}, \frac{8}{64}, \frac{60}{480}, \frac{7}{56}$
2 (a) $\frac{2}{10}, \frac{3}{15}, \frac{4}{20}, \frac{5}{25}, \frac{6}{30} \cdots$ (b) $\frac{4}{10}, \frac{6}{15}, \frac{8}{20}, \frac{10}{25}, \frac{12}{30} \cdots$
(c) $\frac{10}{12}, \frac{15}{18}, \frac{20}{24}, \frac{25}{30}, \frac{30}{36} \cdots$ (d) $\frac{14}{16}, \frac{21}{24}, \frac{28}{32}, \frac{35}{40}, \frac{42}{48} \cdots$
(e) $\frac{6}{40}, \frac{9}{60}, \frac{12}{80}, \frac{15}{100}, \frac{18}{120} \cdots$
3 (a) $\frac{3}{6}, \frac{2}{6}$ (b) (i) $\frac{12}{30}, \frac{15}{30}$ (ii) $\frac{7}{70}, \frac{10}{70}$
(iii) $\frac{3}{12}, \frac{10}{12}$ (iv) $\frac{5}{10}, \frac{6}{10}$ (v) $\frac{16}{24}, \frac{3}{24}$ (vi) $\frac{15}{20}, \frac{12}{20}$

Exercise 4G

1 (a) $\frac{3}{6}$ (b) $\frac{1}{7}$ (c) $\frac{5}{6}$ (d) $\frac{3}{5}$ (e) $\frac{2}{3}$ (f) $\frac{3}{4}$
2 (a) $\frac{2}{10}, \frac{2}{5}, \frac{1}{2}, \frac{3}{4}, \frac{7}{8}$

Exercise 4H

1 (a) $\frac{7}{8}$ (b) $\frac{7}{9}$ (c) $\frac{1}{2}$ (d) $\frac{8}{9}$ (e) $\frac{3}{4}$ (f) $\frac{5}{8}$
(g) $1\frac{3}{8}$ (h) $\frac{5}{6}$ (i) $1\frac{1}{6}$ (j) $\frac{7}{10}$ (k) $1\frac{1}{3}$ (l) $1\frac{1}{10}$
2 (a) $\frac{19}{24}$ (b) $\frac{17}{20}$ (c) $\frac{31}{36}$ (d) $1\frac{31}{40}$ (e) $\frac{17}{30}$
(f) $1\frac{1}{12}$ (g) $\frac{23}{24}$ (h) $1\frac{1}{18}$
3 (a) $\frac{5}{8}$ (b) $\frac{17}{30}$ (c) $\frac{33}{40}$ (d) $\frac{31}{36}$ (e) $1\frac{11}{42}$
(f) $1\frac{13}{70}$ (g) $1\frac{11}{30}$ (h) $1\frac{7}{20}$
4 (a) $3\frac{1}{6}$ (b) $5\frac{3}{4}$ (c) $4\frac{1}{8}$ (d) $9\frac{1}{12}$ (e) $5\frac{3}{16}$
(f) $3\frac{2}{3}$ (g) $7\frac{1}{6}$ (h) $7\frac{4}{15}$ 5 $\frac{1}{2}$ 6 $\frac{49}{80}$

Exercise 4I

1 (a) $\frac{2}{11}$ (b) $\frac{2}{9}$ (c) $\frac{6}{8} = \frac{3}{4}$ (d) $\frac{2}{12} = \frac{1}{6}$
2 (a) $\frac{1}{4}$ (b) $\frac{1}{8}$ (c) $\frac{1}{8}$ (d) $\frac{5}{8}$ (e) $\frac{1}{2}$ (f) $\frac{1}{4}$
  (g) $\frac{1}{2}$ (h) $\frac{1}{5}$
3 (a) $\frac{11}{24}$ (b) $\frac{9}{20}$ (c) $\frac{13}{36}$ (d) $\frac{7}{18}$ (e) $\frac{13}{30}$ (f) $\frac{2}{5}$
  (g) $\frac{9}{20}$ (h) $\frac{7}{40}$
4 (a) $\frac{1}{6}$ (b) $\frac{7}{24}$ (c) $\frac{1}{30}$ (d) $\frac{4}{15}$ (e) $\frac{2}{15}$ (f) $\frac{3}{20}$
  (g) $\frac{11}{30}$ (h) $\frac{3}{20}$
5 (a) $5\frac{3}{20}$ (b) $7\frac{1}{6}$ (c) $1\frac{1}{4}$ (d) $2\frac{1}{5}$ (e) $2\frac{7}{10}$
  (f) $\frac{9}{10}$ (g) $\frac{3}{4}$ (h) $2\frac{4}{5}$
6 $\frac{9}{16}$ 7 $\frac{3}{5}$ 8 $\frac{1}{12}$ acre

Exercise 4J

1 (a) $\frac{3}{8}$ (b) $\frac{3}{32}$ (c) $\frac{8}{25}$ (d) $\frac{9}{32}$ (e) $\frac{5}{36}$ (f) $\frac{21}{40}$
  (g) $\frac{9}{50}$ (h) $\frac{4}{9}$
2 (a) $\frac{2}{5}$ (b) $\frac{3}{5}$ (c) $\frac{1}{2}$ (d) $\frac{6}{25}$ (e) $\frac{5}{8}$ (f) $\frac{1}{8}$
  (g) $\frac{4}{15}$ (h) $\frac{4}{7}$
3 (a) $3\frac{1}{2}$ (b) $3\frac{1}{3}$ (c) $4\frac{4}{5}$ (d) 6 (e) 14
  (f) 6 (g) 4 (h) 10
4 (a) $1\frac{5}{8}$ (b) 3 (c) $1\frac{1}{9}$ (d) $1\frac{3}{4}$ (e) $5\frac{1}{4}$
  (f) $5\frac{13}{24}$ (g) $4\frac{4}{5}$ (h) $5\frac{1}{4}$
5 Jamie $11\frac{1}{4}$, Claire $8\frac{3}{4}$ 6 $82\frac{1}{2}$ mins 7 $7\frac{5}{16}$ cm²
8 $47\frac{1}{4}$ cubic inches
9 (a) $12\frac{4}{7}$ cm (b) $20\frac{3}{7}$ cm (c) $2\frac{5}{14}$ cm

Exercise 4K

1 (a) $1\frac{1}{3}$ (b) $\frac{3}{4}$ (c) $1\frac{1}{2}$ (d) $\frac{5}{7}$ (e) $3\frac{1}{3}$
  (f) $1\frac{7}{8}$ (g) $1\frac{1}{9}$ (h) $\frac{7}{8}$
2 (a) 5 (b) $1\frac{1}{10}$ (c) $1\frac{2}{3}$ (d) $\frac{39}{76}$ (e) $\frac{1}{2}$ (f) 2
  (g) $\frac{17}{27}$ (h) $\frac{21}{40}$
3 (a) $\frac{3}{32}$ (b) $\frac{5}{12}$ (c) $\frac{3}{30}$ (d) $\frac{4}{25}$ (e) $\frac{1}{3}$
  (f) $\frac{13}{24}$ (g) $\frac{17}{60}$ (h) $\frac{1}{6}$
4 (a) 16 (b) 16 (c) 10 (d) $9\frac{1}{7}$ (e) 5
  (f) $1\frac{5}{7}$ (g) 15 (h) 24

Unit 5 Two-dimensional shapes

Exercise 5A

1 (c) 2, 2 (d) 90° (e) 4 (f) 90°, equal
  (g) equal, 90° (h) sides, equal (i) opposite, equal,
  opposite (j) sides, equal, opposite (k) parallel
2 (a) trapezium (b) parallelogram (c) trapezium
  (d) kite (e) rhombus (f) trapezium
3 (b) L (c) B, S, Q, T (d) rectangle (e) E, *M*
  (f) F, K (g) P (h) isosceles (i) L
  (j) C, G, H, U, R

Exercise 5C

6 EG = 5 cm ± 2 mm
7 XZ = 5.8 cm ± 2 mm, YZ = 4.5 cm ± 2 mm.

Exercise 5D

1 A and D 2 B and D 3 B and D
4 A and D, B and C 5 B and C 6 A and B

Exercise 5E

Type of polygon	Sum of interior	Sum of exterior
Equilateral triangle	180°	360°
Isosceles triangle	180°	360°
Parallelogram	360°	360°
Pentagon	540°	360°

Exercise 5F

1 (a) 45° (b) 108° (c) 144°, 36° 2 15 sides
3 8°, 45 sides 4 Rectangle, kite, trapezium, rhombus
5 Rhombus, kite and trapezium

Unit 6 Decimals

Exercise 6A

1

	Tens	Units	.	Tenths	Hundredths	Thousandths
(a)	4	1	.	6		
(b)		4	.	1	6	
(c)	3	4	.	6		
(d)		1	.	4	6	3
(e)		0	.	6	4	3
(f)		1	.	0	0	5
(g)		5	.	0	1	
(h)		0	.	0	8	6

2 (a) Unit (b) Tenth (c) Tenth (d) Hundredth
  (e) Ten (f) Thousandth (g) Hundredth
  (h) Ten thousandth (i) Hundredth (j) Tenth
  (k) Thousandth (l) Hundredth
3 £1.09, £1.13, £1.18, £1.20, £1.29, £1.31
4 Latif, Sheila, Ira, Jean, Naomi, Rachel.
5 52.037, 53.027, 53.072, 53.207, 53.702, 57.320
6 0.0014, 0.0015, 0.002, 0.014, 0.02, 1.5

Exercise 6B

1 (a) 8 (b) 13 (c) 14 (d) 6 (e) 11 (f) 20
  (g) 1 (h) 20 (i) 1 (j) 100 (k) 20 (l) 2
2 (a) 3.6 (b) 5.3 (c) 0.1 (d) 9.3 (e) 10.7 (f) 8.0
  (g) 2.1 (h) 0.5 (i) 2.5 (j) 125.7 (k) 0.1 (l) 9.9
3 (a) 14 mm (b) 80 m (c) 1 kg (d) £204
  (e) 4 lb (f) 0 tonne (g) 11 g (h) 8 min

Exercise 6C

1 6.1 2 3.25 3 68.9 4 126.02 5 1.0
6 18.725 7 19.8 8 11.001 9 158.14 10 1.914
11 118.17 12 5.311

Exercise 6D

1 31.97 2 28.71 3 19.122 4 18.326 5 11.064
6 31.006 7 15.0976 8 178.585

Exercise 6E

1 6.2 2 4.14 3 14.1 4 97.3 5 0.11 6 0.35
7 6.19 8 11.14 9 0.9 10 4.07 11 14.03
12 13.25 13 1.225 14 11.649 15 2.254 16 168.58

Exercise 6F

1	**(a)**	£13.50	**(b)**	£5.48	**(c)**	£5.20	**(d)**	£1.20
2	**(a)**	30.4	**(b)**	3.04	**(c)**	0.304	**(d)**	11.25
	(e)	1.125	**(f)**	0.1125	**(g)**	1.125	**(h)**	0.01125
	(i)	0.001125						
3	**(a)**	172.2	**(b)**	0.0945	**(c)**	0.0144	**(d)**	0.04
	(e)	0.9	**(f)**	0.0012				
4	**(a)**	64.2	**(b)**	642	**(c)**	6.42	**(d)**	562.3
	(e)	56.23	**(f)**	0.5623				

Figures have moved one column left.

5	**(a)**	4.5	**(b)**	45.0	**(c)**	450	**(d)**	2.03
	(e)	20.3	**(f)**	203				

Figures have moved two columns left.

Exercise 6G

1	**(a)**	16.12	**(b)**	0.633	**(c)**	14.84	**(d)**	34.221
	(e)	5.027	**(f)**	0.046				
2	**(a)**	3.45	**(b)**	0.345	**(c)**	0.0345	**(d)**	7.8
	(e)	0.78	**(f)**	0.078	**(g)**	6.5	**(h)**	0.65	**(i)**	0.065

Figures have moved right by number of noughts in the division.

3 15 jugs   **4** £15.40

Exercise 6H

1	3.1	**2**	3.6	**3**	1.7	**4**	1.5	**5**	4.3	**6**	2.7
7	10.7	**8**	1.01	**9**	2.5	**10**	52				

Exercise 6I

1	**(a)**	0.6	**(b)**	0.5	**(c)**	0.7	**(d)**	0.35	**(e)**	0.16
	(f)	0.06	**(g)**	0.875	**(h)**	0.45	**(i)**	0.76		
	(j)	0.3125	**(k)**	0.125	**(l)**	0.54	**(m)**	0.09		
	(n)	0.065	**(o)**	0.6666...	**(p)**	0.95				

2 **(a)** $\frac{3}{10}$ **(b)** $\frac{37}{100}$ **(c)** $\frac{93}{100}$ **(d)** $\frac{137}{1000}$ **(e)** $\frac{293}{1000}$
   (f) $\frac{7}{100}$ **(g)** $\frac{59}{100}$ **(h)** $\frac{3}{1000}$ **(i)** $\frac{3}{100000}$ **(j)** $\frac{13}{10000}$
   (k) $\frac{77}{100}$ **(l)** $\frac{77}{1000}$ **(m)** $\frac{39}{100}$ **(n)** $\frac{41}{10000}$ **(o)** $\frac{19}{1000}$
   (p) $\frac{31}{1000}$

Unit 7 Measure 1

Exercise 7A

1	**(a)**	1.8 m	**(b)**	1.2 m	**(c)**	2.5 m	**(d)**	1.5 m
2	**(a)**	3 m	**(b)**	10 m	**(c)**	6 m		
3	**(a)**	7 m	**(b)**	7 m	**(c)**	0.9 m		
4	**(a)**	3 m	**(b)**	2.5 m	**(c)**	10 m		

Exercise 7B

Question	Metric	Imperial
1	570 ml	1 pint
2	300 ml	$\frac{1}{2}$ pint
3	300 ml	$\frac{1}{2}$ pint
4	100 ml	$\frac{1}{8}$ pint
5	300 ml	$\frac{1}{2}$ pint
6	45 l	12 gallons
7	9 l	2 gallons
8	90 l	20 gallons

Exercise 7C

Question	Metric	Imperial
1	5 kg	11 pounds
2	200 g	$\frac{1}{2}$ pound
3	2 kg	4 pounds
4	100 g	$\frac{1}{4}$ pound
5	1 kg	2 pounds
6	200 g	$\frac{1}{2}$ pound
7	1 kg	2 pounds
8	100 g	$\frac{1}{4}$ pound
9	30 g	1 ounce
10	2 kg	4.5 pounds

Exercise 7D

1	**(a)**	Not sensible, 1.8 m	**(b)**	Not sensible, 1.8 m
	(c)	Not sensible, 7 m by 6 m	**(d)**	Not sensible, 2 kg
	(e)	Not sensible, 300 ml	**(f)**	Could be sensible
2	**(a)**	Sensible	**(b)**	Sensible	**(c)**	Sensible
	(d)	Not sensible, 300 ml	**(e)**	Not sensible, 300 km?
	(f)	Not sensible, 10 g?		
3	**(a)**	Sensible	**(b)**	Not sensible, 80 km/h
	(c)	Not sensible 500 ml	**(d)**	Not sensible, $50 + l$
4	**(a)**	Sensible	**(b)**	Not sensible, 300 m
	(c)	Not sensible, 50 litres	**(d)**	Not sensible, 100 g
	(e)	Sensible		

Exercise 7E

Question	Metric	Imperial
1	metres	feet
2	centimetres	inches
3	kilometres	miles
4	metres	feet
5	kilograms	pounds
6	grams	ounces
7	tonnes	tons
8	litres	gallons
9	millilitres	pints
10	millilitres	fluid ounces/teaspoon
11	millilitres	fluid ounces
12	litres	gallons
13	minutes	minutes
14	seconds	seconds
15	hours	hours
16	days	days
17	metres	feet
18	millimetres	inches
19	kilograms	pounds
20	years	years

Exercise 7F

1	**(a)**	9 o'clock	**(b)**	Quarter past 8	**(c)**	Half past 3
	(d)	Quarter to 6	**(e)**	Ten past 3	**(f)**	Twenty to 3
	(g)	Five to 2	**(h)**	Twenty-five to 9	**(i)**	Twenty-five past 8
	(j)	Ten to 3				

2

Exercise 7G

1 (a) Half past eight   (b) Ten past ten
  (c) Five past eleven   (d) Quarter to five   (e) Five to four
2 (a) 09:15 or 21:15   (b) 03:30 or 15:30   (c) 04:40 or 16:40
  (d) 06:45 or 18:45   (e) 05:00 or 17:00

Exercise 7H

1 (a) 10:00 (b) 22:00 (c) 09:30 (d) 21:30
 (e) 20:20 (f) 08:20 (g) 07:00 (h) 20:00
 (i) 15:30 (j) 04:40 (k) 01:08 (l) 13:08
 (m) 17:50 (n) 05:50 (o) 23:00 (p) 08:00
 (q) 08:15 (r) 20:45 (s) 14:55 (t) 06:40
2 (a) 8 am (b) 9:20 am (c) 9:30 pm (d) 1:10 pm
 (e) 12:10 pm (f) 12:20 am (g) 1:40 am (h) 8 am
 (i) 3:45 pm (j) 6 pm (k) 4:30 pm (l) 9:10 pm
 (m) 11:55 pm (n) 2.02 pm (o) 6:25 am (p) midnight
 (q) midnight (r) noon (s) 10:55 am (t) 8:55 pm

Exercise 7I

1 (a) 6 cm (b) 40 mph (c) 40 ml (d) 100 mph
 (e) 60 ml (f) 80 mm

Exercise 7J

1 (a) 7.7 cm (b) 188 cm (c) 46 mph (d) 22 ml
 (e) 18 mph (f) 8.6 cm

Exercise 7K

1 7.8 2 5.5 cm 3 37 mph 4 82 mph 5 6.7 6 4.4

Exercise 7L

1 (a) 47p first class; 36p second class
 (b) 155p first class; 120 second class
 (c) 205p first class; 145p second class

Exercise 7M

1 (a) 2 cm (b) 3.5 cm (c) 5.5 cm (d) 10 cm
 (e) 7.4 cm (f) 0.8 cm (g) 1.8 cm (h) 6.7 cm

Exercise 7N

1 (a) metres (b) 12 metres
2 (a) 12 seconds (b) 4 minutes
3 (a) 20 feet (b) 6 metres

Unit 8 Collecting and recording data

Exercise 8A

1 (a) Y (b) Y (c) X (d) Y (e) X (f) Y
 (g) X (h) Y

Exercise 8B

Any sensible answer.

Exercise 8C

1 (a) and (b) 2 (a) 3 (b) and (c)

Exercise 8F

1 (a) Alyssum (b) Red (c) Begonia/Dahlia
2 (a) Vauxhall (b) Volvo (c) Volvo (d) 3
 (e) Rover, Vauxhall or VW (f) 1991 (g) Peugeot
 (h) 5 (i) Volvo, Honda, Renault, Ford Escort, Peugeot XT, Ford Sierra, Peugeot GR, Vauxhall, Rover, VW.
4 (a) Cherry (b) Gooseberry and Cherry
 (c) Apple and Pear (d) Pear or Cherry
 (e) Apple and Cherry (f) Pear Espalier

Unit 9 Algebra 2

Exercise 9A

1 (a) Cliffs (b) Lookout (c) Vantage Point
 (d) Landing Stage (e) Tall tree (f) Beach
2 (a) (2,2) (b) (3,0) (c) (8,2) (d) (1,5)
 (e) (7,5) (f) (4,4)

Exercise 9B

1

2 (1,1) (8,1) (8,4) (9,4) (7,6) (2,6) (0,4) (1,4) (1,1).
3 (3,0) (8,0) (9,2) (8,2) (8,3) (7,3) (7,4) (7,5) (9,5) (7,6)
 (7,4) (5,4) (4,3) (3,3) (2,2) (1,2) (3,0)

4
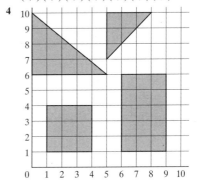

Exercise 9C

1 (b) 75p (b) £1.80 2 (b) (i) £2 (ii) £1.50
3 (b) 60 litres (c) 32.5 litres
4 (c) 8 litres (d) 7.5 kilometres
5 (b) 104 kg (c) 12 weeks

Exercise 9D

1
°C	5	20	**27**	28	**10**	**38**	35	80	**93**	40
°F	**41**	68	80	**82**	50	100	**95**	**176**	200	**104**

2
Kilograms	0	**5**	**9**	45	30	15	**23**	**6**	35	50
Pounds	0	10	20	**99**	66	33	50	14	**77**	110

3

Inches	0	1	2	**4**	**6**	**8**	9	8	**10**	12
Centimetres	0	**2.5**	**5**	10	15	20	**22.5**	**20**	25	30

4

Miles	0	5	**10**	40	**22.5**	30	**45**	**12.5**	24	50
Kilometres	0	**8**	16	**64**	36	**48**	72	20	**38**	80

5

Hectares	0	**8**	**12**	12	15	17	**10**	**18**	3	20
Acres	0	20	30	**30**	**37.5**	**42.5**	24	45	**7.5**	50

Exercise 9E

1 (a) 10 minutes (b) 300 metres (c) 15 minutes
(d) 15 minutes (e) 30 metres per minute or 1.8 km/h
(f) 20 metres per minute or 1.2 km/h

2 (a) David travelled 20 km in 1 hour, he stopped for $\frac{1}{2}$ hour then travelled 40 km in 1 hour. He travelled the 60 km return journey in $\frac{1}{2}$ hour.
(b) First stage 20 km/h, second stage 40 km/h, last stage 120 km/h.

3 (a) Wayne set off from London at 08:00, travelled 75 km in 1 hour and then stopped for 20 minutes. He travelled the remaining 75 km in 40 minutes. He then travelled the 150 km home without stopping in 1 hour.
(b) Tracey set off at 08:20 and travelled 50 km in 40 minutes, she stopped for 10 minutes and then travelled the remaining 100 km in 40 minutes.
(c) Wayne and Tracey passed each other at 75 km from London at 09:20.

4 Between A and B Imran turns a tap off and the water level rose 10 cm in 5 minutes.
Between B and C Imran had turned both taps off and there was no increase in water level for the 5 minutes it took him to undress and get ready for his bath.
Between C and D Imran gets into the bath and the level rises 30 cm immediately.
Between D and E Imran had his bath and the level stayed the same for 15 minutes.
Between E and F Imran let the water out of the bath and the water level dropped 60 cm in 5 minutes.

5

6

7 (a)

(b) 750 metres in 6 minutes
125 metres per minute
7.5 km per hour

8

Exercise 9F

1 A (1, 3); B (3, 1); C (4, 0); D (3, –2); E (5, –3); F (1, –3); G (0, –1); H (–1, –3); I (–3, –2); J (–3, 0); K (–4, 2); L (–2, 3)

2

Exercise 9G

1 (a) $y = 3$ (b) $y = 1$ (c) $y = -1$ (d) $y = -3$
2 (a) $x = -4$ (b) $x = -2$ (c) $x = 1$ (d) $x = 4$
3
4
5

Exercise 9H

1

2

3

4

5

Exercise 9I

1

2

3

4

5

Unit 10 Sorting and presenting data

Exercise 10A

1   **2**

3

Exercise 10B

1 **2**

Exercise 10C

1 **(a)** bar chart of figures in table
   (b) Examples:
       October is warmest in London and Majorca.
       Majorca is always warmer than London.
       January is the coldest month in both places.

2 **(a)** bar chart of figures in table **(b)** Jan and Feb **(c)** £70
(d) Examples
Hotel prices are lowest in October.
Self catering prices are highest in October.
Self catering prices are lowest in January.
Difference in prices is lowest in October.
3 **(a)** bar chart of figures in table
(b) Examples
Norma's range 1500.
Adrian's range 1100.
Norma spent most on Friday.
Adrian spent most on Thursday.

Exercise 10D

1 **(a)** 50 **(b)** Train **(c)** 12
(d) It was only part of the picture.
3 **(a)** **(i)** Tea **(ii)** 30 **(iii)** 15 **(c)** 140 **(d)** 2.19

Exercise 10E

1 **(a)**

2 **(a)**

3 **(a)** Cycleshop **(b)** 17 **(c)** **(i)** 110 **(ii)** 155
(d) Bikeshop **(e)** April
4 **(a)** discrete **(b)** continuous **(c)** discrete
(d) discrete **(e)** continuous **(f)** continuous
(g) discrete **(h)** continuous **(i)** continuous
(j) discrete **(k)** continuous
5 **(a)**

(b)

(c)

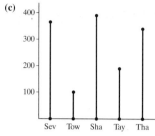

6 **(a)** graph of data in table
(b) Examples
Range of max = 10°C
Range of min = 6°C
Greatest diff (max–min) = 11°C
7 **(a)** 9.00 am **(b)** tank filled up **(c)** slow/steady
8 **(a)** Morgan in multiples of 10, Rees in multiples of 20
(b)

Petrol sales	Wed	Thur	Fri	Sat	Sun	Mon	Tue
Morgan Cars	60	50	60	70	60	80	50
Rees Motors	60	60	80	100	40	60	40

(c) Bar chart of data in table.
(e) Morgan on Mon, Rees on Sat.

Exercise 10F

1 **(a)**

(b)

Unit 11 Three-dimensional shapes

Exercise 11D

Microwave – cuboid
Kitchen roll – cylinder
Biscuits – cylinder
Various packets – cuboids
Rolling pin – cylinder

Ice cream cone – cone
Food cover – square based pyramid
Cheese grater – triangular prism
Orange – sphere
Oxo cubes – cubes

Exercise 11E

1 **(a)** and **(c)** **2** cylinder **3** cube, cuboid

Exercise 11F

1 **(a)** **(b)** **(c)**

2 **(a)**   **(b)**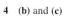

3 **(a)** and **(c)** **4** **(b)** and **(c)**

Exercise 11G

1. (a) (i) cube (ii) 12 (iii) 6 (iv) 8
   (b) (i) triangular prism (ii) 9 (iii) 5 (iv) 6
   (c) (i) squared based pyramid (ii) 8 (iii) 5 (iv) 5
2. (a) (i) 8 (ii) 4 (b) (i) 6 (ii) 3 (c) (i) 4 (ii) 0
3. (A) and (C)
4. Sketches and nets of:
   (a) cuboid (b) cylinder (c) cone (d) tetrahedron
   (e) hexagonal prism.
5. Sketches of:
   (a) square based pyramid base edge 2 cm, slant height 4 cm
   (b) Cuboid 2 cm by 4 cm by 9 cm.
6. Accurate drawing of the nets in the text.
7. (a) cube (b) cylinder
8. (a) 3 cm by 4 cm. (b) (c) 52 cm^2

Unit 13 Measure 2

Exercise 13A

1. (a) 300 cm (b) 3 cm (c) 600 cm (d) 1200 cm
   (e) 10 cm
2. (a) 20 mm (b) 50 mm (c) 120 mm (d) 200 mm
   (e) 1000 mm
3. (a) 5000 m (b) 3 m (c) 10 000 m (d) 20 m
   (e) 60 000 m
4. (a) 5000 g (b) 40 000 g (c) 100 000 g (d) 250 000 g
   (e) 1 000 000 g
5. (a) 3 *l* (b) 8 *l* (c) 50 *l* (d) 75 *l*
6. (a) 6000 ml (b) 40 000 ml (c) 100 000 ml
   (d) 350 000 ml (e) 25 000 ml
7. (a) 3 km (b) 7 km (c) 40 km (d) 45 km
8. (a) 4 tonnes (b) 7 tonnes (c) 30 tonnes
   (d) 55 tonnes
9. (a) 2 kg (b) 3000 kg (c) 50 kg (d) 12 000 kg
   (e) 100 kg
10. 1000 **11** 8 000 000 **12** 1 000 000 **13** 100 000
14. 4000 **15** 1 000 000

Exercise 13B

1. B, C, A, F, E, D **2** 250 kg, 3000 g, 2 kg, 250 g, 25 g
3. 5 mm, 50 mm, 20 cm, 3 m, 3 km
4. 4 cm, 75 cm, 2 m, 3000 mm, 4000 m
5. 200 ml, 600 ml, 1 *l*, 2000 ml, 5 *l*

Exercise 13C

1. (a) 2.5 m (b) 0.5 m (c) 3600 m (d) 0.75 m
   (e) 5 m (f) 0.35 m (g) 4.75 m (h) 600 m
   (i) 40 m (j) 0.005 m
2. (a) 4500 g (b) 400 g (c) 10 300 g (d) 30 g (e) 5 g
3. (a) 35 cm (b) 250 cm (c) 540 cm (d) 0.5 cm
   (e) 8 cm (f) 80 cm (g) 3.5 cm (h) 5 cm
   (i) 8.5 cm (j) 27.5 cm
4. (a) 3500 ml (b) 500 ml (c) 15 400 ml (d) 50 ml
   (e) 3 ml
5. (a) 35 mm (b) 7 mm (c) 0.8 mm (d) 125 mm
   (e) 5 mm
6. (a) 0.3 km (b) 0.05 km (c) 1.25 km (d) 0.075 km
   (e) 0.375 km
7. (a) 0.25 *l* (b) 0.1 *l* (c) 0.05 *l* (d) 3.5 *l*
   (e) 0.001 *l*
8. (a) 0.5 kg (b) 300 kg (c) 0.05 kg (d) 5500 kg
   (e) 6 kg
9. (a) 3.5 tonnes (b) 0.45 tonnes (c) 0.05 tonnes
   (d) 0.003 tonnes (e) 0.075 tonnes
10. 20 glasses **11** 60 pieces **12** 10 batches

Exercise 13D

1. (a) 2.4 cm, 25 mm, 3 cm, 50 mm, 57 mm, 6 cm
   (b) 270 mm, 30 cm, 0.4 m, 45 cm, 500 mm, 1.2 m
   (c) 2 m, 340 cm, 3500 mm, 370 cm, 4 m = 4000 mm
   (d) 0.2 cm, 4 mm, 45 mm, 5 cm, 55 mm, 0.3 m, 36 cm
   (e) 34 cm, 0.4 m, 0.45 m, 50 cm, 560 mm
2. (a) 0.05 kg, 250 g, 0.3 kg, 500 g
   (b) 350 g, 0.4 kg, 500 g, 0.52 kg
   (c) 3000 g, 4 kg, 4.5 kg, 5000 g, 400 kg, 0.5 tonnes
3. (a) 250 ml, 0.3 *l* = 300 ml, 0.4 *l*, 500 ml
   (b) 45 ml, 0.05 *l*, 360 ml, 0.4 *l*, 450 ml, 500 ml

Exercise 13E

1. 640 km **2** 5$\frac{1}{4}$ pints **3** 67.5 litres **4** 220 pounds
5. 0.6 litres **6** 6.7 gallons **7** 0.875 pints **8** 93.75 miles
9. 1.76 pounds **10** 2.625 pints

Exercise 13F

1. 600 g of fat, 1000 g flour, 800 g of dried fruit **2** 6$\frac{2}{3}$ gallons
3. 9.1 kg **4** 10 cm **5** 60 cm by 37.5 cm **6** They are the same
7. 11 pounds of bread and 1.1 pounds of spread **8** 2.86 litres
9. Hazel, her guess was 5.06 pounds **10** 7.7 pounds

Exercise 13G

1. (a) 120 minutes (b) 300 minutes (c) 150 minutes
   (d) 330 minutes (e) 375 minutes (f) 315 minutes
2. (a) 3 hours (b) 4 hours (c) 1$\frac{1}{4}$ hours
   (d) 4 hours 20 minutes (e) 5 hours 25 mins
   (f) 1$\frac{1}{2}$ hours (g) 72 hours (h) 132 hours
   (i) 8 hours 20 minutes
3. 3600 seconds **4** 1440 minutes **5** (i) 31 536 000 seconds
   (ii) 31 622 400 seconds

Exercise 13H

	(a)	(b)	(c)	(d)
1	10:45	10:00	11:55	10:10
2	09:50	11:20	12:30	08:55
3	12:20	13:25	14:30	08:50
4	15:15	20:00	01:35	05:30
5	09:40	11:25	07:55	08:50
6	08:05	10:50	09:40	08:10
7	07:25	09:10	05:40	06:35
8	02:05	04:45	23:15	19:45

Exercise 13I

1. (a) 11th Jan (b) 12th Mar (c) 13th June
   (d) 15th July (e) 20th Sept (f) 30th May
   (g) 5th July (h) 6th Sept
2. (a) 16th Feb (b) 17th Mar (c) 17th Apr
   (d) 21st Dec (e) 29th Nov (f) 2nd Oct
   (g) 6th Apr (h) 9th Dec
3. (a) 5th May (b) 6th July (c) 16th June
   (d) 1st Oct (e) 7th July (f) 19th June
   (g) 30th Dec (h) 4th Jan
4. Wed 10th April **5** Thurs 2nd May **6** Mon 13th May
7. Thurs 25th April **8** Fri 3rd May

Exercise 13J

1. 07:50 **2** 08:35 **3** 07:25 **4** 07:40

5			
Coate	08:35	09:05	09:35
Piper's Way	08:40	09:10	09:40
Old Town	08:50	09:20	09:50
Drove Rd.	08:55	09:25	09:55
New Town	09:00	09:30	10:00
Bus Station	09:05	09:35	10:05

6 Bristol 08:10 08:25 08:40
Bath 08:30 08:45 09:00
Swindon 08:45 09:00 09:15
Didcot 09:05 09:20 09:35
Reading 09:15 09:30 09:45
London 09:40 09:55 10:10
7 07:45 **8** 08:35 **9** 09:15 **10** 08:10 **11** 30 mins
12 20 mins **13** $1\frac{1}{2}$ hours **14** 30 mins **15** 35 mins
16 (a) 07:10 and 07:45 or 08:00 (b) 07:05 and 07:45 or 08:00
(c) 07:50 and 08:15 (d) 08:25 and 09:00
(e) 08:20 and 09:00 (f) 07:55 and 08:15

Exercise 13K

1 (a) 316 km (b) 198 miles
2 (a) 08:20 (b) 25 minutes **3** 76 cm

Unit 14 Percentages

Exercise 14A

1 $\frac{3}{5}$ **2** $\frac{9}{25}$ **3** $\frac{19}{20}$ **4** $\frac{17}{100}$ **5** $\frac{1}{50}$ **6** $\frac{13}{20}$
7 $\frac{39}{100}$ **8** $\frac{9}{50}$ **9** $\frac{9}{10}$ **10** $\frac{7}{10}$ **11** $\frac{9}{20}$ **12** $\frac{1}{200}$
13 $\frac{3}{40}$ **14** $\frac{1}{8}$ **15** $\frac{2}{5}$ **16** $\frac{3}{4}$ **17** $\frac{3}{10}$ **18** $\frac{1}{5}$
19 $\frac{3}{20}$ **20** $\frac{7}{40}$

Exercise 14B

1 0.16 **2** 0.41 **3** 0.99 **4** 0.82 **5** 0.07 **6** 0.55
7 0.38 **8** 0.03 **9** 0.142 **10** 0.987 **11** 0.036
12 0.185 **13** 0.455 **14** 0.0425 **15** 0.19 **16** 0.125
17 0.01 **18** 0.007 **19** 0.005 **20** 0.025

Exercise 14C

Percentage	Decimal	Fraction
40%	0.4	$\frac{2}{5}$
61%	0.61	$\frac{61}{100}$
70%	0.7	$\frac{7}{10}$
35%	0.35	$\frac{7}{20}$
$8\frac{1}{2}\%$	0.085	$\frac{17}{200}$
15%	0.15	$\frac{3}{20}$
12%	0.12	$\frac{3}{25}$
7%	0.07	$\frac{7}{100}$
$1\frac{1}{4}\%$	0.0125	$\frac{1}{80}$
$66\frac{2}{3}\%$	0.666 ...	$\frac{2}{3}$

Exercise 14D

1 99 **2** 414 kg **3** £1190 **4** 72 **5** £25.20
6 £1.68 **7** £28.70 **8** £79.20 **9** £1562
10 0.75 tonnes **11** £43.20 **12** £30 720
13 9 km **14** 3.55 km **15** £669.12 **16** 0.1728 litres

Exercise 14E

1 (a) (i) £0.60 (ii) £11.40 **2** (a) (i) £12
(ii) £68 (b) (i) £111 (ii) £629 (c) (i) £6.09
(ii) £34.51
3 A* A B C D E F G
3 9 18 63 30 9 12 6
4 £112.80 **5** (a) £7560 (b) £5040 **6** £29.25
7 (a) £9.17 (b) £4.90 (c) £346.50 (d) £27.79
8 (a) £306 (b) £142.80
9 (a) £65 (b) £234 (c) £522.60

10 £1700 £2300 £2900 **11** £14.19 £7.92
12 £89.60 + £129.60 + £45 + £50.60 = £314.80

Exercise 14F

1 (a) 5% (b) 12% (c) 15% (d) $7\frac{1}{2}\%$
(e) $41\frac{2}{3}\%$ (f) $8\frac{1}{3}\%$ (g) 3% (h) 1% (i) 50%
2 (a) $7\frac{1}{2}\%$ (b) 20% (c) 20% (d) 4% (e) 4%
(f) 4% (g) $6\frac{1}{4}\%$ (h) $\frac{1}{2}\%$ (i) 21.25% (j) $2\frac{1}{2}\%$
3 30% **4** 6% **5** 55% **6** 16% **7** $3\frac{1}{8}\%$
8 6.4% **9** 8% **10** 42.86%

Exercise 14G

1 £132 £143.40 **2** 15% **3** (a) £3 (b) 5%
4 Nigel £975 Ryan £1125

Unit 15 Algebra 3

Exercise 15A

1 $a = 3$ **2** $b = 3$ **3** $c = 7$ **4** $w = 2$ **5** $m = 1$
6 $y = 0$ **7** $x = 5$ **8** $k = 5$ **9** $n = 6$ **10** $h = 8$
11 $g = 4$ **12** $f = 9$ **13** $d = 5$ **14** $e = 3$ **15** $y = 3$
16 $x = 4$ **17** $m = 4$ **18** $d = 3$ **19** $k = 9$ **20** $y = 10$
21 $t = 10$ **22** $z = 4$ **23** $z = 0$ **24** $n = 5$

Exercise 15B

1 $a = 1$ **2** $y = 2$ **3** $h = 7$ **4** $p = 9$ **5** $q = 10$
6 $d = 8$ **7** $x = 0$ **8** $t = 4$ **9** $r = 3$ **10** $k = 1$
11 $n = 1$ **12** $x = 5$ **13** $m = 5$ **14** $y = 16$ **15** $w = 0$
16 $q = 12$ **17** $p = 2$ **18** $t = 0$ **19** $a = 12$ **20** $x = 0$
21 $p = 38$ **22** $a = 4$ **23** $b = 1$ **24** $y = 0$

Exercise 15C

1 $a = 5$ **2** $p = 11$ **3** $q = 8$ **4** $x = 8$ **5** $y = 13$
6 $s = 3$ **7** $x = 22$ **8** $y = 21$ **9** $s = 27$ **10** $a = 1$
11 $p = 11$ **12** $c = 4$ **13** $a = 1$ **14** $p = 5$ **15** $q = 0$
16 $a = 2$ **17** $b = 2$ **18** $c = 15$ **19** $p = 5$ **20** $y = 21$
21 $t = 5$ **22** $p = 0$ **23** $p = 24$ **24** $p = 0$

Exercise 15D

1 $a = 2$ **2** $p = 2$ **3** $p = 3$ **4** $s = 3$ **5** $k = 2$
6 $u = 4$ **7** $g = 7$ **8** $k = 7$ **9** $j = 2$ **10** $f = 4$
11 $r = 9$ **12** $v = 9$ **13** $t = 2\frac{1}{2}$ **14** $d = 12$ **15** $t = 9$

Exercise 15E

1 $a = 10$ **2** $b = 20$ **3** $s = 12$ **4** $c = 30$ **5** $t = 24$
6 $s = 72$ **7** $h = 72$ **8** $f = 28$ **9** $d = 45$ **10** $a = 45$
11 $b = 40$ **12** $r = 52$ **13** $a = 60$ **14** $b = 32$ **15** $k = 48$

Exercise 15F

1 $a = 1$ **2** $b = 3$ **3** $c = 5$ **4** $p = 9$ **5** $q = 4$
6 $d = 8$ **7** $p = 3$ **8** $r = 2$ **9** $t = 4$ **10** $a = 12$
11 $b = 60$ **12** $s = 20$ **13** $r = 3$ **14** $e = 1$ **15** $p = 0$

Exercise 15G

1 $a = 2$ **2** $a = 3$ **3** $a = 2$ **4** $a = 3$ **5** $p = 0$
6 $p = 2$ **7** $q = 3$ **8** $r = 2$ **9** $t = 5$ **10** $f = 3$
11 $r = 13$ **12** $a = 1$ **13** $a = 0$ **14** $d = 3$ **15** $c = 4$

Exercise 15H

1 $a = 1\frac{1}{2}$ 2 $a = 3\frac{1}{2}$ 3 $a = 2\frac{2}{3}$ 4 $a = 4\frac{1}{3}$ 5 $p = 1\frac{3}{5}$
6 $p = 4\frac{2}{5}$ 7 $e = 0$ 8 $t = 1\frac{1}{2}$ 9 $j = 1\frac{1}{2}$ 10 $c = 1\frac{4}{7}$
11 $k = \frac{1}{4}$ 12 $d = 3\frac{1}{3}$ 13 $u = \frac{2}{9}$ 14 $q = 2\frac{1}{4}$
15 $y = 1\frac{2}{7}$

Exercise 15I

1 $a = -1$ 2 $a = -2$ 3 $a = -4$ 4 $a = -1$ 5 $a = -2$
6 $p = -2$ 7 $s = -5$ 8 $p = -2$ 9 $k = -1$ 10 $h = -1$
11 $y = -5$ 12 $e = 12\frac{1}{3}$ 13 $t = 0$ 14 $w = -1$
15 $c = -2$ 16 $a = 0$

Exercise 15J

1 $s = 3$ 2 $d = 3$ 3 $m = 5$ 4 $h = 4$ 5 $k = 12$
6 $y = 2$ 7 $p = 1\frac{2}{5}$ 8 $f = 3\frac{1}{4}$ 9 $s = 3\frac{2}{3}$ 10 $g = 2\frac{2}{7}$
11 $f = 4\frac{1}{4}$ 12 $k = 3\frac{3}{5}$ 13 $s = 5\frac{2}{3}$ 14 $j = 3\frac{2}{3}$
15 $b = -\frac{5}{9}$ 16 $r = -3\frac{1}{2}$ 17 $t = -5\frac{2}{5}$ 18 $y = -\frac{6}{7}$
19 $e = -\frac{1}{3}$ 20 $f = 1\frac{1}{4}$ 21 $g = -\frac{2}{5}$ 22 $h = -1$
23 $c = 1\frac{2}{3}$ 24 $s = -\frac{5}{8}$

Exercise 15K

1 $p = 1$ 2 $d = 5$ 3 $c = 3$ 4 $b = 2\frac{1}{3}$ 5 $g = 3$
6 $g = 5$ 7 $v = -2$ 8 $s = 1$ 9 $d = -\frac{1}{3}$ 10 $t = 5\frac{2}{3}$
11 $h = 3$ 12 $h = 4$ 13 $s = 3$ 14 $y = 3\frac{1}{2}$ 15 $r = 5$

Exercise 15L

1 $a = 1$ 2 $h = 8$ 3 $g = -2$ 4 $f = 6$ 5 $q = 0$
6 $k = 4$ 7 $g = 1$ 8 $h = -2$ 9 $d = -1$ 10 $v = -5\frac{1}{2}$
11 $s = -5\frac{2}{3}$ 12 $n = 3\frac{1}{2}$ 13 $f = -\frac{7}{8}$ 14 $d = 2\frac{3}{7}$
15 $m = -2\frac{1}{5}$

Exercise 15M

1 $k = 5$ 2 $s = 3\frac{1}{2}$ 3 $p = 4$ 4 $g = -1$ 5 $t = 3\frac{2}{3}$
6 $k = 9$ 7 $d = 7$ 8 $c = 3$ 9 $z = -1$ 10 $b = -4\frac{1}{2}$
11 $p = -1\frac{2}{3}$ 12 $g = 8$

Exercise 15N

1 $h = 12$ 2 $t = -8$ 3 $d = -1$ 4 $f = -3$ 5 $s = 7$
6 $d = 6$ 7 $a = 4\frac{1}{2}$ 8 $q = 4$ 9 $y = -\frac{2}{3}$ 10 $e = -1$
11 $s = -1\frac{2}{3}$ 12 $u = -5\frac{1}{2}$ 13 $t = -1\frac{1}{3}$ 14 $s = -1\frac{3}{4}$
15 $q = -2\frac{3}{4}$ 16 $w = -1\frac{1}{5}$ 17 $h = -1\frac{3}{5}$ 18 $s = -7$
19 $r = -1$ 20 $a = 3\frac{2}{3}$

Exercise 15O

1 $p = \frac{2}{3}$ 2 $h = 66$ 3 $r = 3\frac{8}{9}$ 4 $t = 21$ 5 $g = -3$
6 $d = -7\frac{1}{2}$ 7 $k = 13$ 8 $m = 5\frac{1}{2}$ 9 $d = -12\frac{1}{3}$
10 $j = 23$ 11 $y = -1\frac{4}{5}$ 12 $t = -7$

Exercise 15P

1 $t = 1\frac{1}{2}$ 2 $g = 2$ 3 $s = 4$ 4 $q = 6$ 5 $d = 3\frac{1}{3}$
6 $k = 2\frac{1}{2}$ 7 $a = \frac{1}{2}$ 8 $k = 3\frac{1}{2}$ 9 $d = -2\frac{1}{4}$
10 $p = \frac{5}{7}$ 11 $p = -11$ 12 $r = -4\frac{1}{3}$ 13 $t = 7\frac{1}{3}$
14 $g = 6$ 15 $a = 2\frac{5}{7}$

Unit 16 Pie charts

Exercise 16A

1 IIC English: 180°; Maths: 60°; Science: 45°; History: 45°; Art: 30°.
IIB Maths: 72°; English: 108°; Science: 60°; History: 50°; Art: 40°; French 30°.
IIA Maths: 72°; English: 120°; French: 18°; Art: 36°; History: 54°; Science: 60°.
2 Nesta: 105°; Peter: 120°; Mario: 30°; Gwyneth: 45°; Wes: 60°.
3 (a) Maths: 108°; French: 36°; Other: 54°; Science: 72°; English: 90°.
  (b) Hamster: 50°; Dog: 100°; Cat: 60°; Bird: 40°; Other: 30°; No pet: 80°.
  (c) Car: 144°; Van: 36°; Motorcycle: 48°; Lorry: 60°; Bus: 72°.
4 Tennis, Swimming, Athletics, Football, Hockey.

Exercise 16B

1 (a) 12 (b) 30°
  (c) Fish 150°, Sausages 60°, Salad 90°, Cheese roll 60°.
2 Rice 18°, Apple 54°, Ice cream 144°, Trifle 108°, Fruit 36°.
3 (a) (ii)

  (iii) Tea 108°, Coffee 99°, Milk 63°, Water 36°, Chocolate 54°.
5 Rent 90°, Travel 27°, Clothes 42°, Food 120°, Savings 60°, Spare 21°.
6 (a) Rent £32, Travel £10.22, Clothes £20, Food £49.78, Savings £36, Spare £12 (b) None
7 (a) All their choices (b) chocolate (c) orange (d) 3
8 (a) Bus fares 48°, Going out 100°, Clothes 120°, Records 60°, Other 32°.

Unit 17 Ratio and proportion

Exercise 17A

1 (a) $7 : 2$ (b) $16 : 16$ (c) $8 : 4$ (d) $12 : 15$
2 (a) 80 g, 200 g (b) 120 g, 300 g (c) 200 g, 500 g
  (d) 20 g, 50 g (e) 100 g, 250 g
3 (a) 400 g, 800 g, 800 g, 8 eggs (b) 100 g, 200 g, 200 g, 2 eggs
  (c) 300 g, 600 g, 600 g, 6 eggs
  (d) 500 g, 1000 g, 1000 g, 10 eggs
4 (a) 6 (b) 14
5 (a) 10 kg, 5 kg, 45 kg (b) 30 kg, 15 kg, 135 kg
  (c) 2 kg, 1 kg, 9 kg 6 680 g
7 (a) 12 kg, 38 kg (b) 60 kg, 190 kg (c) 1.2 kg, 3.8 kg

Exercise 17B

1 (a) $1 : 2$ (b) $1 : 3$ (c) $1 : 6$ (d) $1 : 4$ (e) $1 : 3$
  (f) $2 : 3$ (g) $5 : 1$ (h) $7 : 1$ (i) $2 : 3$ (j) $5 : 3$
2 (a) $1 : 5$ (b) $1 : 5$ (c) $1 : 8$ (d) $5 : 1$
3 (a) $7 : 9$ (b) $10 : 11$ (c) $22 : 25$ (d) $1 : 2$
  (e) $9 : 7$ (f) $11 : 3 : 2$
4 £200, £160 5 £160, £200, £120 6 $10 : 25 : 5$
7 (a) 40 mins (b) 1 hour
8 4 lbs   3 lbs   2 lbs
  16 km   12 km   8 km
  28 miles   21 miles   14 miles
  36 t   27 t   18 t
  £64   £48   £32
9 $5 : 3$ 10 7000 kg

Exercise 17C

1 (a) 20 (b) 28 (c) 2.5 (d) 28 (e) 40 (f) 9
2 (a) 18 ft (b) 8 ft (c) 5 ft **3** (a) 135 (b) 84
4 455 **5** (a) 1400 (b) 6 hours **6** 4.8 m
7 (a) 280 miles (b) 77.14 litres
8 (a) £28.80 (b) 15 hours

Exercise 17D

1 £120 **2** £4.50 **3** £10.80 **4** £64 **5** £3.24
6 21 **7** (a) 1 hr 45 mins (b) $5\frac{1}{2}$ hours (c) 8 hours
8 (a) 64 km (b) 10 hours **9** (a) 2.4 hours (b) 2
10 (a) 12 (b) 28.8 (c) 48

Exercise 17E

1 (a) 1.25 km (b) 1.8 km (c) 2.6 km (d) 3.1 km
2 (a) 12 cm (b) 10.4 cm (c) 16.8 cm (d) 51.2 cm
3 (a) 25 cm (b) 276 m (c) 2.19 km
4

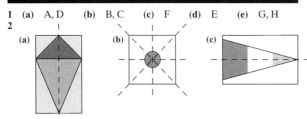

5 (a) 1 : 180 (b) 23.33 cm

Unit 18 Symmetry

Exercise 18A

1 (a) A, D (b) B, C (c) F (d) E (e) G, H
2
(a) (b) (c)

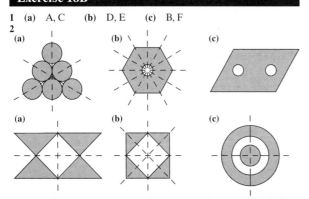

5 (a) A, B, C, D, E, K, M, T, U, V, W, Y (b) H, I, O, X
(c) F, G, J, L, N, P, Q, R, S, Z.

Exercise 18B

1 (a) A, C (b) D, E (c) B, F
2
(a) (b) (c)

(a) (b) (c)

Exercise 18C

1 (a) No (b) Yes (c) Yes (d) Yes (e) No
2 (a) 3 (b) 2 (c) 4 (d) 5 (e) 5

Exercise 18D

1 (a) (i) 3 (ii) 3 (b) (i) 5 (ii) 5

Exercise 18E

1 (a) 2 (b) 3 (c) 4 (d) 1
2 (a) 2 planes (b) 5 planes (c) 6 planes (d) 3 planes
3 (a) isosceles triangular prism (b) cone

Exercise 18F

1 1 **2** **3** pentagon **4**

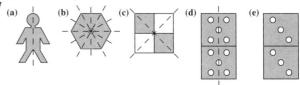

5 8
6 equilateral triangle
7
(a) (b) (c) (d) (e)

Rotational symmetry: (a) 1 (b) 6 (c) 2 (d) 2 (e) 2
10 (a) Infinite (b) 5 (c) 5
11 (a) 3 planes (b) 5 planes

Exercise 18G

1 **2** (a)

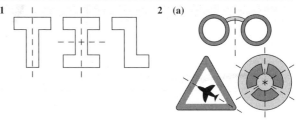

(b) Use a mirror or tracing paper
3 (a) 5 (b) 1 **4** (a), (b), (d) **5** 2 planes of symmetry

Unit 19 Measure 3

Exercise 19A

1 (a) 10 cm (b) 20 cm (c) 9 cm (d) 16 cm
(e) 16 cm
2 (a) 20 cm (b) 12 cm (c) 18 cm (d) 16 cm

Exercise 19B

1 20 cm **2** 22 cm **3** 21 m **4** 22 cm **5** 25 cm
6 22 m

Exercise 19C

1 16.9 cm **2** 13.3 cm **3** 14.8 cm **4** 14.6 cm
5 20.9 cm

Exercise 19D

1 (a) 6.28 cm (b) 9.42 cm (c) 12.56 cm (d) 31.4 cm
(e) 25.12 cm (f) 37.68 cm
2 (a) 62.8 cm (b) 15.7 m (c) 157 cm (d) 7.85 cm
(e) 11.304 cm (f) 25.905 cm

Exercise 19E

1 12.56 cm 2 18.84 cm 3 31.4 cm 4 62.8 cm
5 50.24 cm 6 75.36 cm 7 125.6 cm 8 31.4 m
9 314 cm 10 15.7 cm 11 22.608 cm 12 51.81 cm

Exercise 19F

1 56.52 cm 2 28.26 cm 3 282.6 cm 4 376.8 cm
5 94.2 cm 6 7.85 cm 7 4.71 cm 8 18.84 inches
9 1.884 cm 10 3.14 cm

Exercise 19G

1 3 cm, 1.5 cm 2 4 cm, 2 cm 3 1 m, 0.5 m
4 3.18 m, 1.59 m 5 28.7 cm, 14.3 cm 6 2.39 cm, 1.19 cm
7 1.59 m, 0.796 m 8 1.91 in., 0.955 in. 9 0.318 cm, 0.159 cm
10 0.796 cm, 0.398 cm

Exercise 19H

1 8 cm^2 2 7 cm^2 3 12 cm^2 4 16 cm^2 5 7 cm^2
6 6 cm^2

Exercise 19I

1 $11\frac{1}{2}$ cm^2 2 $7\frac{1}{2}$ cm^2 3 10 cm^2 4 $7\frac{1}{2}$ cm^2 5 15 cm^2
6 $17\frac{1}{2}$ cm^2

Exercise 19J

1 16 cm^3 2 3 cm^3 3 24 cm^3 4 72 cm^3 5 44 cm^3

Exercise 19K

1 (a) 8 cm^2 (b) 15 cm^2 (c) 24 cm^2 (d) 30 cm^2
2 (a) 16 cm^2 (b) 64 cm^2 (c) 100 cm^2 (d) 144 cm^2
3 (a) 4 cm^2 (b) 7.5 cm^2 (c) 24 cm^2 (d) 40 cm^2

Exercise 19L

1 (a) 20 cm^2 (b) 48 cm^2 (c) 51 cm^2 (d) 26 cm^2
2 (a) $7\frac{1}{2}$ cm^2 (b) 16 cm^2 (c) 22 cm^2

3

Shape	Length	Width	Area
(a)	5 cm	6 cm	**30 cm^2**
(b)	4 cm	**5 cm**	20 cm^2
(c)	2 cm	**15 cm**	30 cm^2
(d)	**8 cm**	5 cm	40 cm^2
(e)	**5 cm**	12 cm	60 cm^2

4

Shape	Base	Vertical height	Area
(a)	10 cm	5 cm	**25 cm^2**
(b)	**10 cm**	12 cm	60 cm^2
(c)	**16 cm**	5 cm	40 cm^2
(d)	4 cm	**16 cm**	32 cm^2
(e)	16 cm	**8 cm**	64 cm^2

Exercise 19M

1 (a) 12.56 cm^2 (b) 28.26 cm^2 (c) 50.24 cm^2
(d) 314 cm^2 (e) 200.96 cm^2 (f) 452.16 cm^2
2 (a) 1256 cm^2 (b) 78.5 m^2 (c) 7850 cm^2
(d) 19.625 cm^2 (e) 40.69 cm^2 (f) 214 cm^2
3 (a) 3.14 cm^2 (b) 7.065 cm^2 (c) 19.625 cm^2
(d) 78.5 cm^2 (e) 50.24 cm^2 (f) 113.04 cm^2
4 (a) 314 cm^2 (b) 19.625 m^2 (c) 1962.5 cm^2
(d) 4.91 cm^2 (e) 10.17 cm^2 (f) 53.4 cm^2

Exercise 19N

1 254 cm^2 2 63.6 cm^2 3 6360 cm^2 4 11 300 cm^2
5 707 cm^2 6 4.91 cm^2 7 1.77 cm^2 8 28.3 inches^2
9 0.283 cm^2 10 0.785 cm^2

Exercise 19O

1 6 cm 2 2 cm 3 2 m 4 3.57 m 5 5.35 cm
6 3.09 cm 7 1.26 cm 8 2.76 inches 9 1.13 cm
10 0.892 cm

Exercise 19P

1 24 cm^3 2 36 cm^3 3 108 cm^3 4 64 cm^3 5 125 cm^3
6 512 cm^3 7 160 cm^3 8 250 cm^3 9 288 cm^3

Exercise 19Q

1 £95.40 2 £125
3 (a) 10 tiles (b) 20 tiles (c) 800 tiles (d) £520
4 7 rolls 5 2 tins 6 3750l 7 5.85l 8 2667 tiles
9 400 turves 10 (a) 28.8 m^3 (b) 8 skips

Exercise 19R

1 12 miles 2 25 mph 3 5 hours 4 3.75 mph
5 7 mph 6 8 mph 7 $1\frac{1}{3}$ mph 8 $66\frac{2}{3}$ mph
9 20 mph 10 30 km/h

Exercise 19S

1 26.4 cm 2 (a) (i) 5 m (ii) 2 m (b) 24 m (c) 22 m^2
3 (a) 24 m^3 (b) 68 m^2
4 (a) 500 cm^3 (b) (i) 400 cm^3 (ii) 80% 5 79.8 m
6 (a) 282.6 m (b) 6360 m^2
7 (a) 30 cm (b) 27 cm^2 8 18.9 cm

Unit 20 Averages

Exercise 20A

1 (a) 28 (b) 34, 41 (c) 35 (d) 28, 31
(e) 28, 30 (f) 28
2 (a) 6 (b) 5, 5 (c) 4, 4, 4 (d) 11 (e) 7, 7, 7
(f) 5, 5, 5, 6, 6
3 (a) Maths 8, 17, 8, 5, 20 English 14, 6, 15, 14, 9
(b) Maths 8 English 14 4 (a) 1

Exercise 20B

1 (a) 6 (b) 11 (c) 5 (d) $9\frac{1}{2}$ (e) 6 (f) 12
3 (a) any ⩾ 5 (b) any ⩽ 4 (c) any ⩾ 7 (d) 5
4 (a) $7\frac{1}{2}$ 5 (a) 26 (b) 36

Exercise 20C

1 (a) 13 (b) 24.25 (c) 22.5 (d) 23.75 (e) 19.5
  (f) 25.25
2 (a) £25 (b) £36 3 (a) 162 cm (b) 161.7 cm
4 (a) 560 g (b) 1310 g
5 (a) 13 (b) 16 (c) 6 (d) 25

Exercise 20D

1 (a) History 28, Maths 21, English 14, Art 58, Science 33
  (b) (i) Maths (ii) English (iii) Art

2

Make	Standard	De Luxe	Price range
Ford 1.1	£7145	£7545	£400
Peugeot 1.5	£7460	£9190	**£1730**
Rover 200	£9995	£13 895	**£3900**
Citroen 1.9	£10 220	**£14 205**	£3985
Volvo 1.6	**£11 570**	£15 480	£3910
Audi 1.9	£17 693	**£19 514**	£1821
Porche 3.6	£58 995	£93 950	**£34 995**
Lada 1.3	**£4995**	£6495	£1500
Toyota 1.3	£8040	**£12 767**	£4727

3 (a) London 22, Paris 22, Moscow 29, New York 13, Luxor 14
  (b) Moscow, London and Paris (equal), Luxor, New York

Exercise 20E

1

	Mode	Median	Mean
(a)	6	10	10
(b)	24, 32	28	27.4
(c)	£3.60	£3.60	£4.74

2 (a) £1715 (b) (i) £140 (ii) £155 (iii) £171.50
  (iv) £300
3 2, 3, 4, 5, 7, 10 or equivalent

Exercise 20F

1 (a) 15 (b) 100 (c) 3.66 2 10
3 (a) 10.86 (b) 10.5
4 (i) (a) 8 (b) None (c) 105 (d) 3.1 (e) 4, 8
  (ii) (a) 5 (b) 6 (c) 106 (d) 3.1 (e) 5
5 (a) £3.29 (b) 3 hr 8 min (c) 4.32 m 6 5
7 (a) 14 (b) any number except 1, 3 or 5 (c) 2
  (d) 4 (e) 3.7 (f) 5
8 (a) £13.825 9 (a) 22 (b) 20 (c) 22
10 (a) (i) 24.5 (ii) 31 (iii) 28
  (b) Mean influenced by low figures 4 and 11
11 (a) 20 (b) 14 (c) 14
12 Mean 12, Range 4. Brand B is more consistent.
13 (a)

	Mode	Median	Mean	Range
11A	20	20	18.3	11
11B	17, 18	17	15.9	13
11C	16	16	14.7	12
10A	20, 22, 24	21	19.6	17
10B	18, 19	18	17.3	10
10C	17	13.5	13.2	11
9A	20, 21	19.5	18.5	8
9B	18	17	16.1	6
9C	20	18	18.2	9
9D	10, 11, 16	11.5	12.3	8

  (b) (i) 16, 22 and 17, 18, 21 (ii) 19.5, 19
  (iii) 19.9, 19.4
  (c) (i) 18 (ii) 16 (iii) 14.8
14 (a) See table above for question **13(a)** (b) 20
15 (a) (i) 3.35 (ii) 4 (iii) 3
  (b) Mode – gives highest number of certificates.

Unit 21 Algebra 4

Exercise 21A

1 £130 2 £137.50 3 180 cm 4 150 cm 5 £4.25

Exercise 21B

1 £160 2 £65 3 £172.50 4 £14.40 5 £12
6 £3.36 7 £3.75 8 £3.80 9 £20 10 £41.40
11 12 years 12 5 coins 13 25 bars 14 12 people
15 8 sweets 16 £12.60

Exercise 21C

1 8 2 7 3 10 4 6 5 15 6 0 7 15
8 0 9 16 10 16 11 19 12 32 13 2
14 5 15 1 16 8 17 11 18 0 19 9 20 30

Exercise 21D

1 6 2 16 3 15 4 0 5 6 6 7 7 3
8 9 9 20 10 6 11 7 12 0 13 8
14 12 15 0 16 24 17 4 18 0 19 8 20 6

Exercise 21E

1 (a) 15 (b) 21 (c) 12 (d) 37.2
2 (a) 24 (b) 15 (c) 56 (d) 25.5
3 (a) 160 (b) 75 (c) 210 (d) 79
4 (a) 13 (b) 35 (c) 60 (d) 7
5 (a) 53 (b) 210 (c) 7 (d) 17.5

Exercise 21F

1 −3 2 2 3 −6 4 −4 5 2 6 −8 7 5
8 11 9 0 10 −9 11 8 12 −2

Exercise 21G

1 1 2 −2 3 −7 4 −5 5 5 6 −8 7 3
8 −5 9 −5 10 8 11 −3 12 5 13 −4
14 6 15 1 16 −3 17 0 18 10 19 −5 20 10

Exercise 21H

1 −12 2 −12 3 −10 4 4 5 −21 6 −32
7 30 8 27

Exercise 21I

1 −8 2 −3 3 −6 4 −6 5 −15 6 0 7 15
8 0 9 4 10 −24 11 −11 12 −20 13 −2
14 −5 15 −11 16 8 17 −19 18 0 19 21
20 30

Exercise 21J

1 (a) −7 (b) 25 (c) −60 (d) −7
2 (a) 0 (b) 12 (c) −15 (d) 3
3 (a) −11 (b) −11 (c) −1 (d) 5 (e) 6
  (f) −29

Exercise 21K

1 (a) 4 (b) 8 (c) 4 (d) 20   **2** 9 cm   **3** 2
4 7   **5** 22   **6** 10   **7** 4 chocs   **8** 4   **9** 24

Unit 22 Transformations

Exercise 22A

4 (a) 2 sq right, 2 sq down   (b) 1 sq left, 4 sq up
   (c) 2 sq left, 3 sq up

Exercise 22B

3 (a) $\frac{1}{2}$ turn clockwise or anticlockwise
   (b) $\frac{1}{4}$ turn anticlockwise   (c) $\frac{1}{4}$ turn clockwise
   (d) $\frac{1}{2}$ turn clockwise or anticlockwise

Exercise 22C

2

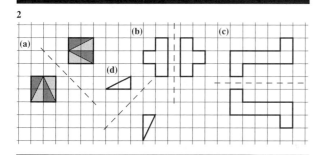

Exercise 22E

3 (b) 2   **4** (b) rotation $\frac{1}{4}$ turn clockwise.

Unit 23 Probability

Exercise 23B

1 (a) $\frac{1}{6}$ (b) $\frac{2}{6}$ or $\frac{1}{3}$ (c) $\frac{1}{2}$ (d) $\frac{1}{2}$ (e) $\frac{1}{3}$
   (f) $\frac{4}{6}$ (g) $\frac{4}{6}$ (h) $\frac{1}{2}$ (i) 0 (j) 0
2 (a) $\frac{4}{52}$ (b) $\frac{1}{52}$ (c) $\frac{1}{4}$ (d) $\frac{8}{52}$
   (e) $\frac{8}{52}$, or $\frac{12}{52}$ if Ace is low (f) $\frac{12}{52}$ (g) $\frac{12}{52}$ (h) $\frac{1}{4}$
   (i) $\frac{1}{2}$ (j) $\frac{3}{4}$
3 (a) $\frac{5}{11}$ (b) $\frac{6}{11}$ (c) 0 (d) 1

Exercise 23C

1 (a) 0 (b) 1 (d) 0 (e) 1 (f) $\frac{1}{2}$ (g) $\frac{1}{2}$
3

	(i) Dice A	(ii) Dice B
(a)	$\frac{1}{6}$	$\frac{1}{6}$
(b)	$\frac{1}{6}$	$\frac{2}{6}$
(c)	$\frac{3}{6}$	$\frac{4}{6}$
(d)	$\frac{1}{6}$	0
(e)	$\frac{3}{6}$	$\frac{2}{6}$
(f)	$\frac{3}{6}$	$\frac{4}{6}$
(g)	$\frac{3}{6}$	$\frac{3}{6}$
(h)	$\frac{2}{6}$	$\frac{2}{6}$

4 (a) (i) $\frac{3}{10}$ (ii) 0.3 (iii) 30%
   (b) (i) $\frac{4}{10}$ (ii) 0.4 (iii) 40%
   (c) (i) $\frac{2}{10}$ (ii) 0.2 (iii) 20%
   (d) (i) $\frac{1}{10}$ (ii) 0.1 (iii) 10%
5 (a) $\frac{25}{100}$, 0.25, 25% (b) $\frac{8}{100}$, 0.08, 8% (c) $\frac{5}{100}$, 0.05, 5%
   (d) $\frac{88}{100}$, 0.88, 88%

Exercise 23D

1 (a) $\frac{1}{2}$ (b) 0.8 (c) 70%
2 (a) $\frac{1}{6}$ (b) $\frac{5}{6}$ (c) $\frac{4}{6}$ (d) $\frac{2}{6}$ (e) $\frac{3}{6}$

Exercise 23F

1 (a) (i) $\frac{4}{36}$ (ii) $\frac{4}{36}$ (iii) $\frac{1}{36}$ (b) (i) $\frac{6}{36}$ (ii) $\frac{6}{36}$
   (c) $\frac{12}{36}$ (d) $\frac{6}{36}$ (e) $\frac{1}{36}$
2 (a) $\frac{1}{25}$ (b) $\frac{4}{25}$ (c) $\frac{5}{25}$ (d) $\frac{9}{25}$ (e) $\frac{16}{25}$ (f) $\frac{9}{25}$
   (g) 1 (h) 0

Exercise 23G

1 (a) HH   HT   TH   TT
   (b) HHH   HHT   HTH   HTT   THH   THT
       TTH   TTT
   (c) EE   EO   OE   OO
   (d)

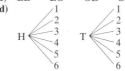

2 (a) 36 (b) 16 (c) 8
4 (b) 7 (c) 1   Has to be 'certain'.   **5** (b) $\frac{1}{2}$

Exercise 23H

2 RR RR RL RR RR RL LR LR LL
3 (a) 4 (b) $\frac{4}{9}$ (c) $\frac{4}{9}$ (d) $\frac{1}{9}$
4 (a)

```
   C
  < C
   C
   T
```

   (b) CC CT TC TT (c) $\frac{1}{8}$
5 (b) (i) $\frac{8}{27}$ (ii) $\frac{1}{27}$ (iii) $\frac{4}{27}$ (iv) $\frac{8}{27}$

Exercise 23I

1 (a) 60 (b) 30 (c) 45
   (d)

	Mon	Tues	Total
Jackie	25	35	**60**
Sam	**30**	**10**	**40**
Total	55	**45**	100

   (e) (i) $\frac{25}{100}$ (ii) $\frac{10}{100}$ (iii) $\frac{60}{100}$ (iv) $\frac{65}{100}$
2 (a)

	Air	Le Shuttle	Boat	Total
July	8	**2**	10	20
Aug	15	5	**30**	50
Sept	**7**	8	15	**30**
Total	30	**15**	55	100

   (b) (i) $\frac{20}{100}$ (ii) $\frac{80}{100}$ (iii) $\frac{30}{100}$ (iv) $\frac{55}{100}$ (v) $\frac{5}{100}$
   (vi) $\frac{30}{100}$ (vii) $\frac{70}{100}$ (viii) $\frac{90}{100}$

3 (a)

	France	Italy	Elsewhere	Total
July	**6**	10	4	20
Aug	18	**24**	8	**50**
Sept	**4**	16	**10**	30
Total	28	50	**22**	**100**

(b) **(i)** $\frac{1}{10}$ **(ii)** $\frac{28}{100}$ **(iii)** $\frac{20}{100}$ **(iv)** $\frac{1}{2}$ **(v)** $\frac{8}{100}$
(vi) $\frac{4}{100}$ **(vii)** $\frac{16}{100}$

4 (a)

	Hotel	Caravan	Camping	Other	Total
July	11	4	3	**2**	**20**
Aug	**22**	14	**8**	6	**50**
Sept	**16**	7	4	3	30
Total	49	**25**	15	11	100

(b) **(i)** $\frac{22}{100}$ **(ii)** $\frac{4}{100}$ **(iii)** $\frac{49}{100}$ **(iv)** $\frac{51}{100}$ **(v)** $\frac{25}{100}$
(vi) $\frac{11}{100}$ **(vii)** $\frac{8}{100}$

Unit 24 Calculators and computers

Exercise 24A

1 `7` `3` `→` `L` `EXE`
`4` `9` `→` `W` `EXE`
`L` `W` `→` `A` `EXE`
`2` `L` `+` `2` `W` `→` `P` `EXE`

$A = 3577\,\text{cm}^2$, $P = 244\,\text{cm}$ $P =$
2 $A = 452.39\,\text{cm}^2$, $C = 75.398\,\text{cm}$
3 $A = 67.5\,\text{cm}^2$
4 $V = 144\,000\,\text{cm}^3$

Exercise 24B

1 `L` `×` `L` `×` `L` `→` `V`
or `L` `x^y` `3` `→` `V`
$V = 125\,\text{cm}^3,\ 216\,\text{cm}^3,\ 343\,\text{cm}^3$
2 `(` `F` `−` `3` `2` `)` `×` `5` `÷` `9` `→` `C`
$C = 30°\,\text{C},\ 10°\,\text{C},\ 20°\,\text{C}$

Exercise 24C

1 `?` `→` `L` `:` `L` `x^y` `3` `EXE`
$L = 4.64\,\text{cm}$
2 $F = 71.6°\,\text{F}$

Exercise 24D

1 `1` `EXE` `Ans` `+` `2` `EXE`
2 `5` `EXE` `Ans` `+` `5` `EXE`
3 `2` `EXE` `Ans` `×` `2` `EXE`
4 `3` `EXE` `Ans` `×` `3` `EXE`
5 `1` `0` `EXE` `Ans` `−` `1` `EXE`
6 `1` `6` `EXE` `Ans` `÷` `2` `EXE`
7 `2` `0` `0` `EXE` `Ans` `÷` `1` `0` `EXE`
8 `(-)` `5` `EXE` `Ans` `−` `2` `EXE`

Examination practice paper

1 (a) Three thousand, six hundred and four **(b)** 3600
2 (a) 17 **(b)** 14
3 (a) **(i)** Isosceles triangle **(ii)** Right-angled triangle
(iii) Rectangle **(iv)** Kite

(b)

(iii) has order 2, the others have order 1.

4 (a)

No.	Tally	Freq.
1	|||	3
2	|||	3
3	⊬||	7
4	⊬||	7
5	||||	4
6	⊬|	6

(b)

(c) **(i)** 3 and 4 **(ii)** 3.8 **(iii)** 5
5 5643, 4904, 3667, 3641
6 (i) 64 **(ii)** 5
7 (a) 18, 23 **(b)** Add 5 to the previous number **(c)** 98
(d) $5n - 2$
8 (b) 82° **(c)** **(i)** 25 cm **(d)** 27.3 cm²
9 (a) $\frac{5}{12}$ **(b)** $\frac{2}{3}$ **(c)** 0
10 37 cm²
11 H1, H2, H3, H4, H5, H6, T1, T2, T3, T4, T5, T6
12 (a) 3456 **(b)** 16 packets
13 (a) $a = 3$ **(b)** $s = 3\frac{3}{8}$ **(c)** $c = 10\frac{3}{4}$
14 Ben's, £22.50; Shoe Box, £23.50; Sale o' Shoes, £22.67; Ben's is the cheapest.
15 (a)

x	−3	−2	−1	0	1	2	3
y	−7	**−5**	−3	**−1**	1	**3**	5

x	−3	−2	−1	0	1	2	3
y	6	**1**	−2	−3	**−2**	**1**	6

(b)

16 (a) 4 hours **(b)** 44.4 mph **(c)** 640 km
17

```
0              1/2             1
├───────────────┼──────────────┤
S               C              B
```

18 (a) Graph A, Good – Negative   Graph B, Good – Positive
Graph C, No correlation
(b) Graph A, Miles per gallon and size of engine
Graph B, Miles per gallon and speed
Graph C, Miles per gallon and number of doors
19 141.3 cm